ENJOYMENT AND UNDERSTANDING

OF THE NATURAL HERITAGE

THE NATURAL HERITAGE OF SCOTLAND

Each year since it was founded in 1992, Scottish Natural Heritage has organised or jointly organised a conference that has focused attention on a particular aspect of Scotland's natural heritage. The papers read at the conferences, after a process of refereeing and editing, have been brought together as a book. The nine titles already published in this series are listed below (No. 6 was not based on a conference).

1. *The Islands of Scotland: a Living Marine Heritage*
    Edited by J.M. Baxter and M.B. Usher (1994), 286pp.

2. *Heaths and Moorlands: a Cultural Landscape*
    Edited by D.B.A. Thompson, A.J. Hester and M.B. Usher (1995), 400pp.

3. *Soils, Sustainability and the Natural Heritage*
    Edited by A.G. Taylor, J.E. Gordon and M.B. Usher (1996), 316pp.

4. *Freshwater Quality: Defining the Indefinable?*
    Edited by P.J. Boon and D.L. Howell (1997), 552pp.

5. *Biodiversity in Scotland: Status, Trends and Initiatives*
    Edited by L.V. Fleming, A.C. Newton, J.A. Vickery and M.B. Usher (1997), 309pp.

6. *Land Cover Change: Scotland from the 1940s to the 1980s*
    By E.C. Mackey, M.C. Shewry and G.J. Tudor (1998), 263pp.

7. *Scotland's Living Coastline*
    Edited by J.M. Baxter, K. Duncan, S.M. Atkins and G. Lees (1999), 209pp.

8. *Landscape Character: Perspectives on Management and Change*
    Edited by M.B. Usher (1999), 213pp.

9. *Earth Science and the Natural Heritage: Interactions and Integrated Management*
    Edited by J.E. Gordon and K.F. Leys (2001), 344pp.

This is the tenth book in the series.

Enjoyment and Understanding of the Natural Heritage

Edited by Michael B. Usher

SCOTTISH NATURAL HERITAGE

EDINBURGH: THE STATIONERY OFFICE

First published in 2001 by The Stationery Office Limited
71 Lothian Road, Edinburgh, EH3 9AZ

Applications for reproduction should be made to Scottish Natural Heritage,
12 Hope Terrace, Edinburgh, EH9 2AS

British Library Cataloguing in Publication Data
A catalogue record for this book is available from the British Library

ISBN 0 11 497290 7

Cover photography: Glen Nant National Nature Reserve, Argyll (inset) and the uplands of Merick and Benyellary, Galloway, by Michael B. Usher

PREFACE

The year 2000 saw significant moves towards new legislation to secure improved arrangements for public access for informal recreation in the outdoors. As in many other areas of life, the new public rights of access are planned to be accompanied by new responsibilities. The concepts of citizenship, personal responsibility to minimise impacts, and a growing recognition of a basic human right to enjoy one's environment, are all playing a key part in the debates on new legal frameworks for countryside access in Scotland and the rest of the UK.

Central to the proposed new legal frameworks is the principle that access to the natural heritage should be undertaken responsibly. Hence, the sub-theme of Scottish Natural Heritage's 2000 Conference, 'finding the new balance between rights and responsibilities', is the theme of the chapters in this book. Increased understanding is also required; only by fostering a sense of value in the right, and of people's roles in securing the conservation of the natural heritage, and of caring for the socio-economic interests of local communities, will that right be maintained. It is important to develop our understanding of how and why people interact with the natural heritage, how their experience and awareness can be improved, and how the negative effects of open-air recreation can be minimised.

The conference provided an opportunity to reflect on two of the early and significant contributors to research into open-air recreation in Scotland. Professors Terry Coppock and Joy Tivy were both geographers with a keen interest in contemporary land-use issues; Joy Tivy as a biogeographer at the University of Glasgow and Terry Coppock in relation to land-use and policy issues at the University of Edinburgh. Each recognised in the late 1960s the degree to which the expansion of open-air recreation was an important social phenomenon with consequences for the rural land-use mix; each led early research programmes whose outputs still contribute to our understanding of these issues; and each contributed to the development of research methods in this field.

Terry Coppock's involvement in recreation lay mainly in the social sciences, beginning with the early surveys of participation which paved the way for today's market research approach to recreation survey. His work provided the starting point for the Tourism and Recreation Research Unit located in the University of Edinburgh, which he led with Brian Duffield. Through the 1970s this Unit became (alongside the Dartington Amenity Research Trust, south of the Border) a main contractor and source of research expertise in open-air recreation, and it was used extensively by the public agencies. The Unit developed, for a group of Scottish agencies, a pioneering tourism and recreation information package (TRIP); we would now label this as a GIS (geographic information system), which integrated both resource and social science data for use in policy and research.

Joy Tivy wrote extensively on biogeography and agricultural ecology. Her recreation research interests lay in the study of the effects of this growing use of land on natural resources. Her first major contribution was the national survey of the recreational use of Scotland's freshwater lochs, their potential for recreation, and the effects and management needs arising from this changing pattern of use. She then developed an interest in the carrying capacity of natural resources for open-air recreation, and she also had interests in the contribution of natural vegetation to landscape appraisal. Human impact on natural resources through recreation, and both the land use and social science aspects of recreation, remain key research themes today.

Both Terry Coppock and Joy Tivy recognised, from their different perspectives, the need to apply academic and research experience in a way which integrated both natural and social science components. They did this at an early stage in the expansion of outdoor recreation and tourism, and did it in ways which made strong, practical contributions to public policy and practice. The directions set by their early research have had sustained influence on later thinking. We applaud their contributions and regret their passing: Joy Tivy died in 1995 and Terry Coppock in 2000.

At the time of the conference there was a considerable degree of excitement about the new possibilities for access, about the rights that might be created, and about the responsibilities that would come with those rights. There were some heated exchanges; perhaps the most controversial topic concerned access by dogs, with very polarised views expressed by the owners and non-owners of these animals. But alongside this excitement the conference focused on the research that has been, and is being, done in Scotland, developing from the pioneering work of Joy Tivy and Terry Coppock. However, the theme of the conference was wider than this in two important respects.

First, what could be learnt from related fields of study and practice? It is not new to seek to find that new balance between rights and responsibilities. Car drivers have had to do it. Health professionals have had to consider it. 'Recreationists do it on paths' might be an appropriate slogan, but how quickly will land managers agree that they 'do it responsibly'!

Second, at a time when new legislation was being discussed, when a new Scottish Outdoor Code was being drafted, there was naturally a focus on the policy issues. In a very real way the conference provided the ideal forum, both for researchers who wanted to explain their results and ideas, and for policy makers who were looking for best practice and for a particularly Scottish approach to open-air recreation.

This book brings together the majority of the contributions at the conference, as well as two further contributions. The book takes a broad view, with a contribution explaining the background to the Norwegian traditions of *Allemannsretten* and *Friluftsliv*, the public right of access to the countryside and the importance of outdoor recreation. Without such traditions, but with increasing demand for outdoor recreation, another contribution focused on the *Leave No Trace* campaign in the United States of America. This campaign is designed to engender understanding of the countryside as well as responsibility for it. Scotland, in developing its new approach, can select from the best of the approaches that are traditional or new in other parts of the world.

A conference and a publication of this nature inevitably involves a tremendous amount of work by many people. In planning for the conference, I should like to thank many members of staff of Scottish Natural Heritage, especially Bridget Dales, Helen Forster, Debbie Greene, Bonnie Maggio, Marion Mulholland and Dougie Pollok, and I am also very grateful for the advice of Richard Davison and John Mackay. At the conference we used the Residence and Catering Services of Strathclyde University, assisted by the staff of the McCance Building. I should particularly like to thank Cameron McNeish, the speaker after the conference dinner, who not only entertained the delegates but also provided much food for thought from his years of experience in the Scottish hills.

The speakers at the conference, and the people who stimulated the conference discussions, have all in their own ways contributed to this book. However, I owe a real 'thank you' to the unseen and generally anonymous referees. As with previous volumes in the *Natural Heritage of Scotland* series, the chapters have generally been sent to two referees – some to more than two, some to fewer. It is the critical comments of the referees that assist in achieving a high quality publication, and although the referees are unnamed it is their hard work that, as editor, I really appreciate. I also owe tremendous thanks to my personal secretary, Jo Newman, who has undertaken all of the editorial changes to the manuscripts, typed countless letters, and ever so gently but with tremendous determination 'twisted the arms' of people who were delivering material past deadlines. Her assistance has been essential. Finally, thanks are also due to Helen Forster for proof reading the manuscript, and to Jane McNair in The Stationery Office who has overseen the whole of the publication process.

Michael B. Usher
Chief Scientist, Scottish Natural Heritage

June 2001

CONTENTS

List of Plates

(between pages 130 and 131)

improved understanding of the relationships between amount of impact and use-related, environmental, and managerial factors can assist managers in selecting and applying effective strategies and actions. Photo shows Jeff Marion taking measurements on a trail in the Howler Monkey Preserve, Belize, investigating the environmental impacts of ecotourism visitation. Photo: Tracy Farrell.

Plate 10   The site is simple though well maintained.

Plate 11   Three stone and turf crescents are arranged to face each other.

Plate 12   The back wall of each crescent is decorated. Judging by the chalk colouring, the walls are popular with visiting children.

Plate 13   Does this sign relate to the pipe in front of it, or to the site in general?

LIST OF CONTRIBUTORS

M. Allison, Research and Evaluation Division, Health Education Board for Scotland, Woodburn House, Canaan Lane, Edinburgh, EH10 4SG

J. Butterfield, Centre for Leisure and Sport Research, Faculty of Cultural and Education Studies, Leeds Metropolitan University, Beckett Park Campus, Leeds, LS6 3QS

J. Carter, 18 Kirkhill Gardens, Edinburgh, EH16 5DF

T. Costley, NFO System 3, 19 Atholl Crescent, Edinburgh, EH3 8HQ

R. Davison, Recreation and Access Group, Scottish Natural Heritage, 2 Anderson Place, Edinburgh, EH6 5NP

A. Fenn, Awareness and Involvement Unit, Scottish Natural Heritage, Battleby, Redgorton, Perth, PH1 3EW

M. Foley, Department of Media, Language and Leisure Management, Glasgow Caledonian University, Cowcaddens Road, Glasgow, G4 0BA

M. Frew, Department of Media, Language and Leisure Management, Glasgow Caledonian University, Cowcaddens Road, Glasgow, G4 0BA

R. Grant, Awareness and Involvement Unit, Scottish Natural Heritage, Battleby, Redgorton, Perth, PH1 3EW

P. Higgins, Department of Physical Education, Sport and Leisure Studies, Moray House Institute of Education, University of Edinburgh, St Leonard's Land, Holyrood Road, Edinburgh, EH8 8AQ

J. Hunt, Woodlands, Strathpeffer, Ross-shire, IV14 9AX

B. Jones, Design and Interpretative Services, Forest Enterprise, 231 Corstorphine Road, Edinburgh, EH12 7AT

J. Lister-Kaye, House of Aigas, Beauly, Inverness-shire, IV4 7AD

J. Long, Centre for Leisure and Sport Research, Faculty of Cultural and Education Studies, Leeds Metropolitan University, Beckett Park Campus, Leeds, LS6 3QS

J.L. Marion, US Geological Survey, Patuxent Wildlife Research Center, Virginia Tech/Dept of Forestry, 304 Cheatham Hall (0324), Blacksburg, VA 24061, USA

D. McGillivray, Department of Media, Language and Leisure Management, Glasgow Caledonian University, Cowcaddens Road, Glasgow, G4 0BA

S.E. Reid, Virginia Tech Dept of Forestry, 304 Cheatham Hall (0324), Blacksburg, VA 24061, USA

M. Scott, Strome House, North Strome, Lochcarron, Ross-shire, IV54 8YJ

R. Sidaway, 4 Church Hill Place, Edinburgh, EH10 4BD

S.G. Stradling, Transport Research Institute, Napier University, 66 Spylaw Road, Edinburgh, EH10 5BR

J. Thomson, Scottish Natural Heritage, Caspian House, Mariner Court, Clydebank Business Park, Clydebank, G81 2NR

O.I. Vistad, Division for Man-Environment Studies, Norwegian Institute for Nature Research, Fakkelgarden, Storhove, N-2624 Lillehammer, Norway

A. Wightman, Department of Physical Education, Sport and Leisure Studies, Moray House Institute of Education, University of Edinburgh, St Leonard's Land, Holyrood Road, Edinburgh, EH8 8AQ

R. Williamson, The Buccleuch Estates Ltd, Estate Office, Weatherhouse, Bowhill, Selkirk, TD7 5ES

S. Wurthmann, Department of Energy and Environmental Technology, Glasgow Caledonian University, Cowcaddens Road, Glasgow, G4 0BA

FOREWORD

The Scottish Natural Heritage Conference 2000 was the ninth in our annual series. Our previous conferences have often had themes associated with both research and review of major natural heritage topics. This year we chose a theme - Enjoyment and Understanding - which has at its centre the delivery of new public policy.

Enjoyment and understanding are key parts of SNH's statutory remit and are essential ingredients in our broader aim of conserving and enhancing Scotland's natural heritage. It is no accident that the first words of our organisation's mission is *Working with Scotland's People*. The people side of our business is central to delivering our strategy and our objectives. Working with people to care for our environment, by fostering understanding and facilitating enjoyment, is vital to achieving our goals.

Rights and responsibilities relating to new access legislation are being debated both in Scotland and in England and Wales. Our conference did not have, as its prime aim, a discussion of the formation of public policy. Rather, it was to provide an opportunity for SNH, with its key partners, to develop ideas as to how the changes ahead could be managed in an effective and fair way. The conference also gave opportunities for those who are critical of some of our proposals to discuss them openly.

We were particularly concerned to see how we could develop the consensus amongst the various parties. Agreement has been forged through hard debate between the parties - landowning bodies, recreational interests and the public sector. We have worked together on the Access Forum to reach agreement and to make recommendations to government. It is particularly impressive to me that the original consensus for a public right for informal recreation and passage, exercised responsibly, over land and water is broadly intact.

When our conference was first planned, we anticipated that our deliberations would take place in the context of a Bill or a draft Bill. For various reasons the publication of a draft Bill has been postponed and its introduction into the Scottish Parliament is not now timetabled until September 2001. Nevertheless, this did not diminish our appetite for seeing how the forthcoming legislation might best be implemented through issues as diverse as information and education programmes, the publication of a Scottish Outdoor Access Code, the development of a broader understanding of the needs of the countryside, staff training, Local Access Groups, and funding packages.

Our main task was to hear and to debate how best we could encourage responsibility to thrive within the context of the new rights. Many participants at the conference were already involved in this process and were well aware of the critical tasks which lay ahead. I hope that the publication of this conference volume in the *Natural Heritage of Scotland* series will make this whole process, and the critical tasks, much more widely known.

John Markland
Chairman, Scottish Natural Heritage

October 2000

PART ONE

UNDERSTANDING AND ENJOYING THE NATURAL HERITAGE

1 THE ENJOYMENT AND UNDERSTANDING OF NATURE AND WILDNESS

John Lister-Kaye

1.1 Preamble

There is a current inclination to view access and recreation as a wholly human subject, about people's rights and recreation opportunities and about changing the *status quo*. Many chapters in this volume rightly address this aspect of what is a very complex subject. But this is only part of the plot. The bigger debate, and the one that is properly emphasised, is about our responsibility toward each other, to the natural environment and to its other occupants, our wildlife, and about effecting balances which properly embrace those responsibilities.

My opinions have been forged over many years of direct experience and involvement both with people and with wildlife. Because they are deeply held I would not wish to bend them to suit the political needs at such an interesting moment in Scottish history. We are facing new wildlife protection legislation, land ownership and land use reform, National Parks for Scotland, and new, clearer public access liberties. Now, more than at any other time in my 35 years of professional involvement with wildlife conservation, it is the time to speak out.

I see myself as one of the last generation to have enjoyed a country childhood where nature and wildness was to be discovered in every field and every ditch. I can vividly recall horses working the land and as a boy I helped farm labourers put wheat sheaves into stooks by hand. I grew up in a world of egg and butterfly collections, of milk still warm from the cow in white enamel cans; and of riding my pony bareback down the Great North Road, the A1, with her foal running loose at foot – something simply unimaginable now. At nine years old I remember great excitement when my father took me to see something truly amazing - a combine harvester. A year or two later I went with him to see a demonstration of a machine called a Dinkum-Digger. This was a prototype of what was to become the great hydraulic earth moving revolution, which was to mark the end of what we looked upon as permanence in the countryside. We had no concept of the power that was about to be unleashed. Hedges, great trees, ditches, banks, stone walls, scrub, woodlands, ponds and wetlands were about to disappear at the push of a lever from a comfortable seat. But I foresaw none of what was to come. For me country life was as yet an idyll closer to *Cider with Rosie* and *Lark Rise to Candleford* than to anything we now know.

Do not be fooled by this nostalgia. The impact of man's activities has been shifting goalposts in front of us for a great deal longer than the last 50 years. In 1851 Henry Thoreau said he was born just in the nick of time. The trouble is that we all make judgements by the standards of our own experience. I can never know the wild woods that Henry Thoreau saw, just as many people now can never witness what I did as a boy. Nothing ever stands still; but, from time to time, it is salutary to look back and ponder at what we have done. It is an unhappy fact of my lifetime that even if the law permitted me to, I could no longer collect many of the birds' eggs and butterflies I did 45 years ago. Anyone who knew the Highlands and Islands in the 1960s will vividly remember how 'other world' those crofting landscapes were. Few crofters would relish that lifestyle now.

However, I do believe that our whole approach to nature and its conservation is incomplete; we are severely hampered by our deep cultural separation from the natural world. The Judaeo-Christian doctrines which have shaped Western society over the last 1,500 years specifically differentiate man from nature and charge him with its conquest. The very first instruction to mankind on the first page of the Bible demands *be fruitful and multiply, and replenish the earth, and subdue it; and have dominion over the fish of the sea, and over the fowl of the air, and over cattle, and over all the earth, and over every creeping thing that creepeth upon the earth.* Well, we have certainly done that.

Our most recent interpretation of subduing the earth has given us 175 years of industrialisation. Removing people from the land and herding them together in cities has completed our separation from the soil. It has caused us to lose sight of the essential quality of wildness. Yet we still hanker after our origins. I suggest that our sometimes-obsessive quest for access and recreation in wild places is symptomatic of that need in us all.

Wild is a quality, not a quantity. It is a word we no longer use freely in nature conservation. It precisely does not mean designated, preserved, protected, measured, annotated and managed; nor does it mean habitats or ecosystems. All of these are quantities based on acreage, species, numbers and other physical properties. We have wedded ourselves to science and the classical concepts of management and containment, the purpose of which is to control and use nature, to subdue it. Wildness gets ignored because we cannot measure it, manage it and contain it. We have actually forgotten what it means because we are no longer a part of it or involved with it in our daily lives; no longer able to participate in its inherent but mercurial spirituality. Perhaps Marcel Proust was right when he wrote *Pour connaître la vraie nature, il faut être amoureux* (to understand true nature you must be in love). Perhaps we simply are not in love with nature any more?

In one sense nature conservation has become like an old-fashioned museum. We have a collection of species here, and another collection there. We call them reserves, national parks and designated areas. But we overlook that you cannot collect the quality of wildness in such areas, just as you cannot make a museum sacred or holy no matter how many sacred artefacts you bring together under one roof.

If I want to see an avocet, I visit a wonderful nature reserve like Minsmere. The avocet is virtually guaranteed along with many other waders, but not wildness. I watch from a hide insulated from the world of the avocet, which paddles about in created lagoons resembling wild wetlands we have destroyed elsewhere. No, if it is wildness my soul craves, I head away from national parks, trails, reserves and the like. I draw a clear distinction between 'wildness' and 'wildlife', although, of course, the two belong together and should be a qualification of each other. I want to insert that notion into our thinking on how we enjoy and understand our natural heritage. A tiger in a cage is wildlife, but it is aeons away from the wildness to which it belongs.

I am not suggesting for a moment that we abandon reserves, national parks and Sites of Special Scientific Interest - far from it. There are excellent reasons for preserving nature in readily quantifiable ways and places. We have little choice these days. This is a race we are already running; there is no turning back. What I am suggesting is that we need to re-write the quality of wildness into our strategic conservation planning, whether it is in nature reserves or other beautiful places. We need to try to learn how to value it and discover it for ourselves all over again, freed-up from the blinding, materialist distractions of all-pervasive modernity.

In 1970 I started a Field Studies Centre in Inverness-shire. My family and I live in the middle of a throughput of a 1,000 adults and 4,000 school children every year. My work with people and nature has never dampened my boyhood passion for natural history, nor has the constant erosion of nature tarnished my commitment to it. Indeed, it could be said that as I have witnessed her suffer so I have come to love her more. Once again, it is quite simply the case that over the last 30 years the wild Highland countryside around me has changed enormously before my eyes and those of our students. We no longer enjoy corncrakes, corn buntings, yellowhammers, skylarks and tree sparrows; we have lost our capercaillie and our black game, and red grouse and hen harriers have almost completely deserted our home moors. If we still have wildcats they are all feral hybrids. Our sea trout and most of our salmon have disappeared. Few curlew, redshank and greenshank now come to our hills to breed, and only a handful of lapwings are left in river fields that used to be vibrant with their mewing, swooping and gyrating antics. Our wildflowers and our butterflies along with a myriad other invertebrates have been pushed aside by industrial agriculture. Huge areas of heather moorland have given way to the sterility of monoculture forestry.

Conversely, buzzards and pine martens are now common, ospreys have returned by accident and red kites and sea eagles have been re-introduced. At long last we have begun to redress the loss of native woodland, although we still have a very long way to go. But in my opinion it is not much of a trade-off. The causality of these very evident changes is complex: shifting climate, industrial air pollution, radically altered land use and greatly enhanced standards of living for people – at least in material terms - are all well-known factors. What is not so openly acknowledged by policymakers is that, for all our designations and doctrinaire notions and deliberations about the environment, the general direction human society has been heading in for the whole of my lifetime is fundamentally hostile to nature and wildness.

So please do not look to this chapter for objectivity or political correctness, or even the ability to see both sides of the argument. I see plenty of other people out there who can, and do, argue very forcibly for human interests and for the many undeniable benefits of materialism. I am for nature.

1.2 The authority of wildness

> *Tyger! Tyger! burning bright*
> *In the forests of the night,*
> *What immortal hand or eye*
> *Could frame thy fearful symmetry?*
>
> *William Blake 1757-1827*

I want to express my concern about the authority of wildness. Although they are all part of the problem, I am not concerned with the usual enemies of nature: chemical agriculture, monoculture forestry, urbanisation and sprawling development, industrial pollution and all the other aspects of people-pressure with which we are all so familiar. My concern lies in the far more insidious threats to the authority of wildness that we conveniently overlook for so much of the time. My personal hit-list of such threats includes five points.

- The constant economic justification for nature as if it has no right to exist on its own. At a time when we are busy writing down our own bill of human rights I find myself asking why nature does not have some too. Who took them away? When did we ever vote on it?
- Cheque-book conservation due to our rush to pay out all the time for things which should be priceless anyway. It is like a suitor who, having failed to woo his love, says 'How about a quarter of a million quid?'.
- Our feeble approach to environmental education because we make such a fuss when our children cannot spell correctly, but it does not seem to matter that they do not understand how the planet works?
- Our obsession for managing nature which has managed itself for thousands or millions of years. It is as though we are not doing our jobs properly if we are not tinkering with it all the time.
- Suburbanisation of nature so that, because of our ignorance and fear that is so prevalent in our largely suburban culture, we often treat nature and wildness like a disease.

I want to concentrate on two aspects, both of which draw together several of these cultural problems endemic in our 21st Century society.

1.2.1 The pursuit of recreation at the expense of wild nature

I have heard it argued that nature reserves should be for people as much as for wildlife. I believe in the primacy of nature as a fundamental principle for nature reserves, which, by definition, are so often a last resort for wildlife; places where we have cornered wildlife because we simply did not want it, or allow it, to exist elsewhere. Recreation must be subordinate to the sanctity of these places. If it is not, we have failed yet again.

We also need to look long and hard at the real justification for recreational facilities in other wild and special places. Is it really wise or necessary to broadcast the wildness of a place for the greater public good? Have we not all seen what happens when we invite commercialism and mass tourism into special places? No amount of packaged exposure to nature is going to make people love it. Rather, it creates an illusion of loving nature that masks our true ignorance of it and the depth of our separation from it. Far too often, in the name of being seen to be doing something, when we open up yet another area we are simply progressing blindly down the route of destroying the sense of discovery and awe which I believe is so important in real countryside recreation. Responsible managers of nature and wild countryside must remember that what wildlife likes best of all is to be left alone.

Just over 100 years ago, in 1895, John Muir, whom we now consider to be the father of National Parks, told a meeting of the Sierra Club

> *"Few are altogether deaf to the preaching of pine-trees. Their sermons on the mountains go to our hearts; and if people in general could be got into the woods, even for once, to hear the trees speak for themselves, all difficulties in the ways of forest preservation would vanish"* (Cohen, 1984, p. 303).

John Muir was wrong. He had failed to understand that designating a Wilderness Area or a National Park would not automatically make people love and appreciate the natural world. If his spirit can now see what recreation has done to his own wilderness paradise, Yosemite Valley, he is surely dying another long drawn out death of a million cuts.

Recently I walked the National Trust's Coastal Trail in North Cornwall. What I experienced filled me with dismay. I found scuffed and scarred headlands with chainlink fencing to stop me falling over the cliffs. Concrete ramps and steps abound. Widespread litter is strewn about by people who evidently thought nothing for that place and were probably only there because they had nothing else to do. When I stopped at the edge of the path to watch a six-spot burnet moth I was pushed out of the way by aggressive, hurrying walkers who cared neither for the moth nor for me. My conclusion was that the very existence of the trail seemed to foster a sense of egocentric right in these people, rather than a sense of enjoyment, discovery and respect. I doubt whether any amount of management can restore the magical wildness of that place as it was for tens of thousands of years before the trail went in.

Surely it is an important principle that people should be able to achieve their own countryside recreation in their own way? Is that not what recreation really is? Was it really necessary for the Speyside Way to cut through Abernethy Forest? Was it wise to invite people with dogs to take their recreation in prime capercaillie habitat? A right to roam should never be allowed to become a right for dogs to roam.

As the Cairngorm Funicular Railway progresses steadily toward the summit of the most precious and fragile mountain ecosystem in Britain, so it concretes itself into Scottish history as an icon of bad planning and fudged responsibility. Do we really believe that it will make people value and appreciate the unique qualities of the Cairngorm plateau? In the name of nature conservation it stands as a signal failure by conservationists to persuade others of the real value of nature in special places. And in the name of contorted economics and recreation, it stands as a triumph of crass materialism over wildness and the authority of nature. Like Gollum in *The Hobbit,* 'I hates it, I hates it, I hates it forever!'.

Some years ago I was involved internally in the access debate within Scottish Natural Heritage. I dared to suggest that there was a fundamental incompatibility between nature conservation and some aspects of public access, and that perhaps we should be honest enough to admit it and adopt two clearly separate but equally robust policies. I was told that I should be searching for the creative synergy between the two. I am still searching. Quite simply, I do not believe that the capercaillie will breed any better for the presence of the Speyside Way in Abernethy Forest. I do not believe that the gondola uplift of tens of thousands of summer tourists onto the summit of Aonach Mor will help protect that already damaged Site of Special Scientific Interest. I do not believe that unrestricted canoeing on Loch Maree will improve the breeding success of the severely threatened black-throated diver. I can find neither creativity nor synergy in these actions. Instead I believe that they are deeply damaging. They simply underline the gross inadequacy of our wildlife protection legislation. I fear that political correctness in its widest and most insidious form – the regularly disastrous desire to please everybody all the time - has often been a critical factor in determining policy.

1.2.2 The compulsive delivery of nature on a plate

I am thinking of the signage, over-interpretation, paths and trails that so often deny the individual a personal, wild experience. I work in environmental education. I help people to discover, understand, and respect nature and their own environment. Over three decades I have witnessed the exhilaration and sheer joy of real wildlife experiences by our public.

People often tell us of their adventures: an otter with cubs popping up beside a lochside picnic, golden eagles tumbling unexpectedly out of the sky locked in a courtship display, a pine marten snatching fledglings from a pipit's nest under the noses of folk sitting quietly beside a burn, and many others. All happen, regularly and perhaps not surprisingly, well away from trails, car parks, interpretation points and view points.   Their impact is immeasurable. They are real discoveries which lift people out of their workaday world and into contact with nature at a level, they have often told me, they thought was not available to ordinary people. Such occasions are precious. They draw people closer to nature. What is vital, I believe, is that we protect that experience of the wild by allowing people to discover it for themselves.

However, we feed it to them without any required effort, and thrust leaflets at them, leaving nothing to the imagination. We waymark their progress so that they know that thousands of other people have been there before them. We destroy any chance of personal discovery by telling them what to expect, and we force them to do so in the company of others who, drawn in by the signs, may have no time or consideration for wildness or the serious visitor. We might as well take them to the zoo.

A word on ignorance and fear. Up to the age of five my daughter Hermione had no fear of insects, frogs, toads and newts, worms and bugs - the happy accident of being brought up in an environmental education centre. She went off to school innocently confident of her personal relationship with the natural world. A few days later she came home tearfully bewildered by the response of other children to an earwig she had allowed to crawl across her hand. Some were petrified and shrank away, others cried out in disgust. They thought she was very strange. She asked me "Why are they all so afraid of nature, Daddy?". The question is profound, the answer complex. But afraid they are, and their fear is rooted in their physical and psychological separation from nature. Many of us are afraid of things outside our sphere of knowledge and understanding. Western society has steadily moved away from nature for centuries; the separation is almost complete. Worse, if it is not furry and cuddly many people do not care whether it exists or not.   I believe we do no favours to children or adults to trivialise or sentimentalise nature. The Disney culture has forced us into an unhappy and unreal association with those creatures with whom we share our world. Children reared on such candyfloss are not likely to become enthusiastic guardians of nature and wildness; they are far more likely to want to tame it and commercialise it.

1.3 Conclusions

So just what am I proposing at this auspicious moment in Scottish countryside management? I am advocating policies that are sustainable. We must take great care that in our often self-indulgent and sometimes over-zealous management of access we do not end up destroying the very qualities of wildness, landscape and nature that people seek to enjoy.

It would be tempting, and, no doubt, politically appealing, to pour our efforts and money into a new network of paths, trails, signage and publicity and into creating a glossy image of the new opportunities and rights which I genuinely hope will assist people to enjoy the Scottish countryside. I am sure that this will be an inevitable consequence of new National Parks legislation. But what I also hope for is that we will look holistically at the implications of public access on wildlife and wildness itself. We have designated our wildlife sites and nature reserves because nature exists in those places. It is also true that for much of this wildlife there is little room in our countryside for expansion. Just because some special plant or bird is not present on a mountaintop does not necessarily mean it is a good place for a path or a trail. We must do better than that. We need to assess the integrity and stability of habitats and ecosystems in order to judge the appropriateness of regular public access. Perhaps for once there is a case for being reactive rather than proactive. Do not create problems where problems need not exist. Perhaps we should watch and wait to see if the demand justifies the supply. I believe we must stand back from the apparent desirability of managed access and look hard and objectively at the long-term implications of our actions and decisions.

I also believe that as well as carefully opening up some new areas we must remove some from disturbance altogether. We must not be afraid to identify and publish 'no-go areas' in particular places on land or at sea where it is clear that people are a negative and a destructive factor in nature conservation. Equally we must explain clearly why these places are essential for nature to be left in peace, or the suspicious public will conclude that the real reason is for the landowner or the fisherman to be left in peace. What is needed is firmness balanced by clarity so that misunderstandings do not occur. We must not shrink from this responsibility, however unpopular it may be with some people.

The counterpoint to this is a comprehensive and well-planned programme of restoration projects which identify and promote corridors for wildlife. This might include community forests and woodlands, wetlands, moorland, heath and scrub where people can experience the outdoors as well as feel a sense of pride and belonging to land restored by their efforts to a semi-natural state.

But, most of all, starting now and persisting indefinitely with great vigour and enthusiasm, we need to re-develop a culture of respect for nature and wildness. We need to be in love again. We need to teach it from the earliest age. Formal teaching qualifications need to include a requirement for delivering environmental education which should be a structured and integral part of the 5 to 14 year old's school curriculum, not the woolly 'now-you-get-it-now-you-don't' add-on to science that it is at present. It needs to preach a discipline and understanding for life, to bring us back into touch with our environment. This is the string missing from the conservation violin. Until we face up to this we stand little hope of producing a whole generation of youngsters who value wild places and the wildlife that depends upon them. In my opinion, for many people countryside recreation and enjoyment will remain a shallow and relatively meaningless exercise – little more than fresh air and fun - without this basic knowledge and understanding of how our cultural and industrial separation from the natural world has brought about the destruction of our natural heritage. We owe it to future generations to do better than that.

I still hope that two strong and parallel policies can emerge clearly from Scottish Natural Heritage and the countryside non-governmental organisations. One of these protects, practices, teaches and respects the authority of nature and wildness – in other words an inalienable conservation ethic; and the other, equally important, which encourages, assists and enables people to discover, understand and enjoy wildness and wildlife for themselves, without threatening it or destroying it for others.

After a speech I once gave to a forestry conference the Chief Executive of one of Scotland's development agencies said to me "When are conservationists going to learn to compromise?". Nature conservation is by definition a compromise. If nature was not already compromised we would not need to conserve it. Yet, I remain an optimist.

I believe in restoration ecology, the process of rebuilding what we have destroyed. Communities must be encouraged and enabled to involve themselves in restoration projects so that they come to love and believe in what they are creating or re-creating. If these are directed specifically at environmental recreation they will help take the pressure off precious wild areas.

I also believe in environmental education, teaching understanding and responsibility to a whole generation of young who will think twice before repeating the mistakes of their predecessors. This means developing an ethic built upon respect for the authority of wildness.

And I believe in doing everything that I can to help people to achieve the psychological, spiritual and physical access needed to discover, understand and enjoy wild nature for themselves.

Tyger! Tyger! burning bright,
In the forests of the night,
What the hammer? what the chain?
In what furnace was thy brain?

Reference

Cohen, M.P. (1984). *The Pathless Way: John Muir and the American Wilderness.* University of Wisconsin Press, Madison

2 *ALLEMANNSRETTEN* – ON ACCESS AND RECREATION IN NORWAY

Odd Inge Vistad

Summary

1.   There is a long historical background in Norway to the public right of access *(Allemannsretten)*. The right is still very important to the people of Norway, and it is now formally protected by the Outdoor Recreation Act of 1957.

2.   There is some evidence of increasing conflict between private and public interests linked to *Allemannsretten*.

3.   Outdoor recreation (*Friluftsliv*) is also very important to people in Norway. Short trips on foot close to home are the most common activities. However, participation in hiking in the mountains, cycling and downhill skiing is increasing.

4.   Urbanisation of society and modernisation of *Friluftsliv* might challenge *Allemannsretten* in several ways.

2.1 The origin of *Allemannsretten* in Norway

The public right of access (*Allemannsretten*) is a part of the Norwegian cultural heritage. *Allemannsretten* represents a continuation of old Germanic traditions and legislation. Today the right of public access has been formally incorporated into statute through the Outdoor Recreation Act of 1957 (see Ministry of Environment, 1985). Growing conflicts along the coastline in Southern Norway in the 1930s and 1940s between the private landowners, cabin owners and the public (privacy versus the public need for recreational areas) was a driving force in the process of creating a specific Act to protect *Allemannsretten*.

During the early settlement of the country, cultivated land close to dwellings (which developed into farms) was occupied for private use only and defined as private property. Outside and between the farms, there were extensive areas in common use (in Norwegian called *allmenning*).

In the 11th and 12th centuries, special rules and laws were written down for both the private properties and the commons. These laws where based on traditional unwritten rights, and this created a common understanding of how the two types of properties should be used and who had special rights over land. The regulation of the commons was developed in later laws (from the 13th to the 17th centuries).

The main rule was that only people living in *bygdelaget* (or the village area) had rights in the commons. This *bygdelag* had to be geographically defined in each case, and not necessarily along other administrative boundaries. There have been many conflicts concerning some of the rights in the commons (grazing, cutting wood, mountain farming, etc.); should these rights be limited to the farmers only or should they include all of the inhabitants in the village area? Other rights, like hunting, fishing, berry picking, etc., have mostly (but not always) been looked upon as rights for anyone in the local area.

Today there are different kinds of common and public properties in Norway, regulated by various laws, for different administrative units, and with different rights for different kinds of users. It is important to distinguish between rights in the commons (*Allmenningsretten*) and every man's rights (*Allemannsretten*). There is no distinction between different kinds of users in *Allemannsretten*.

Allemannsretten is also traditional, but was not specified in a modern law until 1957. *Allemannsretten* has survived the major changes in society, with urbanisation and changed use of the countryside. It can be looked upon as a set of rights which have survived from the older Germanic tradition of rights, where the right to own was primarily a right to use, and the landowner had to give way to other users' rights. In southern Europe (where there is a Roman tradition of rights) it seems that the right to own was superior to the right of other people to use the land.

2.2 *Allemannsretten* today – rights and responsibilities

Allemannsretten includes the right for anyone to travel across or stay for some time on the (uncultivated) lands of others, and to pick natural products for their own immediate requirements. When the ground is frozen it is also possible to walk and stay on cultivated land. The basic principle of *Allemannsretten* is that it must not result in any damage to the land, or disturb domestic animals, wildlife or people – be they owners of the land or other kinds of users.

Norway has very many small properties and small farms. The right of free access is therefore not only a useful right for the public, but also for most of the landowners. A landowner often has to cross other people's land to reach his or her own land.

The principal law defining and governing this right is the Outdoor Recreation Act – *Friluftsloven* – of 1957. Additionally, other laws are important in specifying what is legal, or illegal, in connection with recreational activities in the countryside and other areas of Norway. In converting the rights into statute, a careful balance was sought between the rights of the public and those of landowners. The Outdoor Recreation Act has been amended several times - most recently in 1996. This chapter presents the most important rights and responsibilities stated in the Act. The citations below from the law come from the most recent (1996) version. Peter Scott Planning Services (1998) gave more details, on the legislation, public authorities and the relevant organisations.

When the law was amended in 1996, a section stating the purpose of the law was introduced for the first time (paragraph 1). An unofficial translation is

> *"The purpose of this law is to protect nature as a basis for 'friluftsliv' (outdoor recreation) and to secure the public right to move and stay, etc., in the natural environment; to enable outdoor recreation; to promote health and well-being; and to maintain and encourage environmentally sustainable recreational activity."*

Unofficial translations of other parts of the Act are used in the following sections of this chapter.

2.2.1 Access rights and legislation

The basic public right is defined in paragraph 2 as

"All persons are entitled to free passage on foot over uncultivated land all the year around, when this is done considerately and with due care."

The term uncultivated land (*utmark*) is defined by exception - what is not cultivated is uncultivated. Cultivated land (*innmark*) is defined in paragraph 1a by referring to different categories of cultivated land.

"The following categories come under the heading of cultivated land or its equivalent in this Act: farmyards, houses, plots, tilled land, hayfields, pasture land and forest planting areas, together with similar areas where the free passage of the public would cause unreasonable nuisance for the owner or user."

An information leaflet (Directorate for Nature Management, 1996) used the terms *fenced land* and *unfenced land* (or *open country*), instead of cultivated and uncultivated land. However, a landowner cannot fence uncultivated land to keep the public out. The character and use of the land are the main criteria for differentiating between *innmark* and *utmark*.

The right to travel on foot is the most important and most fundamental public access right. This right is not only connected to recreational activities, but to any purpose - as long as the individual complies with the rules. In winter, the access right includes skiing and using snowshoes. It also includes mountain climbing and other recreational activities. Dog walking is a part of the public access right, as long as the rules about when to keep the dog on a lead are followed.

The access rights in paragraph 2

"... apply to passage on riding-horses, or with farm-horses, to sledging, bicycling, or the like on roads or paths in uncultivated areas and in all uncultivated mountain areas, as long as the municipality has not forbidden such passage in specified areas with the approval of owner or user (a lessee, tenant, lodger etc.). Such a decision must be confirmed by the County Governor."

A bicycle in this context is non-motorised. The municipality can regulate cycling, horse riding, dog teams, etc., in specified areas. Walking on cultivated land is legal when the ground is frozen or covered with snow, but not between 30th April and 14th October. Travel by boat at sea is free for everyone, as is travel on ice-covered sea areas (paragraph 6). Also, anyone has the right to bathe in the sea from a beach in an uncultivated area, or from a boat when this is done at a reasonable distance from an inhabited house (or cabin) and without causing unreasonable inconvenience or nuisance for others (paragraph 8).

Picnicking, sunbathing and overnight camping are permitted on uncultivated land in certain circumstances. These activities must not cause inconvenience or nuisance to others or cause damage to young trees or plantations. A tent must not be pitched so close to an inhabited house or cabin that disturbance is caused to residents, and it must in no case be closer than 150 m. The rule about distance from a house or cabin excludes designated campsites. Camping or any other stay is not permitted for more than two days at a time without the consent of the owner or user. Consent for longer stays is, however, not needed in mountain areas or in areas far away from buildings, unless it is obvious that the stay might entail significant damage or nuisance (paragraph 9). During the summer of 2000 a municipality decided that overnight camping should be forbidden along a very popular cycling road (*Rallarvegen*) in a mountain area in Western Norway. The reason was the large amount of litter from the campers. Generally speaking, the right to stay (e.g. for picnicking, sunbathing and camping) is not as strong as the right of passage or walking.

In connection with outdoor recreation, it is legal to park a car (or another motor vehicle) by a private or public road. However, a landowner may prohibit parking by a private road. By a public road it depends on whether significant damage or nuisance is caused. For some years now there has been a debate in Norway about the overnight parking of camper-vans and caravans alongside roads. The Ministry of Environment interprets the Act as if the rules on parking include camper-vans and caravans, but the regulations concerning camping with tents (maximum two nights; at least 150 m from an inhabited house or cabin) should also apply to camper-vans and caravans. A municipality can regulate such activities, especially when there are large numbers of visitors, and if the activity is to the detriment of wildlife, other users or other kinds of recreational activity.

Although there is no mention of different types of harvesting of natural products in the Outdoor Recreation Act, picking berries, mushrooms, flowers and the roots of wild herbs can still be regarded as a public right on uncultivated land. These activities are regulated by the Penal Code. People are also permitted to pick nuts if they are eaten when and where they are picked. Berries, flowers, roots and mushrooms can even be picked for sale, with some exceptions.

Sea fishing is allowed by anyone, without charge and all-year round, but special rules apply to salmon (*Salmo salar*), sea trout (*Salmo trutta*) and sea char (*Salvelinus alpinus*). Those fishing in rivers and lakes must pay a State fishing fee and usually pay the landowner for a fishing permit. Children, under the age of 16, can fish with a rod or a line without any charge from 1st January to 20th August, even in lakes and rivers, except where there are salmon, sea trout or sea char. This right excludes freshwater crayfish (*Astacus astacus*). Free fishing for children is not a traditional right, but was introduced as a new right in the Act on Salmonids and Fresh Water Fish in 1992.

Generally, the public right of access is available on uncultivated land and is not restricted to linear routes. However, activities like cycling and horse riding are restricted to roads or paths in uncultivated areas, except in the mountains where there are no such limitations. The municipalities may regulate this right. Travelling on foot on a private road is legal all year round, provided it does not cross a farmyard, house plot, fenced garden, etc. All visible paths and roads are defined on topographical maps, and recreational maps usually depict preferred paths with a special colour to encourage the public to use these routes.

2.2.2 Responsibilities for administering the access system

The Ministry of Environment (*Miljøverndepartementet*) is the national authority for environmental and access legislation. The Directorate for Nature Management (*Direktoratet for Naturforvaltning*) is the executive agency of the Ministry. The County Governor (*Fylkesmannen*) represents the State's interests at the county level. The County Councils (County Municipalities) (*Fylkeskommunen*) have only a few responsibilities related to the Outdoor Recreation Act, but they have important outdoor recreation planning functions. The municipalities are the most important authorities in the day-to-day management of access issues. Peter Scott Planning Services (1998) reviewed in detail the responsibilities and actual management aspects of the Norwegian system.

2.2.3 Responsibilities of landowners and recreational users

Allemannsretten is based on responsible behaviour. The relevant text in the Act is translated as *"... considerately and with due care"* (Ministry of Environment, 1985). This encompasses consideration towards the environment, landowners and other users. But the requirements are very much based on common sense.

A landowner can enforce the requirement for responsible behaviour by visitors. The landowner or other user of the property (for example a tenant farmer) has

"... the right to expel a person from his property who behaves inconsiderately or who by inappropriate behaviour exposes the property or rightful interests to damage or nuisance."

This right does not allow the use of physical force in expelling other persons. The owner or user of land must not erect an unnecessary barrier or unauthorised prohibition sign,

"... unless it serves his rightful interests and is not an unwarranted inconvenience to the right of the public to free passage."

as stated in paragraph 13.

2.2.4 Ability of owners to restrict access for certain purposes

The ability to restrict access is partly a question of what are the owner's rightful interests. In general, the owner's right to protect his or her interests is generally covered by the definition of cultivated land (*'innmark'*). Paragraph 3 states that

"The owner or user may – regardless of fencing – prohibit passage over a garden, planting area, autumn snowfields and fallow fields, even when the ground is frozen or covered by snow, in the event that such passage would be liable to cause significant damage."

Certain activities, for example open-air meetings, require the owner's or other users' consent. The critical criterion here is usually the extent of potential impacts, or other consequences of the activity or arrangement, for both the owner and the user.

2.2.5 Differences in access rights between individuals and groups

When the Government was considering amendments to the Outdoor Recreation Act in 1996, the exclusion of commercial activity from *Allemannsretten* was proposed, but rejected. The proposal reflects the current pressures on farming from market forces and from the central authorities. The opportunities for farmers to gain income from *utmark* (uncultivated land) is considered a potential area of economic growth.

In reality, *Allemannsretten,* as defined in the Act, is regarded as including organised activities, and does not differentiate between commercial or non-commercial activities. The critical question is 'What are the consequences of the activity?' and not 'Is the activity commercial or organised?'. However, larger events may require the owner's or user's consent.

It is recognised that groups of people normally cause more serious impacts to the ground and to wildlife than do individuals (Hammitt and Cole, 1998; Liddle, 1997). But many other factors might influence the situation, for example the type of activity, the actual behaviour, the terrain, season, weather conditions, etc. Large sports events (e.g. skiing, running and orienteering events) do not require the agreement of every landowner, but special care is required to avoid possible damage.

Good relationships between recreational organisations and landowners are considered important and Norway has guidelines on how to organise orienteering events to avoid or minimise damage to the environment or other interests. Similar guidelines or agreements apply to ski-tracks, hiking paths and bridleways, and they involve the two farmers' unions and the Forest Owners' Federation.

2.2.6 Additional remarks and issues related to Allemannsretten

Allemannsretten has just as strong a position today as it had earlier. During the 1990s some stakeholders claimed that there was a need for stronger regulation of the use and siting of camper-vans and caravans, but such provision was not included in the 1996 amendment of the Outdoor Recreation Act.

More administrative responsibility and regulatory power has been given to the municipality level in the 1996 revisions. According to these amendments to the Act, those landowners that want to charge a fee to allow access to a facilitated recreational area must have permission from the municipality. The municipalities can now decide on rules for the public's use and behaviour at any type of recreational area, even on state land.

2.3 *Friluftsliv* – outdoor recreation in Norway

Outdoor recreation – *Friluftsliv* – is very much a part of the Norwegian cultural heritage. *Allemannsretten* is looked upon as the most basic premise for *Friluftsliv*. Between 80 and 90 per cent of the Norwegian population participate in different kinds of outdoor sports or recreation. Short trips on foot in those areas (forests, parks, and small roads) neighbouring where people live are the most frequent activity. Hiking in the mountains, biking and downhill skiing are the activities that are increasing most strongly. Most exercise of *Friluftsliv* is non-commercial, in the sense that very few Norwegians participate in any guided trips or other formally organised activities in the outdoors.

Friluftsliv (in Norway) is usually looked upon as two different traditions: the rural tradition based on necessary activities, mostly related to human survival such as fishing, hunting and berry picking, and the urban tradition with more non-utilitarian but appreciative activities like hiking, skiing, swimming and sunbathing. However, today the harvest activities are naturally not relevant only for the rural population, and the urban tradition has for many decades also been a part of the rural recreational pattern. There is also a long-standing egalitarian tradition in Norway towards hunting and salmon fishing policy. The price of a hunting licence or fishing licence should not be so great that only the landowners themselves and rich people can participate. If they are interested and have the skills, anyone should also have the opportunity to go hunting or fishing.

The historical background for the urban *Friluftsliv* tradition goes back to the 18th and 19th centuries. There are several factors involved; some of them are similar for the whole of western Europe, others are more uniquely Norwegian. One factor is the general industrialisation and urbanisation of the society. Fridtjof Nansen later said that *Friluftsliv* (meaning a rich life with simple means in free nature) was one of the important elements in re-humanising this sick society. The coincidental timing of national romanticism, the development of an interest in the natural sciences and early tourism, allured artists, scientists and a foreign elite to the Norwegian fjords and up into the spectacular mountains. They 'discovered' Norway and they appreciated it. In addition Norway was liberated from Denmark, and the Norwegians had a great need to discover or develop something uniquely Norwegian – a national identity. The 'genuine and unspoilt' mountain farmer became the image of the real Norwegian and the mountain area was the real Norway – far away from urban and continental influences and very unlike Denmark (Christensen, 1993; Breivik, 1978). The mountains still have a special position for Norwegians. *Friluftsliv* in the mountains is one aspect of this appreciation, another (which is connected to *Friluftsliv*) is the amount of private cabins that are being built every year in the mountain areas.

Outdoor recreation is popular in Norway. The patterns of participation are quite stable, but there are some trends in how the countryside is being used for recreation, probably similar to those in other western countries. Some activities have increased in popularity through the 1970s and 1980s, especially hiking and skiing in the mountains, hiking in the forests and countryside, running and jogging in the countryside, and downhill skiing. Cycling is the only activity that has increased in popularity during the 1990s, while other activities are quite stable, such as hunting and skiing. Fishing seemed to decrease in the early 1980s, but during the last few years it has increased again. Picking berries is less popular now than it was in the 1970s (Vorkinn *et al.*, 1997).

Only 5 to 8 per cent of the adult population is engaged in hunting or salmon fishing, whereas other kinds of fishing are more popular. The last national study on *Friluftsliv* in the adult population (aged 16–79 years) (Vorkinn, *et al.*, 1997) found that 27 per cent of the population practised inland fishing, whereas 43 per cent fish in the sea. Berry picking has decreased, but still 41 per cent of respondents said that they had picked berries once or more during the preceding year.

The most popular activities are short walks close to home (91 per cent), but these are not to be interpreted as if they all were located in the countryside; many of them are along roads and in towns. Both sunbathing and swimming are very popular (79 and 64 per cent respectively). The figures for other types of outdoor recreation activities are listed in Table 2.1.

Table 2.1. Some countryside activities derived from Vorkinn *et al.* (1997). The activities of fishing, berry picking, taking short walks from home, sunbathing and swimming are discussed in the text.

Percentage of the population	Activity	Average no. of trips per year
63	One or more recreational trips (walked less than 3 hours) in the forests during the last year	26
48	Walking in the summertime (for less than 3 hours) in the mountains	11
42	Cycling in the countryside	22
39	Walking in the summertime (for more than 3 hours) in the mountains	8
35	One or more recreational trips (walked for more than 3 hours) in the forests	17
35	Jogging or running in the countryside	33

In a national study in 1999 (Statistics Norway, 2000) the respondents were asked about the length of their longest walk during the last year. It is interesting to note that 23 per cent had walked less than 5 km, 22 per cent between 5 and 9 km, 32 per cent between 10 and 19 km, and 24 per cent had walked more than 20 km.

A new study indicates that norms concerning *Friluftsliv* might be changing, especially among the young people. The support for official goals concerning *Friluftsliv* (to maintain and encourage traditional *Friluftsliv* in an environmentally sustainable way based on *Allemannsretten*) seems to be decreasing. The new tendency is to favour more specialised, action-like and resource demanding activities like mountain biking, downhill skiing, rafting and even motorised activities (Vorkinn *et al.*, 2000).

2.4 Conflicts and threats

Open conflicts between landowners and the public because of *Allemannsretten* are quite rare. Pressure along the coast is increasing, because the same areas are popular both for private huts or houses, and for public use for picnicking, bathing, walking, boating, etc. This year the Directorate for Nature Management has offered legal support and advice to several municipalities along the coast in order to support public access to the coastline. On the other hand, the central authorities are also discussing how to stop the comprehensive use of dispensations in some municipalities from the building restrictions in the 100 m belt along the coastal edge.

Much attention has been given to a 1998 decision in the Supreme Court about access at the coast. The owner of a beach property (1.3 ha, and with a house 65 m from the sea) had to remove a fence to let the public walk over the property along the shore, because it qualified as *utmark* (uncultivated land). The fence had only had one function and that was to keep the public out; in other words it was an illegal fence. The Norwegian Government has now proposed that there should be a 25 m zone along the coastal edge with open access for the public, if the area can be categorised as *utmark* and the distance from private houses or huts is sufficient such that public use does not interfere with the need for privacy.

One third of Norwegian households own a summer house or a cabin for recreational use. Even 40 per cent of those who do not own a cabin have the opportunity to use one. There are 350,000 cabins and summer houses in Norway (Statistics Norway, 2000). Around 3,000 new cabins are being built every year – an increase close to 40 per cent compared with the early 1980s.

The largest number of huts is in the mountains and inland areas and this is also where most of the new cabins are being built. There is an on-going debate about fences around the huts in the mountain areas. While their purpose is mainly to keep grazing sheep away from the hut, fencing has led to a growing conflict with the public recreational interests, in addition to conflict with those holding legal grazing rights. New cabins are usually planned and built as cabin estates. In some existing cabin estates with an open structure and big cabin sites, there are condensation plans: new cabins are being planned in-between the existing ones. There are often good environmental reasons for this, but there is fear of an increasing conflict between new and old cabin owners and with other kinds of visitors to the mountains. The new cabin estates, or 'hut villages', are often located in or near to popular hiking and skiing areas. Good planning is needed to avoid both access problems and reduced aesthetical and social quality for the different user groups.

The management of one of Norway's most popular tourist attractions, the North Cape, has also challenged *Allemannsretten*. A private company owns the North Cape plateau and has also developed a tourist centre, restaurant, etc., under ground. However, the same company requires a fee of around 150 kr on entry to the North Cape plateau by car, irrespective of whether or not the visitor wants to use the tourist centre. This entrance fee appears to be in conflict with the Outdoor Recreation Act, and the environmental and recreational organisations have been fighting it for several years. They argue that the company can charge for parking and for entering the centre, but not for entering the plateau and taking a walk.

Another example of conflict arose when the owner of a hotel wanted people to pay for the use of the ski tracks he had prepared. This was strongly resisted by the local people because they had used the ski tracks for decades, with or without special preparation. This conflict did not really develop into a court case because the local arguments were accepted. In many municipalities there is a system of voluntary economic support for the preparation of ski tracks.

This kind of conflict is typical of the potential conflicts between farmers and recreational interests. Today there is an urgent need by farmers and landowners, in a situation of fierce international competition, to find alternative incomes to traditional farming (food and fibre production). The farmers and their organisations, and even the politicians, are now looking at the opportunities on uncultivated land, and the possibilities of making an income from tourism and recreational services. In a commercial sense, a conflict arises because both access to nature and enjoyment of nature are free and protected by law. Therefore, some people look upon *Allemannsretten* as a hindrance to making money from nature-based tourism. There is, however, a legal possibility of charging a fee for the use of facilities or services provided, but the scale of the fee must be in accordance with the provision.

In modern society there is probably an ongoing change in people's attitudes and feelings towards nature and the countryside. Urbanisation increases the physical (and possibly perceptual) distance between people and nature, reduces people's knowledge about nature, and often induces a more romantic view of the countryside. Urbanisation, combined with difficult economic times in farming, can induce new conflicts between the urban and rural populations concerning how the forests and mountains ought to be used and managed. These can be expressed in different views about motorised traffic and attitudes to noise and quietness; in different perspectives about whether the forests and mountains are primarily agricultural landscapes (for production) or aesthetic landscapes (for recreation); and in different views about conservation issues, for example on how to manage the big predators such as wolf (*Canis lupus*) , bear (*Ursus arctos*), wolverine (*Gulo gulo*) and lynx (*Lynx lynx*).

2.5 Concluding remarks

Allemannsretten, the public right of access, is not a right that only applies to *Friluftsliv*, outdoor recreation. The purpose for the access is irrelevant, as long as the person behaves according to the rules. But different kinds of *Friluftsliv* are obviously the most important motive when the public spend time in the countryside and the wildland. The statistics indicate that participation in *Friluftsliv* is high and quite stable, but new types of activities arise. Despite the fact that mountains have a specially attractive position, the majority of *Friluftsliv* is taking place quite near people's homes; in other words, in and around the highly populated areas. The result is a geographical concentration of the recreational activity, combined with a broader spectrum of physical activities.

My forecast is of a situation with more internal conflicts in the '*Friluftsliv* family'. Several activities can be accepted according *Allemannsretten*, but there might still be social conflicts between different kinds of activities, for instance between family walking and high speed cycling along the same paths. In Norway there is as yet very limited experience in handling such conflicts. With some exceptions the *Friluftsliv* policy in Norway can be summed up like this: Norway has a small population with a strong and living *Friluftsliv* tradition, in a big country with a long coastline, and with lots of forests and mountains, and Norwegians have free access to the countryside. In other words, there is room for any legal, recreational activity. The need for a special *Friluftsliv* plan has been limited, except the need to protect the collective *Friluftsliv* interests in areas with other strong exploitational interests (the coastline from Sweden to the Kristiansand area, and the forests and countryside around the biggest cities, are examples). A relevant question today is whether *Allemannsretten* can be a hindrance in trying to handle social conflicts between different legal recreational activities.

References

Breivik. G. (1978). To Tradisjoner i Norsk Friluftsliv [Two Traditions in Norwegian *Friluftsliv*]. In *Friluftsliv. Fra Fridtjof Nansen til våre dager [Friluftsliv. From Fridtjof Nansen until today]*, ed. by G. Breivik and H. Løvmo. Universitetsforlaget, Oslo. pp. 7-16.

Christensen, O. (1993). *Skiidrett før Sondre. Vinterveien til et Nasjonalt Selvbilde.* [Skiing before Sondre Norheim. The Winter Road to a National Self-image]. Ad Notam Gyldendal, Oslo.

Directorate for Nature Management (1996). *Right of Access – from the Sea to the Sky: an Information Brochure.* Directorate for Nature Management, Trondheim.

Hammitt, W.E. and Cole, D.N. (1998). *Wildland Recreation: Ecology and Management, 2nd edition.* Wiley, Chichester.

Liddle, M. (1997). *Recreation Ecology: the Ecological Impact of Outdoor Recreation and Ecotourism.* Chapman and Hall, London.

Ministry of Environment (1985). *The Open-Air Recreation Act* [*an English translation and explanation of The Outdoor Recreation Act – 'Lov om friluftslivet*]. Ministry of Environment, Oslo.

Peter Scott Planning Services (1998). Access to the Countryside in Selected European Countries: a Review of Access Rights, Legislation and Associated Arrangements in Denmark, Germany, Norway and Sweden. *Scottish Natural Heritage Review* No. 110.

Statistics Norway (2000). *Statistical Yearbook.* Statistics Norway (Statistisk Sentralbyrå), Oslo.

Vorkinn, M., Aas, Ø. and Kleiven, J. (1997). Friluftslivutøvelse blant den voksne befolkningen – utviklingstrekk og status i 1996. [Participation in outdoor recreation activities in the adult population – tendencies and status in 1996]. *Eastern Norway Research Institute, Lillehammer, ØF-report 07.*

Vorkinn, M., Vittersø, J. and Riese, H. (2000). Norsk friluftsliv – på randen av modernisering. [Norwegian *Friluftsliv* – on the edge of modernisation]. *Eastern Norway Research Institute, Lillehammer, ØF-report* 02.

3 How Do People Enjoy the Natural Heritage? Patterns, Trends and Predictions of Recreation in the Scottish Countryside

Jo Hunt

Summary

1.   There is no consistent and long running measure of recreation in the Scottish countryside. This review draws evidence from a wide range of sources in order to build a picture of activity over the past 15 years.

2.   Countryside recreation is characterised in four ways: numbers of people participating, the range and popularity of activities followed, the profile of active participants (and, by inference, those who are not), and satisfaction levels with available access, recreation provision and personal enjoyment.

3.   It is anticipated that new rights of access will lead to changes in demand, including both the release of latent demand and the continuation of current trends of rising participation. However, it is likely that any 'access dividend' will be predominately enjoyed by those who are already taking part.

4.   Walking is the most popular and fastest growing form of countryside recreation, and opportunities exist to enhance its availability. Increased participation may arise from wider access rights and good access facilities, but individuals' awareness, leisure time, transport and income will also need to be considered if the natural heritage is to be enjoyed by a wider cross section of Scottish society.

5.   There will also be a need to measure the changes in countryside recreation, and the profile of those taking part, as new rights and provision are extended.

3.1 Introduction

In a very urbanised society, with relatively easy access to varied farmland, woodland, lochs, coast and mountains, access to the countryside is one of the main forms for informal recreation in Scotland. The countryside can be viewed as an antidote to the pressures of indoor work, as a place to pursue a hobby or sport, or as somewhere to do very little, slowly. Rights of access enable people to enjoy a more natural heritage, in what is often, for them, an unusual environment. New rights of access, whether confirming or extending the extent of land in the countryside over which we all may traverse, will offer the opportunity for increased access, potentially enabling a greater number of people to pursue a more diverse range of activities in the location of their choice. However, whilst new rights will undoubtedly enable greater access, will new access legislation release a currently unfulfilled and latent demand and lead to greater access participation?

   This chapter examines the take-up of informal outdoor recreation over the past 15 years, using four broad indicators, namely participation (how many participate?), activity (what do they do?), profile (who are they?) and satisfaction (will they be back?). The patterns and trends for each indicator are reviewed in the light of their potential impact on the take-up of access. In particular, four topics are addressed.

- Will the numbers of people accessing the countryside increase (latent demand)?
- Are the range and types of activity changing (long-term trends)?
- What are the costs and benefits of new access (is access highly valued)?
- Will the same people or will new participants join in (who gains)?

These questions are examined using data gathered across a range of sources, from national surveys of leisure, sport and tourism activity between 1987 and 1998, to the specific views of walkers, cyclists and horse riders; and from the experience of visitors to a national trail, a community path network and a popular mountain area, all in Scotland. The focus is on informal countryside recreation in predominately rural areas, often enjoyed by people from urban areas. The chapter does not look at private or paying countryside pursuits, nor the use of urban greenspaces for outdoor recreation.

The limitations of the information are threefold. First, the relatively small sample sizes of the various monitors of leisure activity, of between 1,500-2,000 respondents per survey, scaled-up to represent the population, have confidence limits of around 3 per cent variation (Greene, 1996). Using a range of indicators may help corroborate the significance of trends.

Secondly, recreation is a very individual and personal, almost private, activity. During my own leisure time in the past 20 years I must have been counted many times by people-counting machines, and answered more than a handful of visitor questionnaires, but those data only represent a tiny portion of my participation. I can recall both a very damp form in 1981, in which I detailed my spending on food whilst walking the West Highland Way, and over the winter of 1997/1998 I patiently completed five, 22-page questionnaires on mountain activities in the Cairngorms. But these forms did not ask about the solid week of rain and my companion's departure on day two; nor did they ask about a display of sea-green and magenta northern lights, viewed from the entrance of a snow-hole. It may be crudely possible to estimate levels of activity, but this does not even start to account for the experiences.

It is also very difficult to predict the likely impacts of the new access legislation on countryside leisure demand in Scotland. Looking to the future, there has been no specific research on the potential uptake and patterns of recreation in the countryside resulting from new rights of access in Scotland, although this has been researched in relation to open spaces access in England and Wales. Whilst the new bill can potentially create greater opportunity and a larger available resource, it may or may not result in greater use and activity. The take-up, quality and experience of access also depends on many factors from income and transport to fitness and household size. We cannot legislate to create inherently good or inherently bad access experiences.

3.2 Recreation indicators

3.2.1 Participation

Participation, the number and pattern of people accessing their natural heritage, is most commonly measured using one of three different techniques. First, there are population studies, interviewing a representative sample of people, who may or may not have taken part, by questionnaire and extrapolating behaviour to the whole population. Second, there are selective studies, which do the same, but focus on people in a selected area or interest group. Finally, people counting, manually or more usually using concealed machines, records numbers on the ground.

Day visits between 1987 and 1998 show the very high volume of recreational participation, in trips from home lasting more than three hours (Centre for Leisure Research, 1985, 1996, 1997, 1999; System Three, 1988, 1989, 1990, 1991, 1992a, 1992b). During a typical four week period most Scots currently enjoy 3.5 day visits. This has increased steadily from 2.5 day visits, 10 years ago, but has levelled in the past four years. As recently as 1973, the day visit was a rare treat, with considerably less participation, focused on stays away from home.

Visits to urban facilities are most frequent, including cinemas, art galleries, shopping and visiting friends. Countryside and seaside visits combined account for around one-third of all day outings, 140 million day visits out of a total of 420 million in Scotland each year (Figures 3.1 and 3.2). The level of countryside and seaside visits is roughly equivalent to the combined visits to all built facilities for sport, culture and amusement, about the same as the total for visits to family and friends, and for recreational shopping.

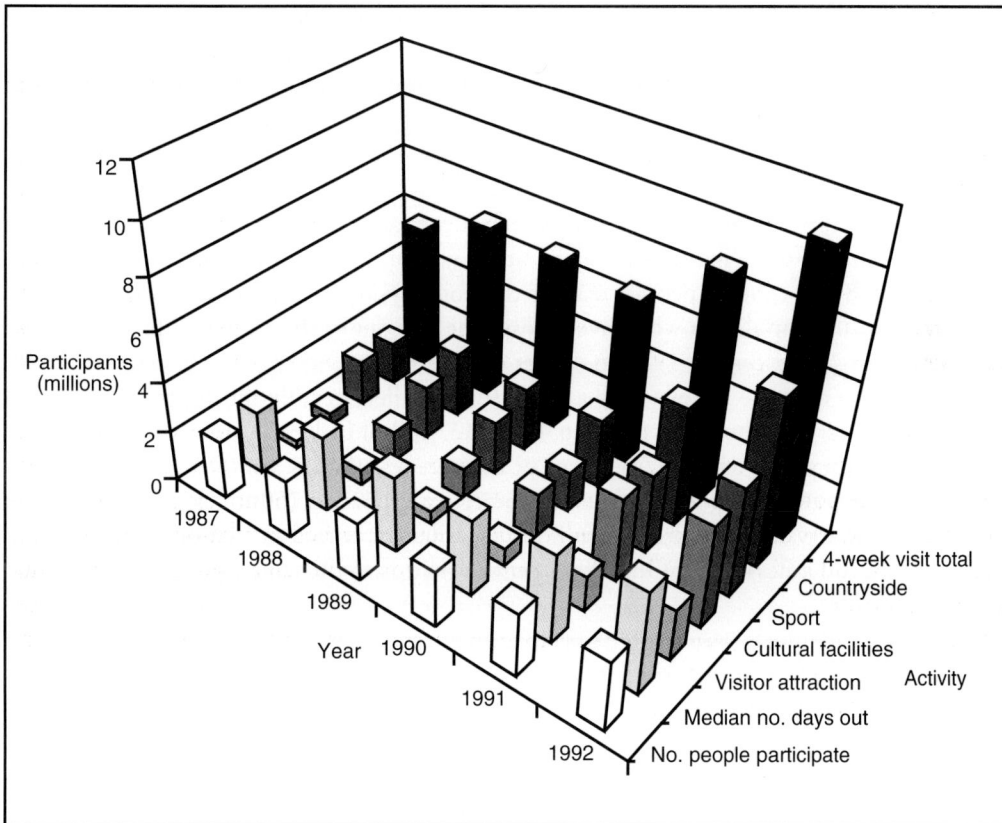

Figure 3.1. Scottish day visits from 1987 to 1992. The columns show four-weekly participation totals.

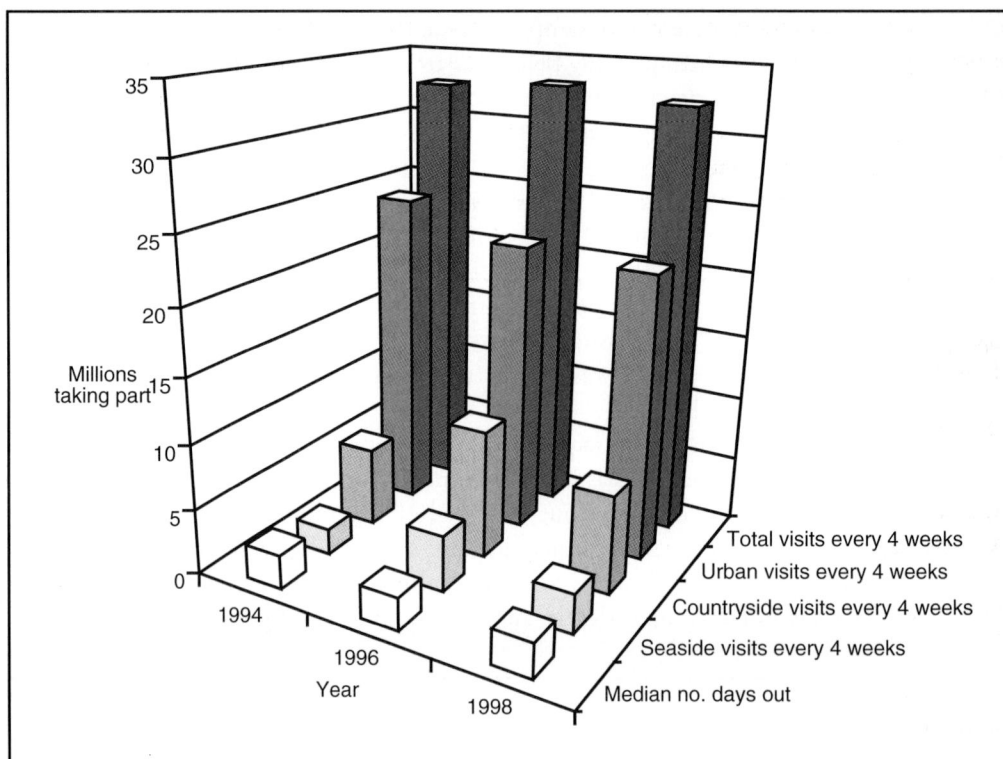

Figure 3.2. Scottish day visits from 1994 to 1998. The columns show four-weekly participation totals.

Of these sectors, countryside visits have seen the greatest increase over the past 10 years, with a doubling of participation, sustained at an annual growth rate of around 8 per cent, with about 68 per cent of people visiting the countryside at least once in a year. The proportion of the population who have at least one day out in the countryside each month has risen from 25 per cent in 1987 to 40 per cent in 1998.

The average distance travelled for a day visit has fallen steadily during this time, from 61 km (38 miles) from home in 1987, to 43 km (27 miles) in 1998. However, this is more marked in urban visits, where 57 per cent of trips are less than 8 km (5 miles) from home and only 12 per cent to another urban area more than 100 km (60 miles) away. Only 31 per cent of countryside visits are within 8 km (5 miles) of home, and 26 per cent are more than 100 km (60 miles) away. Only 2 per cent of visitors to the countryside travel there on public transport.

Looking at temporal patterns of participation at several different, managed countryside access areas, there are strong similarities at a range of sites. There are more visitors in summer months, mostly at weekends and at predictable time peaks during the day. Participation in mountain areas is concentrated into a shorter visitor season (Hunt and Dearden, 1996), with stronger weekly and diurnal peaks. This would be expected in areas which are further away from urban centres, have more extreme climatic variation, and involve longer, active days (Table 3.1). In contrast, country parks (Duffield and Long, 1977) and community path networks (MacPherson, 1999), which are closer to home, more hospitable all year, and offer facilities for shorter activity periods, have a more even spread of participation over the year, but are still strongly peaked for certain times and days (Table 3.1).

Table3.1. Seasonal and daily timing of participation at selected outdoor recreation sites.

	Community path network	National Trail	Mountain area
Season (percentage of year's visits)			
Spring	13	47	42
Summer	34	34	46
Autumn	38	11	4
Winter	15	7	8
Day			
Weekday	29	19	37
Weekend day	71	81	63
Duration (percentage of all visits)			
under 2 hours	78	6	18
2-4 hours	18	24	11
over 4 hours	4	39	70
multi-day	0	31	1
Peak use time (24 hour clock)	16.00	11.00	10.00
Total annual use			
No. of users	35,000	23,000	125,000
No. of visits	120,000	105,000	560,000
Change over 2 years (per cent)	+ 61	- 19	+ 9

This diurnal and seasonal pattern has implications for the capacity of any particular site to receive or accommodate a large number of visitors (Barrow, 1976). The comparable level of visits to a single short walk adjacent to the A9 trunk road, at The Hermitage (National Trust for Scotland, 2000), with the total annual use of a 50 km (30 mile) path network around nearby Dunkeld (Ekos Economic Consultants, 1998), indicates that location is paramount. The physical limitations, such as car parking, restrict gross participation levels more than the extent of the access area itself. The similar orders of magnitude of use in the different areas shows that countryside access is widespread and that differing market segments exist. However, the total levels of use probably say more about what we think is a manageable access unit, be it dispersed or highly concentrated, than the relative popularity of one type of facility over another.

There will, of course, be impacts arising from increasing concentration and use. The potential for damage to the site, pressure on other uses of the land, impairment of enjoyment of users, and the resource consumption to fuel the activity, will all increase. However, the scope to absorb greater numbers of people participating in informal recreation in the countryside is still open to major expansion, but physical saturation, on the vast majority of sites, is unlikely. The balance to be struck between the desirable level of participation and the acceptable level of impact is more likely to limit capacity, as will the available level of management intervention both to support the participation and to manage the balance.

3.2.2 Activity

The large and increasing number of participants is spread across a diverse range of activities, from walking, cycling and sailing to telemark skiing, kite flying and Tai Chi. Only the major and generalised activities are monitored. There is much specialisation within each activity and there is scope for a wide range of conduct within each group. After a static and slowly declining period of activity in the late 1980s, there has been a long term increase in activity of visitors to the countryside during the 1990s, with a growth rate of 2 to 3 per cent each year in most activities.

The three most popular main activities in the natural heritage, pursued by between 25 per cent and 35 per cent of visitors for each activity, are short walks, longer walks and driving or sightseeing (Figures 3.3 and 3.4). The levels of cycling, heritage centre visits and outdoor sports are similar at about 5 per cent. Cycling (7 per cent), mountaineering (2 per cent) and horse riding (1 per cent), all have an increasing participation, but their segment of the market remains fairly constant. Fifty-five per cent of Scots have been for a walk in

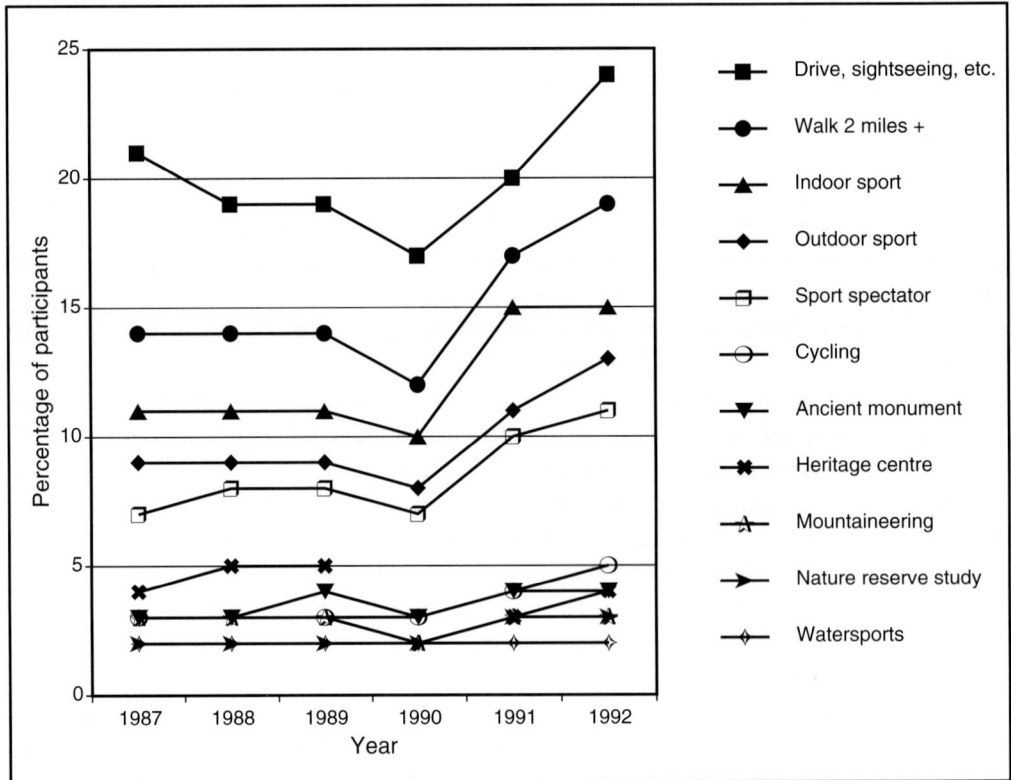

Figure 3.3. The range of recreational activities in Scotland during day visits, 1987-1992.

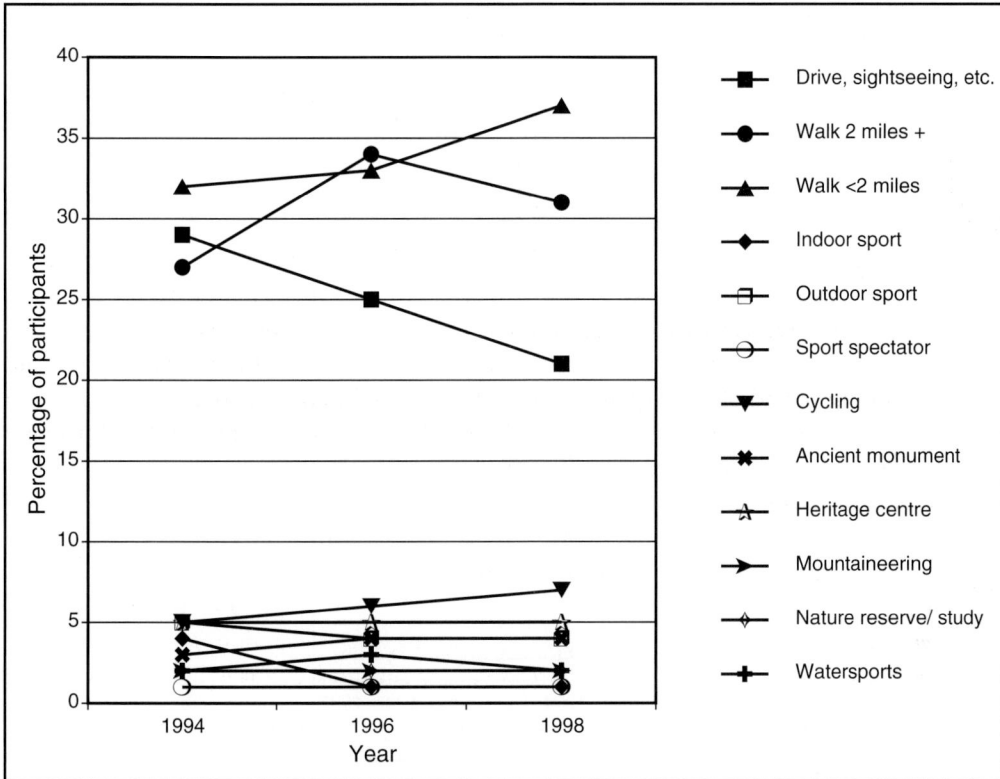

Figure 3.4. The range of recreational activities in Scotland during day visits, 1994-1998.

the countryside in the past year, 52 per cent of households own a bicycle, 4 per cent have been on a horse and 3 per cent in a boat. Self-propelled countryside activities are the most popular forms of recreation, coming behind watching television in popularity, and are all more popular than cultural activities outside the home.

More passive sightseeing and drive-only excursions are declining markedly (Scottish Tourist Board, internal reports). This may be due to increased fuel costs, but also represents overall higher physical activity levels as people still drive and enjoy the view, but also walk some of the time, and join in other activities. Overall, the relative popularity of different pursuits changes little as numbers of visitors increase.

Sports activities show very similar patterns. After declines in the 1980s, sports activity has shown continuous growth throughout the 1990s (Coalter, 1998). During the two most popular months of each year, 28 per cent of people go for a long walk and 23 per cent for a swim. The numbers walking are increasing by 4 per cent and swimming by 2 per cent, each year. Cycling has a popularity similar to football, with 10 per cent active each month. Mountaineering is steady at 5 per cent as is horse riding at 1 per cent of population. Sports activity corroborates day visit surveys, and also shows that informal, individual and non-competitive 'sport' is enjoyed by the majority of the population, whilst organised, team, competitive sports are pursued by a minority, after schooling has ended. A greater number of people watch competitive sport than take part (Figure 3.5).

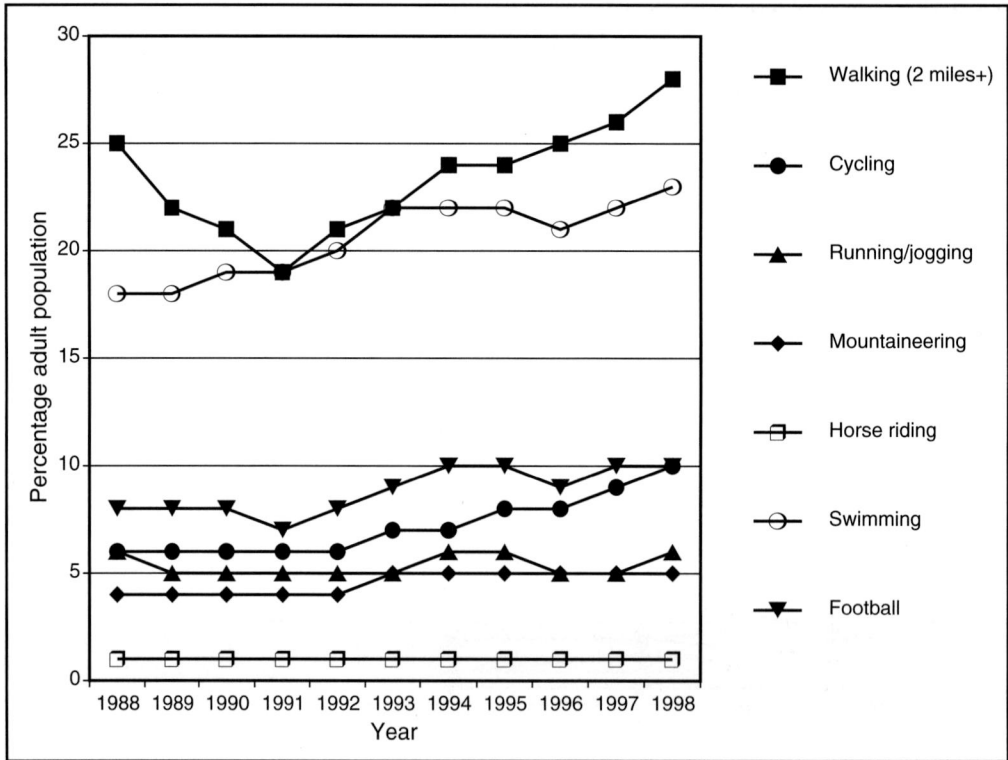

Figure 3.5. Three year running averages of the activities for Scottish sports participants, 1987-1999.

Tourist visits in the countryside are a smaller, but significant, component of total activity. In 1998, 6.7 million holidaymakers each spent an average of 4.5 nights on holiday. Of the 30 million tourist nights, 4.8 million were following natural heritage related special interest holidays, particularly going walking, mountaineering, sailing and visiting heritage sites (Figure 3.6). About 500,000 walkers and mountaineers spent over 2 million days on active holidays. This is a very important niche market, often concentrated in areas that are both economically and environmentally fragile (Jones Economic Consultants, 1996). Activity holidays represent about 5 per cent of all countryside participation.

Looking at all holidays, activities based on the natural heritage form a part of two-thirds of all holidays. The levels of interest in visiting heritage sites and in going for a walk are both around 20 per cent, swimming 13 per cent, though swimming in the sea is less popular in the UK than in other European countries. Golf, nature study, watersports and cycling all attract around 3 to 4 per cent each. Twenty million holiday days are spent outdoors, representing one-fifth of domestic participation. Six million days are spent walking whilst away on holiday; this represents one-eighth of all walks in Scotland. Evidence also points to outdoor activity and special interest markets showing more resilient demand, as overall tourism numbers wane.

Looking beyond the general groupings by mode of activity, the range and take-up of activities varies greatly between different access areas (Table 3.2). Whilst it is to be expected

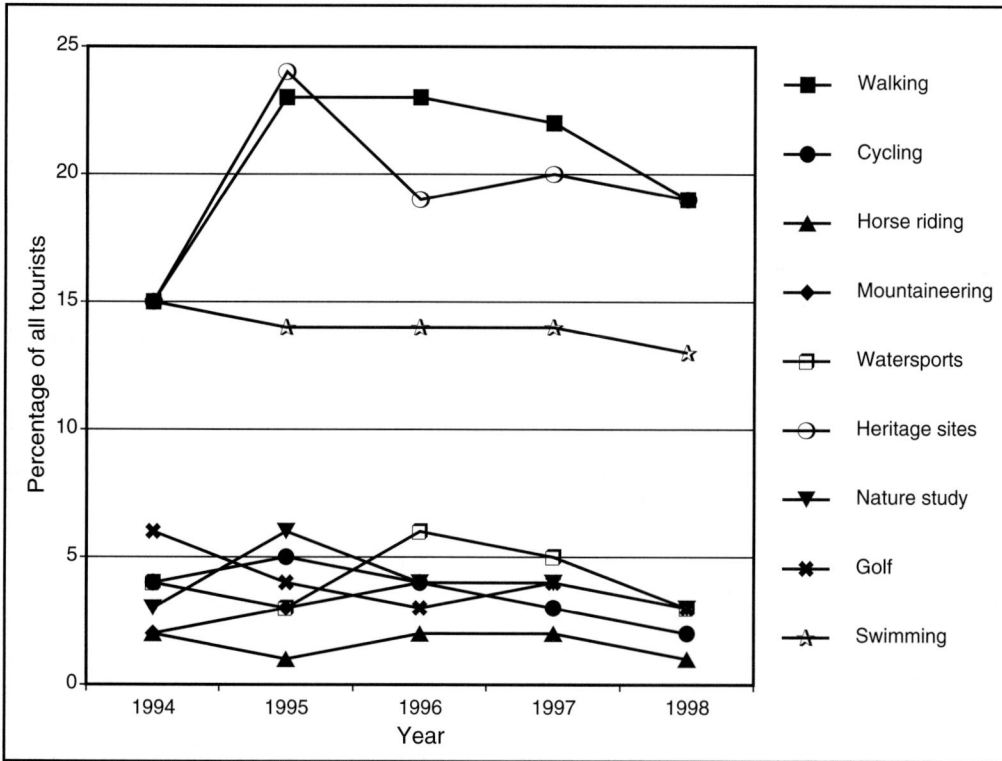

Figure 3.6. Annual participation of tourists in Scotland, 1994-1998.

to find multi-day walks on the West Highland Way, summit ascents in the Cairngorms and off-road cycling around Dunkeld, there are also strong overlaps with a surprisingly large number of hill summits that can be reached around Dunkeld, and many short glen walks in the Cairngorms. This may offer opportunities to re-direct activities between areas to balance use, although allegiance to local and favourite areas is strong. Participation substitution may also take place, with one developed and promoted area only attracting use at the expense of other areas or activities (Argyll Associates, 1993). Strategic development and marketing are needed at both a local and a national level.

Table 3.2 Activities pursued at selected outdoor recreation sites.

Ranked activities		*Area*	
	Community path network	*National Trail*	*Mountain area*
First	Short/family walk	Whole day walk	Walk to summit
Second	Walking the dog	Walk in stages	Long walk in glens
Third	Long/hill walk	Part day walk	Short walk in glens
Fourth	Cycling	Whole route walk	Winter climbing
Fifth	Bird watching	Several-day walk	Mountain biking
Sixth	Picnic	Cycle	Rock climbing

3.2.3 Profile

Enjoying the outdoors is not evenly distributed across all sectors of the Scottish population. This can be seen to some extent by comparing the profile of access groups, their location, gender, age and social class make-up (Figure 3.7). Surprisingly, there is little data at a population level on ability, income and ethnicity profiles.

There are broadly equal numbers of men and women who walk in the countryside (System Three, 1996). Men are, however, strongly over represented in mountaineering and cycling. Most participation in activities by gender is within 10 per cent of the population balance. The exceptions are the 85 per cent of horse riders who are women, also correlated to high income (System Three, 1999). By contrast, 90 per cent of football players are men, the majority of whom are under 24 (Coalter, 1998).

Age information is only collected in questionnaire based surveys. Both walking outdoors and swimming indoors have age distributions close to the population, though these tend to attract fewer under 24s and over 55s, but more in middle years. This pattern is exaggerated and skewed to younger people in both cycling and mountaineering. Visiting the natural heritage is more evenly spread across all ages than most sports and cultural activities. The frequency of participation is more telling: the younger you are the more frequently you will go walking, and this is repeated for most other pursuits (Figure 3.7).

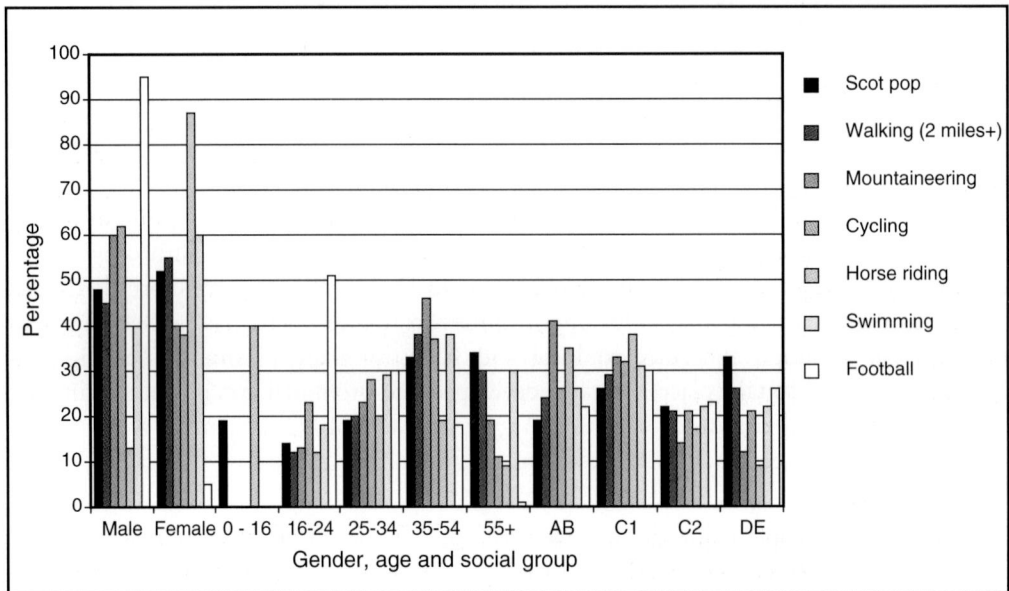

Figure 3.7. Profile of activity in Scotland, 1999, related to gender, age and social group.

This is even more apparent among young people (Figure 3.8). In a typical four week period, over half of all under 18s will go swimming, over one-third will go running and three-quarters of boys play football. Only one-quarter will go for a long walk, compared with a population average of 55 per cent. This, in part, reflects school-organised games, as well as safer and group activities close to home. More monitoring of youth participation is required to understand if they will become the next cohorts of walkers.

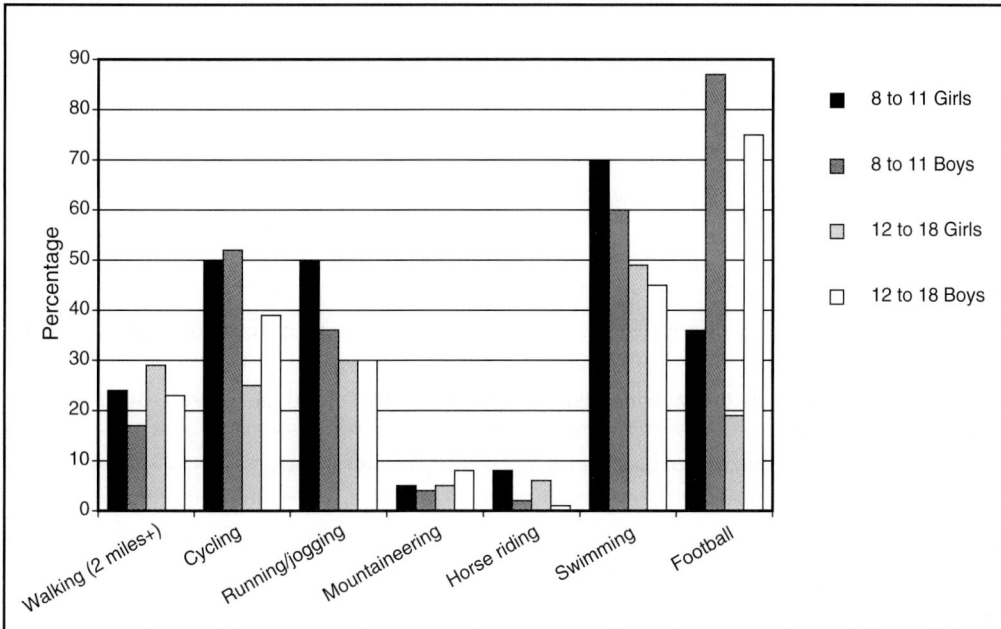

Figure 3.8. Sports activities for young people, 1996-1998.

Similarly, the higher your occupation and income status, the more frequently you will take part in sport. It is not surprising that advertising frequently uses images of outdoor activities to sell to young people with high disposable income. The skewed distribution is more pronounced for social class than for age: the minority pastimes of mountaineering and horse riding are followed by professionals (Figure 3.7). The majority activities of walking and swimming by managerial and skilled-manual workers.

Broader appeal and more informal pastimes are very much more likely to be taken up casually. Club membership is only 1 per cent for walkers, 3 per cent for cyclists and 12 per cent for mountaineers; this compares with at least 35 per cent for football and other more organised sport. The ability to use club networks to influence peer behaviour and 'good practice' is clearly much weaker among the large participation activities.

3.2.4 Satisfaction

Do all of these people enjoy the natural heritage? The levels of satisfaction with current provision are extremely high (ASH Partnership, 1985, 1987; Forgewood Market Research, 1995; Inglis, 2000; Mather, 1998, 2000). In most site surveys users rate their visit as 75 to 90 per cent enjoyable or very enjoyable; 10 to 20 per cent quite or not very enjoyable, and only 2 to 4 per cent have not had a good experience (Table 3.3). These satisfaction ratings are very high in comparison with visitor attractions and cultural facilities (Scottish Enterprise, 1999). However, the latter are often paying for provision whereas outdoor provision is free at the point of use. Repeat visitors account for 80 to 90 per cent of visitors to most access areas.

There are detractors and barriers to access, both real and perceived, and these can be grouped by where the barrier lies (Table 3.4). Some are 'personal', including ability and mobility, skills, affordability and fitness; some 'behavioural', including fear (of others),

Table 3.3. Satisfaction rating (percentage) for outdoor recreation activities at selected sites.

Satisfaction rating	Area		
	Community path network	*National Trail*	*Mountain area*
Enjoyable	85	89	75
Quite enjoyable	13	8	22
Not enjoyable	2	2	4

speeding traffic, impacts of other activities in the area, and confrontation; whereas others are 'physical', about location, quality of provision and environmental factors. The concerns that detract most are predominately personal, whereas the behaviour and conduct of others is significant, and physical provision is only a minor impediment.

The enablers and improvements, that are sought to gain more and better access, can be similarly grouped (Table 3.4). 'Physical' changes to signs, surfaces, facilities and information are important; as are 'behavioural' changes through involvement and facilities to modify others' behaviour; and changes to 'personal' circumstances, particularly available time and income, are included.

Table 3.4. Detractors and barriers, and enablers and improvements, to recreational enjoyment, by activity and selected sites. Listed in descending order of importance to visitors.

Walking	Cycling	Horse riding	Community path network	National Trail	Mountain area
Detractors and barriers					
Fear of attack	Traffic safety	Not interested	Too far from home	Muddy path	Low flying aircraft
Fear of an accident	Not fit enough	Fast traffic	Do not know about it	Rough path	Cyclists on paths
Personal disability	No cycle routes	Too expensive	Wet and muddy	Eroded path	Poor weather
Might get lost	Poor surfaces	Not available	Speeding cyclists	Inadequate signs	Eroded paths
Do not like walking	Cannot afford a bike	Too busy	Not interested	Fallen trees	Competitive events and sponsored walks
Might meet owners who object	Too busy	Locked gates	Dog mess	Midges	
Enablers and improvements					
More signposts	More cycle routes	Lower cost	More seats	More information	Advice on deer and access
Better surfaces	Better surfaces	More time to ride	More toilets	More signs	Manage eroded paths
All ability provision	Better weather	Better tracks	More litter bins	Path improvements	Advice on minimal impact
Public transport	Cycle lanes on roads	More access to local routes	More shelters	Improved or more visitor services	Remove vehicle tracks
Involve community	Signing and information		More signs	Completion certificate	Repair damaged ground
Good behaviour	More time to cycle				Discourage bikes on tracks

It is evident that different types of survey tend to lean toward questioning that elicits certain types of response. The walking responses are very personal, being derived from a population study conducted in people's homes. Outdoor questioning on a path network brought responses about the physical structures for access.

The most frequent solutions suggested by users are generally associated with better physical provision, with only minor calls for more social solutions. This could be interpreted as reinforcing the demand for more and better provision, which is the current emphasis of management. It could also reveal that physical solutions provide more for existing beneficiaries and fail to address the underlying personal barriers to access to the natural heritage, such as time, cost (indirect), ability and confidence.

3.3 Future patterns of countryside recreation

3.3.1 Latent demand

'Would you spend more time in the natural heritage if you were able to? Do you want to access it closer to home? Are you sure of your right to be there?'. There has been no direct research to measure unrealised demand for access, or the likely demand effects of the forthcoming legislation. It is very difficult to measure. Several studies in different activity groups have found high levels of latent demand, with 30 to 50 per cent of current participants wanting to do more, in different places, and to try other activities.

Recent research in England and Wales has looked at the likely influence on patterns of use arising from a statutory right of access, for open air recreation on foot, to mountain, moor, heathland, downland and commons (Le Mesurier, 2000). This research also extended to the support and demand for similar access to forest and woodland, to rivers and waterside, and to cliffs and foreshore.

Le Mesurier (2000) found that 30 per cent of respondents already felt able to go where they wished, whereas 60 per cent felt that their access was restricted and 10 per cent felt that access was not available to them. Only one in five interviewed realised correctly that they have access only along Rights of Way, even on unenclosed ground. In support of extended rights of access, 85 per cent supported a right to walk in open spaces, 65 per cent thought that this should extend to taking a dog too, only 25 per cent supported the extending of this right to cycle, and 14 per cent thought that no additional access was desirable. For rights of access over water, 69 per cent supported rights by canoe and rowing boat, whereas 16 per cent thought that this should extend to powered craft, and 19 per cent wished to see no greater access to water.

On latent demand and the changes that they might make to their pattern of use as a result of a right of access over open spaces, Le Mesurier (2000) found that 70 per cent felt that it would have little or no impact, and 26 per cent a positive impact. Of the positive impacts, 12 per cent would spend more time or go more often, 9 per cent felt more comfortable to wander from the path or to change their route, and 4 per cent would pursue new or different activities, particularly on water. The profile of those doing more mirrors current participants and would not therefore change the profile of future visitors. To assess the influence of awareness, respondents were informed of their current and proposed future rights. Levels of positive impact increased from 26 per cent to 37 per cent: with 16 per cent increasing use and 26 per cent changing the way that they use the outdoors.

Whilst these findings are not directly applicable to the situation in Scotland, they do highlight a potentially significant release of new access participation as a result of enhanced rights. However, the increased activity will be enjoyed largely by existing users. The influence of better provision, available closer to home, and increased leisure time and income, would all have greater positive impacts on levels and spread of use. There is urgent need similarly to assess the support, awareness and demand effects of free access in Scotland, including both rights and responsibilities.

3.3.2 Long-term trends

The large body of research measuring the participation, activities, profile and satisfaction of people at leisure in the natural heritage, shows trends which are of importance to the way in which new access rights may be taken-up.

The two key trends are that outdoor access numbers are increasing by 3 to 4 per cent per year. The proportion of the population which goes into the countryside is rising only slowly, with most of the growth coming from increasing frequency of activity of existing users. Walking is the most popular outdoor pastime and is the fastest growing activity (8 per cent), with the widest appeal across Scottish society. Other, more active pursuits have a secure niche, and appeal to younger and higher income groups.

Among existing activities, latent demand is high. Between 15 and 45 per cent of users would like to do more, with only one-quarter getting outdoors for active recreation more than once a week, one-half every month, and one-third not at all. The proportion of the population who is just not interested in getting out is small, at around only 5 to 8 per cent.

The direct impact of new access rights on how people enjoy the natural heritage is likely to be modest, probably less than in England and Wales due to the existing access by implied consent. It will most likely be through changing patterns of activity amongst existing participants. Clear understanding of the practical implications of new legislation could significantly enhance the marginal uptake of access, as may the provision of good facilities of all types. However, even very significantly increased uptake will do little to change the profile of those benefiting.

3.3.3 Is access highly valued?

Access is highly and consistently enjoyable and will require new resources for implementation. Does access provide a good return and would those taking part be willing to pay for the experience? The contingent valuation question – asking people to say how much they would be prepared to pay to keep the service – has not often been asked. There is usually a reluctant response from those asked, with almost a half refusing to give a price. Cost benefit analyses have been made (Hanley and Spash, 1993), but have not been found to be very meaningful or provide useful assistance during access planning.

Asked how much users would pay as a 'one off payment to a charitable trust', for access to an existing community path network (Ekos Economic Consultants, 1998), the most common 'bids' were £1.00 from day visitors and £5.00 from tourists and local residents. When adjusted for protest and income constrained bids, the average value priced was £10.71. By comparison, the actual most common contributions made to a charity appealing to 'restore the balance', on a prominent and eroded mountain, was £1.00 from day visitors and £5.00 from regular users (The Footpath Trust, pers. comm.). The theoretical valuation would have covered the costs of development and maintenance of the network by around 140 per cent, whereas the actual donations to the mountain site met only around 15 per cent of the erosion control and maintenance costs!

A more positive indication is the interest of many users to play an active part. Research shows a demand for involvement in community access (Inglis, 2000), which has been one of the real innovations in access development in recent years. There is also a willingness to understand and reduce the users' own impacts (Taylor and MacGregor, 1999), a key tool in American wilderness management (see Marion and Reid, this volume), but much less widely applied in Scotland. This bodes well for the balance between rights and responsibilities.

3.3.4 Who gains?

All people may have equal access rights, but access opportunities vary greatly depending on where you live, and the take-up is influenced by many factors such as free time and income, ability and confidence, education and custom. Even though access is free, it still requires leisure time, disposable income and skills to make use of the opportunity.

Walking appeals to the widest spectrum of people. In general, the more specialised and sport-orientated the activity, the narrower the range of appeal. Those who enjoy themselves most often in the outdoors are more likely to be male, in their 30s, in professional or managerial employment, be agile and have a car. Additionally, research continues usually only to ask those who are already active, and misses those who are not.

Access solutions usually focus on physical management of sites and information, rather than tackling the personal barriers to participation. The long-term nature of many of the factors influencing activity creates a strong inertia, and habits create a resilience to changing individual patterns. If the benefits of the natural heritage are to be universalised, a concerted and innovative emphasis will be needed to overcome social and economically based exclusion from participation. Without a change in current methods of promotion, provision, involvement, and strong connections to related agendas, new access will be consumed in greatest quantity by those who already take part.

The outlook for access to the natural heritage is buoyant. The numbers of people enjoying walking, in particular, is high and increasing. Significant latent demand remains untapped, both among existing and potential users, and can be released by both increased investment in high quality paths and locally focused promotion to widen awareness. The challenge is the more equitable distribution of the likely and potentially very sizeable access dividend. This needs to be realised both spatially, affecting where the benefits and potential conflicts arise, and socially, affecting who gains and who loses out.

3.4 Measuring progress

Finally, there is also a minor challenge. This is to measure, effectively and simply, the changing patterns of use and behaviour, and the changing profile and attitudes of those who join in. This requires a long-term commitment to target monitoring and analysis carefully – and dissemination of findings to provide feedback to access managers and user groups.

Building a picture of long-term comparison requires a combination of measuring changes in participation at the population level, studying in detail the take-up on selected path networks, and identifying the profile and motivations of users and non-users. There are five recommended targets for data capture. First, we must continue the biannual Day Visitor Surveys, with additional questions on barriers to access for those who currently do not take part. Second, we should continue broad questioning, area and interest based surveys across a variety of types of access facilities, areas and activities, and extend them to seek out those who could, but are not yet, taking part. Third, it would be valuable to identify and run a strategic network of people counters, and then both analyse and model the data. Fourth, we need to use the time during the passage of the Land Reform Bill to research the likely take-up, awareness and response to new rights and new facilities. The results should be very positive. Finally, there will be a requirement to disseminate a selective slice of the information gathered, both new and historical, to a wider audience on a regular basis.

The introduction of a system akin to *Allemannsretten* (Vistad, this volume) into a modern, leisured and urbanised society is a unique and far-reaching cultural event. We need to measure and report on the impact and take-up of wider access rights in Scotland.

References

Argyll Associates (1993). *Glencoe Visitor Survey.* Unpublished report, National Trust for Scotland.

ASH Partnership (1985). The Southern Upland Way: visitor survey. Unpublished report, Countryside Commission for Scotland.

ASH Partnership (1987). The West Highland Way Survey, 1986. Unpublished report, Countryside Commission for Scotland.

Barrow, G. (1976). Balancing use and capacity: Tarn Hows. Unpublished report, Centre for Environmental Interpretation, University of Manchester.

Centre for Leisure Research (1985). *Patterns of countryside recreation trips. Scottish Leisure Survey, volume 4.* Countryside Commission for Scotland, Battleby.

Centre for Leisure Research (1996). UK day visits survey 1994. Unpublished report, Countryside Recreation Network.

Centre for Leisure Research (1997). UK day visits survey 1996. Unpublished report, Countryside Recreation Network.

Centre for Leisure Research (1999). UK day visits survey 1998. Unpublished report, Countryside Recreation Network.

Coalter, F. (1998). Sports participation in Scotland 1987-1996. Scottish Sports Council Report No. 54.

Duffield, B. and Long, J. (1977). *Patterns of outdoor recreation in Scotland.* Tourism and Recreation Research Unit, University of Edinburgh, Edinburgh.

Ekos Economic Consultants (1998). Establishing the overall value of a path network. Unpublished report, Paths For All.

Forgewood Market Research (1995). West Highland Way users survey 1994. Unpublished report, Scottish Natural Heritage.

Greene, D. (1996). Leisure day trips to the Scottish countryside, 1987-1992. Scottish Natural Heritage Research, Survey and Monitoring Report No. 10.

Hanley, H. and Spash, C. (1993). *Cost-Benefit Analysis and the Environment.* Edward Elgar, Cheltenham.

Hunt, J. and Dearden, M.A. (1996). Ross and Cromarty Footpath Survey: annual patterns of use and spending. Unpublished report, Scottish Natural Heritage.

Inglis, A. (2000). Appraisal of community management of access in mid-Ross and Black Isle. Unpublished report, The Footpath Trust.

Jones Economic Consultants (1996). The economic impact of hillwalking, mountaineering and associated activities in the Highlands and Islands of Scotland. Unpublished report, Highlands and Islands Enterprise.

Le Mesurier, P. (2000). Access to other open countryside: measuring the potential demand. Unpublished report, The Countryside Agency.

MacPherson, C. (1999). Survey of use of community path networks in mid-Ross and Black Isle. Unpublished report, The Footpath Trust.

Mather, A. (1998). East Grampians and Lochnagar visitor survey 1995: overview. Scottish Natural Heritage Research, Survey and Monitoring Report No. 104.

Mather, A.S. (2000). Rothiemurchus and Glenmore recreation survey 1998-99: final report. Scottish Natural Heritage Research, Survey and Monitoring Report No. 166.

National Trust for Scotland (2000). Visitor statistics 1999. Unpublished report, National Trust for Scotland.

Scottish Enterprise (1999). Visitor attraction statistics. Unpublished report, Scottish Enterprise.

System Three (1988). Leisure day trips: 1987. Unpublished report, Countryside Commission for Scotland.

System Three (1989). Leisure day trips: 1988. Unpublished report, Countryside Commission for Scotland.

System Three (1990). Leisure day trips: 1989. Unpublished report, Countryside Commission for Scotland.

System Three (1991). Leisure day trips: 1990. Unpublished report, Countryside Commission for Scotland.

System Three (1992a). Leisure day trips: 1991. Unpublished report, Countryside Commission for Scotland.

System Three (1992b). Leisure Day Trips: 1992. Unpublished report, Scottish Natural Heritage.

System Three (1996). Walking in the countryside in Scotland. Scottish Natural Heritage Research, Survey and Monitoring Report No. 11.

System Three (1999). Survey of horse riding in Scotland. Scottish Natural Heritage Research, Survey and Monitoring Report No. 136.

Taylor, J. and MacGregor, C. (1999). Cairngorms Mountain Recreation Survey 1997-8. Scottish Natural Heritage Research, Survey and Monitoring Report No. 162.

Note: a complete set of references on which this review is based can be obtained from the author.

4 THE EFFECTS OF RECREATION ON THE NATURAL HERITAGE: THE NEED TO FOCUS ON IMPROVING MANAGEMENT PRACTICE

Roger Sidaway

Summary

1.   This chapter reviews research on the environmental effects of recreation in order to assess its coverage and value to recreation managers and decision-makers. It is considered that the effects of informal recreation are only rarely important at national levels and that it is at the local level that research and development effort should be directed.

2.   However, the evidence on which this conclusion is based is far from satisfactory. Hitherto, research has been limited to a narrow range of impacts, has often been methodologically weak, and has rarely been undertaken or disseminated in a way that is helpful to managers and decision-makers.

3.   The need to provide practical advice to safeguard sensitive habitats and vulnerable species following the introduction of statutory rights of public access reinforces the case for further research and development. Guidance is needed so that managers can both gauge the importance of recreational effects and know which management measures are likely to be effective.

4.   Recommendations are made for future research and for the more systematic evaluation of impact management.

4.1 Introduction: assessing the problem

Concerns about the potential impacts of recreation were fuelled for many years by perceptions of increased pressures on the British countryside. These were stimulated by undoubted growth in outdoor recreation in the 1960s but arguably could be traced back to reactions to rural change in the nineteenth century (Sidaway, 1998a). However, these more recent concerns have been put into perspective by a number of investigations, which have reached broadly similar conclusions. For example, Sidaway (1988) considered a series of case studies of recreational effects undertaken in England and Wales and observed that

"overviews of ecosystems and species groupings have concluded that recreational disturbance and damage are relatively insignificant to the survival of the species when compared to the major environmental threats of pollution or loss of habitat. Nevertheless, local impacts can be serious and should not be minimised" (Sidaway, 1988, p. iii).

Sidaway and Thompson (1991) also commented on the potential effects of recreation in the uplands, observing *"that there are impacts is undeniable, but whether they present serious conservation problems is questionable. When compared to the major factors which influence the survival of habitats, such as climatic variation, grazing or fire, the recreational impacts are of little long-term conservation significance. However, in some situations they may be the critical last link in a chain of limiting factors"* (Sidaway and Thompson, 1991, p. 32).

A general review of recreational effects in the Scottish environment considered the problems of traffic congestion, visual intrusion and user conflicts associated with tourism and day visits in the Scottish countryside (PIEDA, 1991). It specifically considered footpath damage, the visual impact of caravans, ski areas, intrusive activities (water sports, motor sports and mountain biking) and wider environmental disturbance. The overall conclusions of this review were that *"in general, however, land use changes and associated habitat loss have stronger influences than recreation"* and that where tourism influences ecological change, such changes are *"confined to specific areas, are not severe and appear to be manageable"* (PIEDA, 1991, p. 21).

Even in England, where higher population pressures might be expected to have more pronounced effects, evidence submitted by English Nature to the House of Commons Environment Committee came to similar conclusions.

"Leisure related impacts should be assessed in the context of other activities which have an impact on the countryside or coast. Leisure activities do not in themselves represent the greatest threat to nature conservation. Direct impacts on nature conservation include disturbance, trampling and erosion but these are often localised or short-term in duration and can be managed. Impacts from associated development often represent a greater threat" (House of Commons Environment Committee, 1995b, p. 105).

Such evidence was instrumental in leading the Environment Committee towards a similar conclusion in undoubtedly the most comprehensive review of the topic in recent years.

"We note that on the balance of evidence we have received, compared to other activities, leisure and tourism do not cause significant widespread ecological damage to the countryside. However, there is no need for complacency. We believe there are important issues to address, involving transport, rural culture and leisure management, as well as local conflicts in specific areas" (House of Commons Environment Committee, 1995a, p. xiv).

However, there are four important qualifications to be made to these assessments.

* When sport and recreation are coupled with the development of facilities, their construction can lead to significant loss of habitats in sensitive areas, notably coastal development of resorts in Britain in the nineteenth century and, more recently, estuarine marinas.
* When applications of new technology result in new activities (such as jet skiing and mountain biking), although these effects are usually temporary until management measures are developed to deal with them.

- Where habitats lack resilience due to low dynamic and long recovery cycles, for example many alpine systems.
- When cumulative changes in environmental quality result from small-scale incremental effects which are not significant in themselves. The harmful effects on wildlife may be low but the associated visual and social effects give an impression of an eroded countryside.

While these overviews have helped to re-frame the problem, by suggesting that local considerations were likely to be of more pressing concern than national policy considerations, the introduction of access legislation both in England and Wales and in Scotland has moved the policy agenda forward. Both pieces of legislation contain, or are likely to contain, some environmental safeguards which will operate at the local level. Thus there will be a pressing need to provide practical advice on when and how these safeguards will apply. This chapter addresses the implications of this changing agenda.

4.2 Approach

This chapter is largely based on reviews of research into the environmental effects of recreation, undertaken for Scottish Natural Heritage (SNH), most recently by Sidaway (1994, 1997), supplemented by more recent material supplied by SNH staff.

Seven general headings are used in this chapter to classify the potential effects of recreation. These are: disturbance to fauna, damage to vegetation and soils, removal of biota, pollution, hydrological effects, habitat loss and habitat creation. The term habitat loss is particularly associated with the development of facilities for recreation. For consistency, the use of the word 'damage' has been confined to effects on vegetation, whereas 'disturbance' is used to describe the effects on fauna. It is also useful to differentiate between short term *effects* (e.g. observed responses of disturbed birds) and long term *impacts* (e.g. reductions in population sizes), although clear criteria have not been established for judging when cumulative short term effects result in a long-term impacts (Brown and Langston, 2000).

It should be emphasised that recreation activities can have positive as well as negative environmental effects. For example, improved awareness and understanding of nature conservation or the generation of visitor income for reserve management are both positive. Other environmental benefits include habitat creation (e.g. landscaping of golf courses, which can also be beneficial to wildlife) campaigns by angling and surfing organisations to improve water quality, or protection of the countryside more generally by rambling and mountaineering groups.

Table 4.1 explores the relationships between recreation activities and the impacts that they may cause in more detail. It sets out the characteristics of the activity and relates them to the potential impacts. Some of these characteristics could be a feature of most activities, for example disturbance to fauna. Some are more specific such as the removal of specimens or quarry by various forms of collecting, shooting or fishing. An example of an indirect impact of that type is predator control, which selectively removes species and is a feature of some forms of game shooting management.

Table 4.1. Recreation behaviour, including both its direct and indirect biological effects.

Behavioural characteristics		Examples of recreational activities	Potential impacts
Direct effects	Human presence – numbers, frequency of occurrence, duration, periodicity, proximity, noise	All activities	Disturbance to fauna
	Physical contact e.g., trampling at access points	All land-based activities, and air and water sports	Damage to vegetation and soils
	Removal of specimens or hunting quarry	Collecting, game shooting, fishing	Removal of biota
	Deposition of alien material, e.g. oil, gas, litter, excreta, lead shot	Motorised water sports and all other activities	Pollution
	Water movement	Motorised water sports	Hydrology and geomorphology of inland water bodies
Indirect effects	Associated development of paths and tracks, car parks, building, and earth moving	Most activities including walking, game shooting, golf courses, marinas, and downhill ski-field development	Habitat loss
	Habitat management, e.g. predator control	Game shooting, angling	Removal of biota
	Accidental fires	Land-based activities	Habitat loss (especially on heathland and woodland)
	Associated tree and woodland planting	Game shooting, golf	Habitat creation (positive impacts)

4.3 The assessment of local importance

UK Centre for Economic and Environmental Development (1993) drew attention to the confusion that is caused by the failure to distinguish between the apparent lack of impact at the national level and potentially serious problems at the local level. The report comments that recreation interests tend to stress the national effects whereas conservation interests focus on the local effects. However, assessing the importance of recreational effects at a local level is critical on two counts. A manager needs to know both when an effect matters and whether it is possible to mitigate a potentially harmful impact. At this second stage, armed with a detailed understanding of both the recreational activity and its effects, and the habitat of the species that has been affected, it should be possible to design efficient solutions to well-defined problems.

However, as Hockin *et al.* (1992) point out, assessing the importance of recreational impacts is largely a matter of judgement. In making that judgement, recreation managers have to balance the possible harmful effects that recreation might have on wildlife, relative to the considerable range of benefits which so many people derive from enjoying the countryside. Thus a large part of the problem confronting managers is the lack of clear criteria by which the importance of impacts can be judged.

As serious damage to vegetation is usually all too evident to the manager, the researcher and the user, it is quite defensible to take a pragmatic approach and categorise these effects according to their need for treatment (e.g. Bayfield and Aitken, 1992). Where the evidence of change is less tangible and the causal relationships are uncertain or unknown, it is far more difficult to decide when remedial action is required. Such is the case with the potentially damaging impact of disturbance to birds because of the subjectiveness that is apparent in interpreting ecological importance (Hockin *et al.*, 1992; Brown and Langston, 2000).

UK Centre for Economic and Environmental Development (1993) also highlighted the problems with other effects, such as noise, as there are marked differences between perceived and actual noise levels, and certain pollution effects, when again reliance has to be made on subjective judgements. The problems of providing guidance to local management are further illustrated by considering in more detail two effects of primary concern to countryside access - disturbance to birds and damage to vegetation – where the approach is somewhat different. A strategic view is developing on when disturbance effects on birds matter, whilst more local considerations apply to effects on vegetation and the major emphasis is on improving management.

4.4 Disturbance to birds

Activities which have disturbing effects on birds, such as recreation, can be considered along a spectrum ranging from short-term behavioural responses, which may be designed to distract or lure a potential predator away from nest or young, to longer-term effects, such as reduced breeding density or permanent reductions in population. The range and relationships are set out in Table 4.2. It is particularly important to distinguish between these short-term and long-term effects as short-term responses, which are easily observed, may not be reliable indicators of long-term consequences at the population level.

Table 4.2. The range of effects that disturb birds (from Sidaway, 1994).

Stimulus (dose effects)	Level of behavioural response (ethological effects)	Intermediate effects (ecological effects)	Long-term implications (population level effects)
Characteristics of activity	Characteristics of species	Wintering population	Impact on survival
• level of activity • duration • frequency • predictability • proximity • presence of dogs • noise	• alarm behaviour • avoidance action • habituation	• temporary disruption to feeding or roosting • temporary redistribution of population	• permanent redistribution or decline of population
		Breeding population	Impact on reproduction
		• abandonment of pre-breeding site • abandonment of nest • desertion of eggs or young • predation of eggs or young	• breeding density • breeding success

The short-term effects of disturbing activity are most likely to be serious if they occur at a crucial period, such as the breeding season, when most species adopt a nesting territory. Disturbing activity can have noticeable effects when the birds are prospecting for territories or during incubation, particularly if eggs or chicks are left exposed and are taken by predators.

Reductions in population sizes have been recorded in ground nesting shorebirds. Recreational disturbance has been found to be more significant than predation in reducing the breeding success of a local population of ringed plover (*Charadrius hiaticula*) on the Norfolk coast over the period 1995-9 (quoted by Brown and Langston, 2000). The decline in the national population of the little tern (*Sterna albifrons*) has been attributed to recreational disturbance on its shoreline breeding sites (Nature Conservancy Council, 1984). However, in the latter case, the special protection subsequently given to these sites during the nesting season has apparently contributed to an increase in the population (Sidaway, 1994).

In some cases where recreation impacts have previously been considered to be important, e.g. Batten *et al.* (1990), more recent research has suggested otherwise. Intensive monitoring of dotterel (*Charadrius morinellus*) over 12 breeding seasons on the Cairn Gorm–Ben Macdui plateau has not detected significant effects on breeding distribution, hatching or fledgling success, brood movements, or the return of breeding adults or young, due to hill walking. Nor was there substantial evidence of any link between avian predator numbers or activity on dotterel due to recreation during that period (D.P. Whitfield, pers. comm.).

It seems likely that certain activities can be more disruptive than others. For example, it is useful to distinguish between the brief disturbance effects caused by passing walkers compared to those of longer-term duration when people may remain in or around a breeding territory for several hours while angling or picnicking. Walkers' dogs running out of control may seek out nests and disturb adult and young birds. More determined behaviour can have more lasting consequences, such as the activities of wildlife photographers and over-enthusiastic bird-watchers.

In some situations, birds or mammals respond to predictable (either in time or space) activity by displaying a low level of response, usually because they become habituated to it. However, it cannot be assumed that birds will necessarily habituate. A survey of research ornithologists' field experience of disturbance revealed considerable variation among species and individuals of the same species, which are also affected by the proximity of settlements; associated human activity was also reported (Sidaway, 1995). However, the relationship is not linear: animals in very remote areas where human presence is rare may be tame, but as human activity increases they become wary and take refuge, although they may become habituated when human activity is frequent and predictable (Hockin *et al.*, 1992).

In England and Wales guidance is being prepared for assessment, on a site by site basis, of the implications for nature conservation of a statutory right of access. A precautionary approach has been taken to assessing disturbance to birds which takes into account the uncertainty over the circumstances in which disturbance may be significant (Brown and Langston, 2000). The risk is considered to be greatest to vulnerable species in one or more of the following categories, for which Britain has international conservation obligations, namely

- birds of conservation concern;
- the European Union's Birds Directive 79/409, Annex 1 species;
- regularly occurring migratory species;
- Wildlife and Countryside Act 1981, Schedule 1 species; and
- Biodiversity Action Plan priority species.

This exercise in risk assessment assumes that aggregations of feeding, roosting, lekking or breeding birds will be more vulnerable to disturbance and that these are likely to occur in predictable locations. Special protection will also be afforded to extremely rare species. By considering these aggregations on a habitat by habitat basis, it is then possible to identify species which are potentially vulnerable to more dispersed recreational access on foot. This approach takes a vital first step in quantifying the potential problems of increased access. What is now needed to complete the equation is an assessment of where increased demand for access will occur and to identify where demand places vulnerable species at greatest risk.

Management options for reducing disturbance to birds outwith sanctuary areas or reserves are not well-developed. In many circumstances, the only achievable mitigating measures may be the creation of disturbance free zones or total restriction of access. Typical measures used within reserves are the creation of banking, screens or hedges to give concealed access to observation hides, increased nesting cover by planting, creation of islands or spits, creation of buffer zones or zoning of areas to prohibit access (Hockin *et al.*, 1992; Rehfisch *et al.*, 1996).

4.5 Damage to vegetation and soils

Some of the different problems of recreational use in upland Britain were identified by Bayfield and Aitken (1992). Steep slopes, high rainfall and erodible soils in mountain areas, coupled with poor recovery of vegetation because of the short growing season and infertile soils, typify mountain areas. Mountain vegetation shows relatively low resistance to recreational use and soils have low resistance to wear under the wet ground conditions; peaty soils are particularly vulnerable in such conditions. In drier conditions, dense stands of heather can reduce the dispersal of walkers and fewer paths may be formed. The major problems in woodlands stem from the general dampness of the ground. The overhead cover provided by trees means that footpath surfaces are slow to dry and are easily damaged. Tree cover tends to reduce the dispersal of recreational use, particularly where there is a dense understorey.

The process of vegetation change that follows continued trampling is well documented (e.g. Brotherton *et al.*, 1977; Bayfield and Aitken, 1992). Trampling may initially affect the distribution and abundance of relatively sensitive species and lead to the loss of vegetation, eventually producing bare ground. Prolonged trampling is likely to be accompanied by a reduction in the height of vegetation, an increase in soil compaction, a reduction in infiltration capacity and an increase in run-off. The major damage occurs where drainage is lacking. Soil is removed along footpaths, causing gullying, the loosening of soil by frost action and further trampling producing a surface that is unpleasant to walk on. People then tend to walk to the side of the path, widening it and extending the affected area. The sequence of changes is further described by Cole (1985), who reviewed the effects on germination, the establishment, growth and reproduction of plants, because of the removal of organic matter and changes in soil conditions.

Bayfield and Aitken (1992) also drew attention to studies of the proliferation of footpaths in upland areas (for example, Watson, 1984 and 1991). They described the visual impacts of hill tracks, cairns and litter and how the intrusion of such features into a landscape arouses more comment than localised effects on habitats. Where damage to vegetation occurs on an appreciable scale, this can have an indirect effect on animal populations, principally by affecting food supplies (Cole and Landres, 1995).

Although vegetation changes may be well documented and measured, and their local importance recognised, objective means of assessing their significance is lacking. As Cole (1985) commented

> *"Lack of theoretical work and the short time frame of most studies leave us with little ability to evaluate the significance of most of the impacts that have been described"* (Cole, 1985, p.135).

Even where different dimensions of impacts have been categorised according to, for example, their extent or severity, the categories used have been necessarily arbitrary. For example, Bayfield and Aitken (1992) categorised the extent of the impacts as

- local, when it is confined to less than 10 per cent of most sites, and
- extensive, when more than 10 per cent are affected.

They classified severity as

- low, when formal management is required at sensitive sites,
- moderate, when management is needed for heavy use, and
- severe, when management is needed even for light use.

Thus in the absence of clear and agreed criteria, professional judgements on the severity of the impacts may vary and may not accord with visitors' perceptions which were observed to have been lower than those of professionals (Brotherton *et al.*, 1977).

Regarding management measures, Bayfield and Aitken (1992) provided one of the relatively few advisory manuals which concentrated on practical techniques of restoring damage to vegetation, although its main focus was the effects of trampling on routes and paths. The manual covered the techniques of protecting soil, constructing paths, drainage and reinforcing or reinstating vegetation. Bayfield and Aitken (1992) emphasised different strategies at the planning and management stages. During planning, emphasis was given to site and route selection in order to minimise potential impacts at the outset, although they recognised that managers were frequently constrained by previous decisions and the need to repair previous mistakes. At the management phase, the emphasis was on site or route restoration and modification, ideally providing different surfaces for different recreational users and selecting the most appropriate surface for increasing levels of use.

4.6 The role of research reviews in guiding decision-makers

Recreation managers are largely dependent on secondary sources for information on local effects or secondary sources, notably reviews of the scientific literature. In the case of well-reviewed fields, such as damage to vegetation and disturbance to birds, these may provide a reasonably comprehensive picture, but this is less likely for other topics, such as the polluting effects of recreation. Thus, for some effects, it may not be possible to say whether there are impacts; alternatively, the effects might not have been researched, or the relevant literature might exist but is only available in less accessible literature sources.

While recreational impact management appears to have been covered by a series of 'good practice' guides (e.g. Sidaway, 1991; Elson *et al.*, 1995; Sidaway, 1994), these guides are also limited by the nature of the source material. The four main limitations of the reviews and guides were identified by Sidaway (1994).

- The tendency to focus on particular habitats and relatively few species with little if any replication over time or in different parts of the country. Consequently many of the research reviews have had to rely on research from overseas, yet do not consider whether it is justified to extrapolate research results from different habitats and social systems to British conditions.

- The relatively small number of studies, which specifically examine the relationship between the recreation activity and the habitat or species. As a result the reviews draw on vegetation or habitat surveys, which may be conducted as part of a management plan, or trend analysis of bird populations, which establish the breeding status of species in particular areas. There is always the danger when using such surveys that inferences drawn about the impacts of recreation may not be well-substantiated as recreational activity *per se* did not form a part of the investigation.

- A reliance on description without critical evaluation of the methods used in individual research studies means that their reliability and relevance are not assessed. Without clear criteria to assess research studies, apparently conflicting results are confusing and reviewers tend to conclude that the relationships are complex and not understood. Yet criteria for assessing disturbance research, on the basis of research design and statistical analysis, have been suggested (Sidaway, 1990, 1994; UK Centre for Economic and Environmental Development, 1993; West *et al.*, 2000).

- Little research has been done that is pertinent to management needs or has been interpreted in a way that is helpful to recreation managers. This appears to be because there has been little dialogue between the research community and recreation managers.

More recent work on inland lochs in Scotland (Dickinson *et at.*, 1998) and marine Special Areas of Conservation (UK Centre for Economic and Environmental Development, 1999) has begun to remedy some of these deficits for these habitats by providing more focused inquiry and more specific management advice.

4.7 Future research into recreational effects

4.7.1 *Recreational disturbance to fauna*

Although there has been a considerable British research interest in disturbance to birds, the theoretical basis of the work is generally weak and the relationships between behavioural responses and longer-term effects at the population level are not understood. There is a major gap in comprehension between the scientific community and recreation managers.

The former have given the topic low priority and have not addressed many of the technical difficulties of undertaking such basic research. Meanwhile, recreation managers see the topic to be of increasing political importance.

The four topics where there is greatest uncertainty, but not necessarily a major risk to wildlife, are public access to moorland in upland Britain, public access and angling to river and waterside areas, watersports and estuaries, and canoeing and salmon spawning grounds. What is apparently needed is a concerted effort to find the resources for a research programme of monitored experiments and some carefully designed basic research. As this will take some time to achieve, there is a short-term requirement to develop consensus on interim management approaches. Priorities are needed not only for research but also on assessing areas and species at risk, following the approach taken by Brown and Langston (2000) while the limited range of management approaches should be evaluated for their effectiveness.

4.7.2 Noise

Research on the impact of noise caused by recreational activities has been confined to motorised land or water sports and the problems surrounding venues or events. There appears to be no need for basic research *per se* although the methods used to test noise levels have not been applied in a consistent way and could be standardised (UK Centre for Economic and Environmental Development, 1993). There is, however, a major discrepancy between actual and perceived noise levels and it seems likely that further research on the public perception of noise levels around recreational sites would be valuable.

At established sites or approved venues, noise levels are controlled by event management. In these situations, and at other established venues, e.g. small airstrips, joint management schemes could pave the way towards establishing better relationships with local communities, as suggested by Elson *et al.* (1989). Limited trial schemes could be established. There appears to be a continuing process of technical development by manufacturers, of which the public are unaware, and the requirement is for wider dissemination and application of management techniques.

4.7.3 Damage to vegetation and soils

Most basic relationships concerning physical damage from trampling are reasonably well understood and the research requirements have been spelt out by Bayfield and Aitken (1992). They advocated a series of vegetation and soil sensitivity studies which would examine the susceptibility of different vegetation types, predict rates of deterioration and allow the selection of appropriate impact management techniques. They also suggested that further research is required on the effects of different types of recreational use, which would also assist in the selection of appropriate techniques.

Although considerable development work has been undertaken on path construction, the appropriate techniques are not necessarily systematically applied or evaluated. Bayfield and Aitken (1992) suggested that some technique development is required in demonstrations and field trails which would integrate research and development projects. Thus their overall priorities are demonstration schemes, the wider application of existing techniques and renewed emphasis on monitoring and evaluation. Educational programmes would be helpful for those sports whose impacts are localised but widespread, e.g. horse riding and off-road cycling.

4.7.4 Removal of biota

A broad range of effects result from recreationists collecting or removing biota. Most activities, such as divers collecting marine life for consumption or as souvenirs; bait digging, bramble picking and mushroom gathering, are either not practised on a scale to warrant research or have been modified by codes of practice. Some independent work has been done on the effects of wildfowling (Bell and Fox, 1991) and grouse shooting (Redpath and Thirgood, 1997). In the latter case, considerable emphasis is being placed on improving the biodiversity of moorland management (Moorland Working Group, 1998; UK Raptor Working Group, 2000) and it is doubtful whether further research on effects is warranted.

4.7.5 Pollution

This is potentially a very broad field in which relatively little assessment has been made of recreation effects. An assessment has been made of gaseous discharges from power boats used in water skiing (UK Centre for Economic and Environmental Development, 1993), but these impacts are relatively trivial compared to the use of cars in recreational travel. This chapter has concentrated on the effects of recreation activities at the places where they occur, yet most activities entail considerable travelling from home or holiday location. Car-based, recreational travel, in particular, can have substantial environmental impacts, which have been little studied, let alone ameliorated.

If other polluting effects such as discharges of sewage or litter were taken into account the total impacts of recreation could be greater then has been supposed. It is generally assumed that effects on water quality are likely to be low but the public health literature has not been examined to confirm this. It would be safer to assume that the effects are at the moment unknown because no systematic evaluation of research across the full range of recreational activities has been undertaken. It is suggested that an environmental audit of recreational areas in the countryside, where use is concentrated, is required to assess whether there are potential problems. If key areas are identified this would provide the necessary focus for a research review or studies. A similar audit approach to recreational travel would re-emphasise the need to develop alternative modes of transport.

4.7.6 Hydrology and geomorphology

Research reviews have been undertaken which assess the effects of increased water turbidity and bank erosion from water skiing (e.g. UK Centre for Economic and Environmental Development, 1993) and inland lochs in Scotland (Dickinson *et al.*, 1998), which developed a more rigorous approach to the topic. This approach could be more widely applied; further work on the management of Scottish freshwater lochs could be undertaken in an integrated way, rather than on a site by site basis. This suggests that higher priority should be given to the development of management plans and application of management techniques than to further research on these effects

4.7.7 Habitat loss

This is potentially a very wide field when all associated developments, e.g. golf courses, marinas and airstrips, are taken into account. The processes are covered by development control but a stocktaking exercise, which considers recent developments, might be useful. The problem may not be with the number of developments as much as with their location in, or adjoining, nature conservation areas. A review of golf course development, for example, might reveal that most land has been taken from agricultural use with some eventual benefit to nature conservation as new habitats are created.

4.7.8 Positive environmental benefits

There appears to be very little explicit documentation of the positive impacts of recreational activities, which may be direct, in the form of habitat creation or site protection, or indirect, in the form of the campaigning activities of recreation organisations. A combined exercise, which considers the balance sheet of habitat loss and habitat creation and other positive impacts of recreation, could be worthwhile.

4.7.9 Improved research methods and standards

The main research and development needs have been summarised in Table 4.3, but coupled with this agenda is a general need to improve research methods and standards. In particular,

Table 4.3. A summary of research and development requirements (based on Sidaway, 1994).

Effect	*Research undertaken*	*Research required*	*Development undertaken*	*Development required*
Disturbance to birds (and the fauna)	Limited research, many basic relationships not understood	Basic research and monitored experiments	Limited range of exclusion measures	Evaluation of management approaches
Noise	Relationships understood	Research on perceptions of non-users	Event management	Trials of joint management schemes; wider application
Damage to vegetation	Most relationships understood	Limited research requirement	Techniques not systematically applied or evaluated	Some technique development; demonstration schemes; evaluation trials
Removal of biota	Limited research on impacts	Unlikely that further research warranted	Statutory and voluntary restrictions	-
Pollution	No systematic evaluation of research	Environmental audit to assess potential impacts, especially of recreational travel, and provide focus for research	Control of anti-fouling paint, refuse disposal; low emission engines for water ski boats, personal watercraft	Dissemination of standards
Hydrology/ geomorphology of inland water bodies	Limited research on turbidity and bank erosion	Problem assessment	Engineering solutions known	Integrated management
Habitat loss and benefits to conservation	No systematic study	Stocktaking exercise	-	-

a relatively neglected aspect of this work has been the testing of hypotheses and the use of theoretical models, which help to clarify whether common-sense prescriptions and subjective assessments have any scientific basis (Legg, 1999). Other authors have commented on the lack of experimental designs to assess causal relationships (Flather and Cordell, 1995).

Anderson (1995) argued that effects on populations will only be clarified when groups of investigators, working on different research questions, work together, whereas Cole (1985) argued for more integration of associated projects in the social and natural sciences. These points equally apply to British research where one of the major problems of assessing the significance of recreational impacts is a lack of understanding of the dynamic processes of ecosystems over reasonably long periods of time and where little work has been replicated. Managers are likely to require information on site conditions, including species diversity, climatic factors and human disturbance, as well as the social environment of noise, perceptions of crowding and possibly conflicts between different user groups. The implications are that research programmes will need to be integrated within a framework of theory and have a clear contribution to integrated management.

The increasing specialisation of scientific research makes communication difficult between researchers and practitioners or, even more importantly, between researchers and recreation organisations and participants. Relatively little is done to apply research by promoting its findings to lay people, on the lines of the *Save our Sandpipers* leaflet produced to raise the awareness of anglers to the risk of disturbance (Holland and Yalden, undated). Relatively few scientists write or are asked to write popular articles for mountain bikers' magazines or anglers' journals. Perhaps researchers feel their task is completed when their research findings eventually enter the scientific research literature. The national agencies, in particular, should ensure that funds are earmarked for the wider dissemination of research results.

4.8 The need for critical evaluation of management practice

Research is by no means the only solution to the problems of managing recreational impacts. A variety of approaches to impact reduction have been taken, covering regulation, planning, management and education as well as research. If good practice is to be extended effectively, there needs to be an assessment of which problems are amenable to which approach. However, what is very striking is the lack of critical evaluation of management initiatives (UK Centre for Economic and Environmental Development, 1999). Indeed, in relation to vegetation effects, Bayfield and Aitken (1992) gave higher priority to demonstrations and field trials than to more basic research.

Set against this is the need to think more strategically, for example whether to concentrate or disperse use or whether, as suggested by Brotherton *et al.* (1977), to maintain or rehabilitate the resource, reduce use of problems areas or reduce use of the entire site. In practice, a limited range of management options have been considered in Scotland.

> "*Management measures have inclined towards hardening the site, simply because it has usually proved much easier to manipulate the resource than to manipulate visitor numbers or behaviour*" (Dargie *et al.*, 1994).

Pending further research and the assessment of management techniques, there is a need for interim guidance on conservation and habitats. For example, while there are listings of the characteristic species to be conserved on each of the main habitat types in Britain, there is little published information on their sensitivity to human disturbance from a variety of causes. One example of the type of guidance needed is the calculation of the optimum distances between refuges to limit disturbance for over-wintering waders. Rehfisch *et al.* (1996) have calculated that by placing refuges at 2, 4 and 7 km apart for grey plovers, 2.5, 5 and 10 km apart for dunlins and 3.5, 5.5 and 9.5 km for redshanks, these refuges were within reach of 90, 75 and 50 per cent of the respective populations of these species during their normal roost movements. This provides a preferable approach to the crude rules of thumb used hitherto, but it needs to be replicated for other species and more widely disseminated.

4.9 Broadening the basis of decision making: involvement, ownership and responsibility

A marked feature of previous conflicts between recreation and conservation has been the uncertainty about the importance of recreational effects (Sidaway, 1988). But given the time it takes to agree, design and conduct a research programme, and that situations change relatively rapidly, it is important to recognise that management frequently has to proceed on imperfect knowledge. In which case, rather than rely solely on their own judgement, it is preferable that managers involve recreation users and conservation bodies to provide a collective judgement on how to minimise potential impacts. This collaborative approach to management should begin as early in the process as possible, so that problem definition, the selection of management options, and monitoring and evaluation are all based on collective decisions (House of Commons Environment Committee, 1995a).

The principles of collective decision making to reach consensus are well known and can be paraphrased as – get the right people there, with the right terms of reference, share what information there is, develop common ownership of the problem, agree how to proceed and assess performance (Sidaway, 1998b). This approach to access management planning was developed for moorlands in the Peak District National Park (Sidaway, 1998c) and could provide a useful model for the proposed local access forums to be introduced as part of the forthcoming access legislation.

One recent example of this form of decision making has been the involvement of user groups and the local community in determining the priorities for traffic management in Glen Muick. A partnership of public bodies, including SNH, and local landowners formed a charitable trust and carefully assessed a series of schemes, giving their reasons for preferring certain options over others. By brokering these proposals at a facilitated workshop, the Upper Deeside Access Trust (UDAT) has been able to gain the agreement of user groups to the introduction of parking charges which will contribute to local environmental management. Five years earlier, before the Trust began its work, such a proposal would probably have been rejected out of hand. What makes the UDAT distinctive in highland Scotland is the open and positive manner in which it approached a potential problem.

Many recreation organisations have developed environmental awareness, have developed conservation policies, and have secured funding for, or encouraged volunteers to, work on management measures (Sidaway, 1991). Alternative approaches to minimising recreation effects, which depend on ethically based self-regulation by users, have been developed in the USA are well described elsewhere in these proceedings (Marion and Reid, this volume). There is considerable scope for similar ethical practices to be developed by recreation organisations in Britain.

4.10 Monitoring and evaluation

Monitoring provides the essential feedback loop which ensures that management is effective. Indeed, in the context of uncertainty about the effects of recreation, site monitoring has the added advantage of providing an opportunity to build trust locally between the relevant interest groups.

Put in the context of providing information on which management decisions will be based, the logic of monitoring is inescapable, yet current practice leaves much to be desired. All too often monitoring is an afterthought with the inevitable result that its aims are generalised and vague, with little effort made to relate monitoring to management problems and objectives (Bayfield and Aitken, 1992), while few, if any resources, have been dedicated to the exercise. Little thought has been given to defining objectives in measurable terms or stating hypotheses about proposed changes in use, so that findings cannot be related to management action. There are few sites where there is sufficient information on how recreational use is distributed or where there is reliable information on trends in use over time.

'Regulatory' monitoring, designed to compare changes to quality standards in order to trigger a management response when unacceptable change occurs, addresses some of these problems. There has been an understandable hesitancy to adopt the most elaborate versions of planning and monitoring schemes, such as the 'limits of acceptable change' (Stankey *et al.*, 1985) in Britain, because of the cost and intrinsic problems of measuring changes in some of the most crucial impacts. It may also be difficult to get representatives for some informal activities and to maintain their involvement over long periods (Sidaway, 1997). However if the alternative is continuing conflict then a joint approach to management problems, even on limited scale, is a preferable approach. The challenge is to devise a planning exercise which meets these needs and is commensurate with the scale of the problem; some options were suggested by Sidaway (1997).

4.11 Conclusions

Hitherto, most research on recreation effects has been driven by academic rather than practical goals. It has clarified the absence of a major threat to the natural heritage but revealed disappointingly little that is of direct relevance to resource managers. There has been a gross lack of investment in the research and evaluation which would be used to underpin sound management. The new access legislation should reinforce the case for giving higher priority to the topic.

There is a need to look strategically at the gaps in research, and to determine where resources can be used to best effect. It should be possible to identify the 'hot-spots', those habitats and species that are most vulnerable and liable to major recreation demands. Equally the relative costs and returns of more basic research, or the evaluation of management techniques, could be calculated, with the latter probably providing better value for money in the short-term.

Hitherto it is as though the research and conservation community has been addressing the implicit question 'how do we justify excluding recreation from environmentally sensitive areas?'. A more constructive approach will be to invest in collective management and to initiate discussions at a local level between researchers, managers and user groups. Instead, the issue to be addressed is 'how do we manage recreation to ensure that the wildlife interest of areas, that is important both to recreation and nature conservation, is both maintained and enhanced?'.

Recreation effects have been a quasi-political issue in Britain for far too long. Many of the original concerns have proved to be unjustified. Now is the time to sort out the real issues and to take the time and trouble and devote the resources to providing sound advice to local managers. Failure to do so will prolong the uncertainty and lead us back into unnecessary conflict.

Acknowledgements

I should like to thank Des Thompson for his valuable comments and encouragement during the preparation of this chapter, and also Phil Whitfield for his contribution of information.

References

Anderson, S.H. (1995). Recreational disturbance and wildlife populations. In *Wildlife and Recreationists: Coexistence through Research and Management*, ed. by R.L. Knight and K.J. Gutzwiller. Island Press, Washington, D.C. pp. 157-168.

Batten, L.A., Bibby, C.J., Clement, P., Elliott, G.D. and Porter, R.F. (1990). *Red Data Birds in Britain: Action for Rare, Threatened and Important Species.* Poyser, Calton.

Bayfield, N.G. and Aitken, R. (1992). *Managing the Impacts of Recreation on Vegetation and Soils: A Review of Techniques.* Institute of Terrestrial Ecology, Banchory.

Bell, D.V. and Fox, P.J.A. (1991). *Shooting Disturbance: an Assessment of its Impact and Effects on Overwintering Wildfowl Populations and their Distribution in the United Kingdom.* Wildfowl and Wetlands Trust, Slimbridge.

Brotherton, I., Maurice, O., Barrow, G. and Fishwick, A. (1977). *Tarn Hows: an Approach to the Management of a Popular Beauty Spot.* Countryside Commission, Cheltenham.

Brown, A. and Langston, R. (2000). Assessing the potential impacts on wild birds in England and Wales of a statutory right of access to the countryside. Unpublished report.

Cole, D.N. (1985). Soil and vegetation in wilderness: a state-of-knowledge review. In *Proceedings of the National Wilderness Research Conference: Issues, State-of-Knowledge, Future Directions,* ed. R.C. Lucas. USDA, Gen Technical Report INT - 220, pp. 135-177.

Cole, D.N. and Landres, P.B. (1995). Indirect effects of recreationists on wildlife. In *Wildlife and Recreationists: Coexistence through Research and Management*, ed. by R.L. Knight and K.J. Gutzwiller. Island Press, Washington, D.C. pp. 183-202.

Dargie, T., Aitken, R. and Tantram, D. (1994). Trossachs Tourism Management Programme: environmental monitoring, Unpublished report.

Dickinson, G,. Drummond, J., Murphy, K. and O'Hare, M. (1998). An Approach to Measuring Recreational Impacts on Inland Lochs. Unpublished report.

Elson, M.J., Buller, H., Thorpe, I. and Lloyd, J. (1989). *Providing for Air Sports.* Sports Council, London.

Elson, M.J., Heany, D. and Reynolds, G. (1995). *Good Practice in the Planning and Management of Sport and Active Recreation in the Countryside.* Sports Council and Countryside Commission, London.

Flather, C.H. and Cordell, H.K. (1995). Outdoor recreation: historical and anticipated trends. In *Wildlife and Recreationists: Coexistence through Research and Management*, ed. by R.L. Knight and K.J. Gutzwiller. Island Press, Washington, D.C. pp. 3-16.

Hockin, D., Ounsted, M., Gorman, M., Hill, D., Keller, V. and Barker, M.A. (1992). Examination of the effects of disturbance on birds with reference to its importance in ecological assessments. *Journal of Environmental Management*, **36**, 253-286.

Holland, P. and Yalden, D. (undated). *Save our Sandpipers*. Peak Park Planning Board, Bakewell.

House of Commons Environment Committee (1995a). *Session 1994-5, Fourth Report: The Environmental Impact of Leisure Activities. Volume I, Report, together with Proceedings of the Committee leading to the Report.* HMSO, London.

House of Commons Environment Committee (1995b). *Session 1994-5, Fourth Report: The Environmental Impact of Leisure Activities. Volume II, Minutes of Evidence.* HMSO, London.

Legg, C. (1999). Review of published work in Relation to Monitoring of trampling Impacts and Change in Montane Vegetation, Unpublished report.

Moorland Working Group (1998). *Good Practice for Grouse Moor Management.* Scottish Natural Heritage, Perth.

Nature Conservancy Council (1984). *Nature Conservation in Great Britain.* NCC, Peterborough.

PIEDA (1991). *Review of Tourism in the Scottish Environment.* PIEDA, Edinburgh.

Redpath, S.M. and Thirgood, S.J. (1997). *Birds of Prey and Red Grouse.* HMSO, London.

Rehfisch, M.M., Clark, N.A., Langston, R.H.W. and Greenwood, J.J.D. (1996). A guide to the provision of refuges for waders: an analysis of thirty years of ringing data from the Wash, England. *Journal of Applied Ecology*, **33**, 673-687.

Sidaway, R. (1988). Sport, Recreation and Nature Conservation. *Sports Council, Research Study* No. 32.

Sidaway, R. (1990). *Birds and Walkers: a Review of Access to the Countryside and Disturbance to Birds.* Ramblers' Association, London.

Sidaway, R. (1991). Good conservation practice for sport and recreation. *Sports Council, Research Study* No. 37.

Sidaway, R. (1994). Recreation and the natural heritage: a research review. *Scottish Natural Heritage Review* No. 25.

Sidaway, R. (1995). Field experience of disturbance to birds: a pilot study. *Scottish Natural Heritage Research, Survey and Monitoring Report* No. 25.

Sidaway, R. (1997). Recreation planning for the care of natural resources, Unpublished report,

Sidaway, R. (1998a). Recreation pressures on the countryside: real concerns or crises of the imagination. In *Leisure Management: Issues and Applications,* ed. by M.F. Collins and I.S. Cooper. CAB International, Wallingford. pp, 85-96.

Sidaway, R. (1998b). *Good practice in rural development No. 5: consensus building.* Unpublished report.

Sidaway, R. (1998c). Access management by local consensus. *Rights of Way Law Review,* Section **13.1**, 7-12.

Sidaway, R. and Thompson, D. (1991). Upland recreation: the limits of acceptable change. *ECOS*, **12**, 31-39.

Stankey, G.H., Cole, D.N., Lucas, R.C., Peterson, M.E. and Frissell, S.J. (1985). The limits of acceptable change (LAC) of wilderness planning. USDA *Forest Service General Technical Report* Int - 176.

UK Centre for Economic and Environmental Development (1993). *Water Skiing and the Environment: a Literature Review.* UK Centre for Economic and Environmental Development, Cambridge.

UK Centre for Economic and Environmental Development (1999). *Framework for Reviewing and Managing Potential Recreational Impacts on Annex I and II Features within UK Marine Special Areas of Conservation, Final Steering Group Review.* UK Centre for Economic and Environmental Development, Cambridge.

UK Raptor Working Group (2000). *Report of the Working Group.* Department of the Environment, Transport and the Regions and the Joint Nature Conservation Committee, Bristol and Peterborough.

Watson, A. (1984). A survey of vehicular hilltracks in north-east Scotland for land use planning, *Journal of Environmental Management,* **18**, 343-353.

Watson, A. (1991). Increase of people on Cairn Gorm plateau following easier access. *Scottish Geographical Magazine,* **107**, 99-105.

West, A.D., Goss-Custard, J.D. Stillman, R.A., Caldow, R.W.G., Lee S.E.A., Dit Durell, V. and McGrorty, S. (2000). Predicting the impacts of disturbance on wintering wading birds using a behaviour-based individuals model. Unpublished report.

5 BEHAVIOUR ASSOCIATED WITH ACCESS TO THE COUNTRYSIDE

Tom Costley

Summary

1. Access to the countryside for walking represents a major recreational activity in Scotland.

2. The majority of participants do not encounter any problems with access and do not cause difficulties or problems for farmers and land managers.

3. The urban fringe is the area where conflicts are most likely to occur with gates being left open, litter and problems with dogs being the major concerns, as well as illegal activities such as fly tipping, drugs and poaching.

4. The development of networks of local paths will be an important feature in managing public access to the countryside.

5. A wide-ranging promotional campaign and education programme will be necessary to support the launch of the Scottish Outdoor Access Code.

5.1 Introduction

The Scottish Outdoor Access Code (SOAC) will be a central feature of new legislation in Scotland concerning arrangements for access to the countryside. Within this legislation, a public right of access for informal recreation and passage is proposed, accompanied by a duty on those exercising the right to behave responsibly. Responsible behaviour is required to prevent damage and disturbance to the outdoors, to those who live and work in the outdoors, and to those who visit the outdoors for enjoyment and other purposes. Responsible behaviour by the public will be defined in the new legislation and will be guided by the SOAC, which will be referred to in the legislation.

Scottish Natural Heritage (SNH) will be required to review the effectiveness of the SOAC every three years or so and report to Government. With regard to this duty, SNH wished to obtain a detailed understanding of current views on issues relating to behaviour and of the types of actual behaviour associated with access to the countryside. In essence, prior to the introduction of the legislation and the publication and promotion of the SOAC, it is necessary to establish a 'baseline' against which changes over time can be compared.

SNH therefore commissioned NFO System Three to undertake this baseline study of the views, perceptions, values and actual behaviour associated with access and informal recreation in the countryside. It was imperative that the methods adopted for this study were capable of replication so that, in the future, it would be possible to monitor the effectiveness of the SOAC in influencing behaviour. This chapter reports the results of this baseline study.

5.2 Method

The programme of research comprised a number of distinct elements, including both qualitative and quantitative approaches. The focus of this chapter is on the results which emerged from the two main quantitative surveys.

5.2.1 Scottish Opinion Survey

Questions regarding behaviour in the countryside and attitudes towards access-related issues were inserted in the July 2000 wave of the Scottish Opinion Survey. This was carried out during the period 27th July to 1st August 2000. In addition, during this period, 170 additional interviews were carried out in the Highlands and Islands and in Southern Scotland so as to ensure an adequate representation of rural areas within the overall sample.

At the analysis stage the data obtained from the additional interviews were combined with those obtained in the Scottish Opinion Survey, giving a total sample size of 1,165. At the 95 per cent level of confidence, the results are accurate to ±2.9 per cent. To ensure that the sample was representative of the Scottish adult population in terms of age, sex and social class, the data were weighted to match population estimates.

5.2.2 Telephone survey of farmers and land managers

During the second half of August and early September 2000, a representative sample of farmers and land managers were interviewed by telephone. A total of 475 interviews was completed and the key characteristics of the sample were that 68 per cent of respondents were owners and the remainder tenants or managers; and that 30 per cent had land holdings of less than 100 ha, 43 per cent had holdings of 100 to 300 ha and the remainder had a farm or estate of more than 300 ha. The sample included farmers and land managers from all parts of Scotland and covering all types of activity – arable, lowland livestock (beef and dairy cattle and sheep), less favoured areas and other activities.

5.3 Setting the context – use of the countryside

In the survey of the general public, a number of questions were asked in order to establish

- some contextual information on the volume of use of the outdoors for informal recreation,
- the public's attitudes towards behaving responsibly in the outdoors, and
- the extent to which the public encountered problems in seeking access to the countryside.

About 60 per cent of the respondents had undertaken an outdoor activity in the countryside during the previous two months. The most popular activities were short walks of up to 3 km in length (42 per cent), longer walks (30 per cent) and cycling on surfaced roads (14 per cent). The only other activity which was undertaken by more than 3 per cent of respondents was off-road cycling (9 per cent).

Within the population as a whole, certain types of people were more likely to have taken part in these outdoor activities and these included those aged between 35-54 years; those in the professional, managerial and non-manual occupations (social classes A, B, and C1s); dog owners; and those with access to a car.

On the last occasion that these participants had taken part in these outdoor activities, over a quarter had visited a coastal or cliff top area and a similar proportion had visited a forest or woodland area. A fifth had been on a path/track in the countryside and a similar proportion had visited a river or lochside. Smaller proportions had been in farmland areas (16 per cent) or in the mountains or on moorlands (15 per cent). A third of participants visited that particular location on at least a weekly basis with a further 17 per cent doing so at least once per month. A quarter were accompanied by a dog on their last visit to the countryside. The majority (65 per cent) claimed that they allowed their dog to run free but within sight, with most of the remainder stating that they had the dog on a lead, evenly divided between those who said that the dog was on a lead all or most of the time.

The majority of participants in outdoor activities (82 per cent) claimed that they had not had any reason to alter their route on their last visit to the countryside. Amongst those who had changed their route there were three main reasons. There was a 'no entry' or 'private' sign, an informative sign, or a field with livestock. Each one of these reasons was mentioned by around 5 per cent of all participants.

Similarly, 80 per cent of respondents claimed that they did not encounter any problems during their last visit to the countryside. Amongst the one in five who had encountered problems, the main examples were a 'keep out' or 'no entry' sign, a barbed wire or electric fence, a blocked or overgrown path, or a locked gate. Amongst those whose last visit was to farmland, a third claimed that they encountered some sort of difficulty with access.

On their last visit to the countryside, a fifth of participants stated that they had crossed a field or fields – 43 per cent stated that they had followed a path or track in doing so, 30 per cent said that they had walked around the edge, and 31 per cent said that they had taken the shortest route across the field. Note that this sums to over 100 per cent because some respondents had undertaken two of the three options.

When asked to indicate how important it was that people should behave responsibly in the countryside, nine out of ten respondents stated that it was 'very important'. In terms of knowledge of the Country Code, 71 per cent claimed to have heard of it but a significantly lower proportion had more than a superficial knowledge of its main messages. The two elements of the Country Code which respondents were most likely to recall were related to taking litter home (70 per cent) and leaving gates as they were found (63 per cent). In addition, nearly two-fifths of respondents referred to keeping dogs under control (39 per cent) – a figure which increased to 45 per cent amongst dog owners. Other aspects of the code were mentioned by less than a quarter of respondents.

The respondents were also asked to select from a list of 11 access-related issues the ones that are most likely to have an effect on farmers and other land managers. Figure 5.1 highlights the range of responses to each of the issues on this list.

5.4 Setting the context – farmers and land managers
Eighty per cent of interviewees in the survey of farmers and land managers stated that there was some degree of use of their land by the public. Those activities mentioned by more than a fifth of respondents were

- walking less than 3 km (33 per cent),
- dog walking (31 per cent),

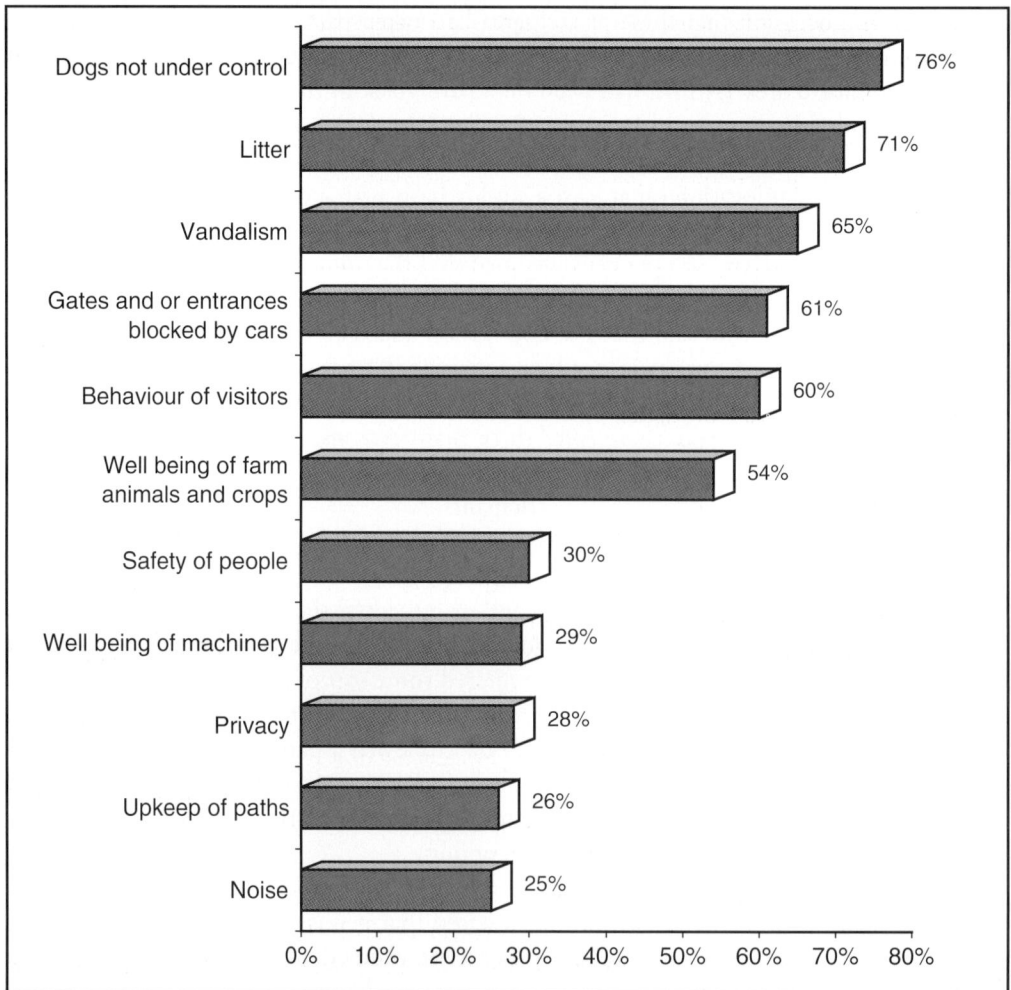

Figure 5.1. The 11 issues relating to access which affect farmers and land managers. The data show the percentage of respondents in the Scottish Opinion Survey of 1,165 members of the general public in summer 2000.

- shooting (27 per cent),
- fishing (24 per cent), and
- walking between 3 km to 13 km (22 per cent).

Amongst those interviewees who described their properties as being in the urban fringe, dog walking was cited by 41 per cent compared to 29 per cent in rural areas.

Two-thirds of interviewees claimed that there had been 'no change' in the amount of public access to their land over the last five years. Around one in ten believed that there had been a 'major increase' and about one in five felt that there had been a 'minor increase'.

A number of examples of behaviour or problems were identified by the interviewees as directly affecting their own land and the main issues are outlined in Table 5.1. Without exception, those farmers and land managers who regard themselves as being located in urban areas were much more likely to cite these various examples of behaviour and problems as directly affecting their land. In most cases, the proportion of farmers in urban areas mentioning each of these issues was 15 to 20 percentage points higher than the equivalent figure featured in Table 5.1.

Table 5.1. Activities or problems which directly affect farmers. The data show percentages of the 475 interviewees included in the telephone survey of farmers and land managers.

Issue	*Percentage of interviewees*
Gates left open	39
Litter	38
Problems with dogs	31
Fences or walls damaged	17
Gates or entrances blocked with vehicles	15
Vandalism of property or machinery	11
People starting fires	11
People camping without permission	10

When asked directly, around four in ten interviewees stated that they were affected by at least one of three illegal activities – fly tipping (28 per cent), poaching (21 per cent), and drugs or glue sniffing (7 per cent). Once again, those farmers in the urban fringe areas were much more likely to be affected by at least one of these activities – 64 per cent compared to 38 per cent in rural areas and this was especially the case with fly tipping, with 57 per cent affected in the urban fringe compared to 23 per cent in rural areas.

The interviewees were presented with a series of statements to do with public access to land and asked to indicate the one which best described their own attitude. The distribution of responses is shown in Table 5.2. The majority of interviewees chose one of the two statements which focused on the need for public access to be accompanied by responsible behaviour and, ideally, from the farmers' perspective, the courtesy of asking for permission, where practical. Just under a third of interviewees were of the opinion that public access to land caused additional costs for the farmer or land manager; in urban areas, this was 51 per cent compared to 24 per cent in rural areas.

Table 5.2. Attitude of interviewees relating to public access to land. The data show percentages of the 475 interviewees included in the telephone survey of farmers and land managers.

Statement relating to public access to land	*Percentage of interviewees*
I don't mind people coming on to my land as long as they cause no damage, act responsibly and ask permission first	42
I don't mind people coming on to my land as long as they cause no damage and act responsibly	38
I would prefer to exclude all public access from my land	9
I don't mind people coming on to my land for certain activities as long as they cause no damage and act responsibly	8
I welcome people on to my land because I feel that providing for public recreation is a useful alternative source of income	2

5.5 Control of dogs

Litter, gates being left open, and problems with dogs were the three main access-related issues or problems which directly affected farmers. To establish the extent to which farmers, land managers and the general public held similar opinions and attitudes towards the control of dogs in the countryside, the same question was asked in both surveys. Different scenarios were presented and the respondents were asked to indicate what level of control would be appropriate in each situation ranging from excluding dogs completely, through being on a lead, to being under close control.

Amongst farmers and land managers, there were two situations where the majority (70 per cent) believed that dogs should not be allowed at all – in a field with cattle and/or calves and in a field with sheep and/or lambs. In comparison, amongst the general public, the proportions in favour of excluding dogs completely were 39 per cent in fields with cattle and/or calves and 43 per cent in fields with sheep and/or lambs. In both cases around 50 per cent of the general public felt that keeping the dog on a lead would be appropriate; a feeling that was shared by almost four in ten of farmers in relation to fields with cattle and/or calves, reducing to around a quarter for fields with sheep and/or lambs.

In fields planted with crops and where there are ground-nesting birds, the differences between the general public and the farmers and land managers were less significant. In both cases, around 45 per cent of the farmers believed that dogs should not be allowed at all compared to just over 30 per cent of the general public.

In the other situations – meeting horse riders, meeting cyclists, when close to farm buildings and houses, and when in the hills and mountains - around 60 per cent of farmers and land managers believed that keeping dogs on a lead would be appropriate. For the first three of these situations, the comparable figures for the general public were between 50 and 70 per cent who felt that having the dog on a lead was appropriate. However, in the hills and mountains, less than one in five of the general public thought that it was necessary to have a dog on a lead.

5.6 Crossing fields

In a similar vein, a question was asked in both surveys regarding the most appropriate choice for crossing a field in different situations. There were two main situations where there were significant differences between the general public and farmers and land managers. First, in a field with sheep and lambs, just over half the general public felt that they should find an alternative route and a third would go around the edge of the field. In comparison, over 70 per cent of farmers would prefer the people to find an alternative route and a quarter would prefer them to go around the edge of the field.

Second, in a field with cattle and calves, the general public indicated similar courses of action, as was the case with sheep and lambs. Amongst farmers and land managers, 80 per cent would prefer the people to find an alternative route, with 16 per cent content that they walked around the edge of the field.

In other situations where the field was planted with crops, including grass, or if it was ploughed or when the farmer was working in the field, the general public and farmers and land managers held similar views as to the preferred course of action. In the majority of these situations, the preferred option was to go round the edge of the field. However, if the farmer was working in the field, the preferred option would be to find an alternative route.

5.7 Influencing behaviour

There were some interesting differences between the general public and the farmers and land managers with regard to the best means of attempting to influence the public's behaviour in the outdoors (Figure 5.2).

The primary difference is that, whereas the general public believed that information presented on signs at the start of trails and paths would be a significant means of communication, farmers were more inclined to favour a longer-term education programme targeted at children which would seek to inform them of the various functions of the countryside, both as a recreational space and as a working environment. The high level of support for television advertisements amongst both the general public and the farmers may well reflect the fact that it is such a pervasive medium. Also, previous experience of the communication of the Country Code through the medium of television may well have influenced this choice.

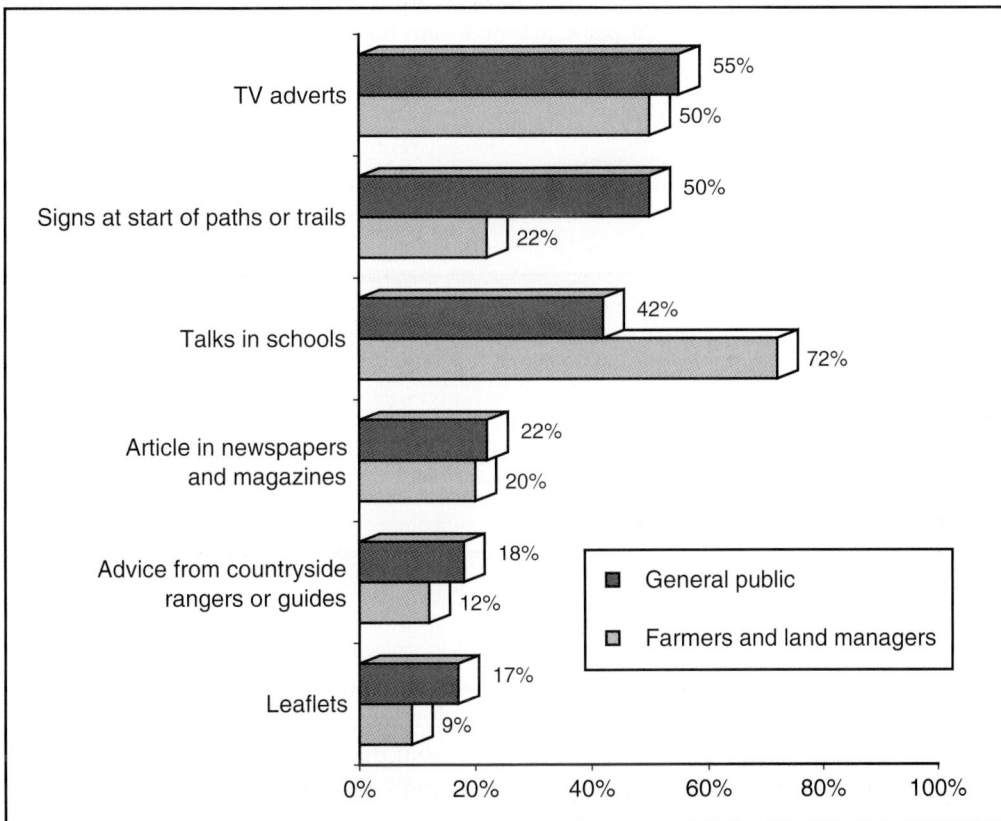

Figure 5.2. Means of influencing behaviour (per cent). The data show the percentages of all 1,165 Scottish Opinion Survey of the general public in summer 2000 and of all 475 interviewees in the telephone survey of farmers and land managers in autumn 2000.

5.8 Management of public access

A number of options for managing public access were presented to the respondents in the farmers' and land managers' survey in order to determine which were being implemented currently and which would be considered in the future. Table 5.3 summarises the main findings. No other measure was mentioned by more than 10 per cent of those interviewed.

The control of dogs was the main measure currently being taken by farmers and land managers. Looking to the future, the idea of working with local authorities and other bodies to promote responsible public access to the countryside was the one most likely to be undertaken. Providing gates and stiles and maintaining paths were also areas where a significant proportion of respondents believed that more could be done to encourage the management of public access to the countryside. It is worth noting that, at present, 97 per cent of the interviewees did not receive any financial assistance directly related to providing or managing public access to their land.

Seven measures were identified as being the most important to help manage public access to the countryside in the future. These are grant-aid to cover the costs of providing access facilities such as gates and paths (51 per cent), additional payments for time and effort spent managing access (36 per cent), compensation for loss or damage (31 per cent), public education programmes (29 per cent), grant-aid for access-linked diversification (22 per cent), information leaflets (14 per cent), and ranger services (10 per cent).

Table 5.3. Managing public access. The data show percentages of the 475 interviewees included in the telephone survey of farmers and land managers.

	Currently taken	Consider taking in the future
Make sure that any dogs are kept under control	71	1
Provide gates and stiles to prevent damage to field boundaries	29	11
Keep animals in fields which are not crossed by paths	25	1
Make sure there are no obstructions on paths which might affect walkers	23	8
Work with local authorities and other bodies to promote responsible access	15	24
Maintain paths to encourage walkers to use them	12	11
Leave a field margin to allow access	11	8
Prohibit access by locking gates	11	5

5.9 Some final thoughts

While public access to the countryside for recreation does generate a number of difficulties for farmers and land managers, especially in the urban fringe, there is a general recognition that many of these problems are created by a small minority. This is particularly the case for those farmers (around 40 per cent) who suffer from the impact of illegal activities such as fly tipping, poaching and drug-taking. Legislation already exists to deal with these particular problems but remedial action will be dependent on the resources available to the police to address these illegal activities compared to other crimes.

The majority of problems affecting farmers and land managers are generated, by general consensus, through the ignorance of a large section of the population in relation to the dynamic of the countryside in general and farming in particular. Two-thirds of farmers and land managers claim to suffer difficulties produced by access to the countryside. It is recognised that the majority of these difficulties are a direct result of a limited understanding of how the visitor's actions impact upon the farmer and countryside activities rather than any malicious intent. For this reason, it is understandable why there is a significant level of support, especially amongst farmers, for an extensive education programme to be developed and promoted to coincide with the launch of the SOAC.

The two sets of survey findings have highlighted a number of areas where there are considerable differences between the views and opinions of the farming community and the general public towards management of access to the countryside. One of these areas of divergence is in relation to the control of dogs. Walking a dog is one of the primary motivators for people to go into the countryside for informal recreation; around one in four of those walking in the countryside are accompanied by a dog. Significantly, these people were more likely to choose to walk on farmland as opposed to country parks or other designated areas, possibly as a result of increasing control over dogs in these areas.

In the majority of situations on farmland, the public believed that keeping dogs on a lead would be sufficient control – the one exception is in the hills and mountains where over 60 per cent thought that it would be acceptable to let the dogs off the lead but under close control. The farmers and land managers had a similar opinion to the general public with regard to dogs in the hills and mountains. They also had a similar opinion in relation to meeting participants in other types of activities in the countryside, such as cycling and horse-riding. However, their position was more towards excluding dogs completely from farmland, especially in fields with cattle and sheep, but also to a lesser extent in fields with crops.

Another area of divergence related to fields with grass. To the person on a walk in the countryside, an empty field with grass was not considered to be a reason for adjusting their route; to the farmer, such a field is a valuable element of the farm and an asset which should be looked after. Consequently, the farmer would prefer the walker to take another route or walk around the edge while a significant proportion of walkers do not see any problem in walking across the field by the shortest route. This reflects another example where a greater degree of understanding of farming by the individual walker could minimise the potential for conflict.

One of the major issues to emerge from this study is the important role which the further development of local networks of paths could play in managing access to the countryside. From the perspective of the public seeking opportunities to access the countryside for recreation, such facilities would address a significant volume of demand, especially amongst the majority whose access to the countryside is for walks of 3 km (2 miles) or less and who are happy to restrict their routes to a limited number of areas. Apart from meeting the recreational needs of these 'users', the path networks could also act to limit the direct impact on farming enterprises. From a land manager's perspective, this managed provision would also minimise the costs which might fall to the landowner or manager in terms of providing the necessary infrastructure for outdoor activities. It would also direct the need for such investment to designated areas where the primary responsibility would lie with local authorities and other similar organisations.

The predominance of walking as the main access activity does tend to dominate the other pursuits such as cycling, horse-riding and water-related sports. While some degree of shared use of areas and paths is recognised, the prevalent situation is more likely to feature the participants in these activities making their own arrangements with farmers and land managers where appropriate.

There is little evidence from the qualitative elements of this study that the new legislation and the launch of the SOAC will have a significant impact on the volume of demand for access to the countryside. If anything, the opportunities presented by this legislation may well result in a better quality of access, by informed participants. This, naturally, depends on the provision of adequate resources, allocated to the promotion and education phases of the implementation of the SOAC. It is evident that the promotion of the SOAC will require to use a range of media aimed both at the general public and also at children through schools and youth organisations, but also directly at those seeking access to the countryside. It is vital that the content and tone of any communications is tested so as to ensure that it is appropriate to the audience being addressed (see Allison, this volume).

6 IMPACTS OF RECREATION ON LAND MANAGEMENT

Richard Williamson

Summary

1.   Any scan of recent broadsheet newspapers will show just how polarised views can become when talking about access to the countryside.   The language and iconography of warfare is used – 'battlelines are drawn', ramblers are on the 'warpath', and images are of barbed wire.

2.   People are pigeonholed or categorised into comfortable stereotypes. Integrated land management is a goal, but it is forgotten when talking about access.

3.   Ask land managers about access problems and they will mention the 'unholy trinity' of dogs, litter and vandalism. These are not access problems; they are social problems.

4.   The biggest change required will be in attitude. Stop thinking in stereotypes and get on with the business of achieving a multi-benefit countryside.

6.1 Introduction

"What beside increases the attractions of the district to the visitor is the almost absolute and unrestraint freedom to be enjoyed. Notices of trespassers will be prosecuted, keep to the road and others of a like nature by which a selfish and exclusive landlordism would seek to deprive the general public of enjoyments which have a heritage of humanity are no where to be seen. In this respect The Duke of Buccleuch in following his example the other landed proprietors of the district have allowed to all the liberty to roam wheresoever they list" (Brown, 1891, p. 10).

As this extract from the History of Sanquhar demonstrates, the Buccleuch Estates have a long tradition of open access. People in the 21st century can still wander wheresoever they 'list'. However, managing them nowadays is a little more complicated. Recreation is more than a country walk; estate management is a 'high tech' business; successfully to integrate recreation, estate management requires an approach that is both flexible and tolerant.

6.2 Integration and compartmentalisation

Integration is about how things fit together, and about joining them up. Integrated access is about fitting the needs of walkers, cyclists, horse riders, canoeists and many others into the plans for timber felling, barley harvesting, pheasant shooting, salmon fishing, and many other estate management operations. Integrated access is a fine aspiration, but yet it is one which collectively we are nowhere near reaching yet.

On the other hand, our thinking on access is perhaps the opposite to integration. Disintegration is about fragmentation, about everything being in pieces, and about nothing being joined up. Much of the debate about access focuses on compartmentalised issues. It boxes the issues into neat subsets. There are problems caused by walkers, problems caused by farmers, or problems between cyclists and horse riders. It is a reductionist approach that prevents progress towards integration. This lazy, boxed thinking fuels people's preconceptions about each other. Factors think and act like factors, foresters like foresters, ramblers like ramblers, and so on. Because society produces stereotypes that exaggerate differences, in effect almost creating caricatures, there is no surprise that access is still disintegrated.

Life really is not that simple. Farmers shop in supermarkets, factors visit swimming pools, and gamekeepers enjoy the cinema. Similarly, office workers shop at farmers' markets and accountants cycle in forests. Everybody uses products from the countryside. Where is the real divide? There is plenty of evidence for the disintegrated approach. The planning systems shows how society loves to work in nice, neat, cosy boxes. There are structure plans, local plans, tourism strategies, access strategies, local forest frameworks, indicative forest strategies, forest strategies, local economic strategies, biodiversity action plans, species action plans, habitat action plans, and community plans. Do all of these plans and strategies fit together? Are they all integrated? Everybody seems to want to have a say in how land is managed. The list of communities with an interest in the countryside is almost endless. It is a list, though, of nicely boxed organisations and interest groups.

In order to be able to develop an integrated approach to access we need to be clear about our objectives. What do we want of countryside access? Are we searching for a political ideal or do we want practical access for real people?

6.3 A land management perspective

At the moment there is much emphasis on land reform. However, lack of clarity of objectives is producing muddled thinking and creating mixed expectations. There have been four land reform consultation papers. Originally land reform was seen as being needed both on the grounds of fairness and to remove land-based barriers to rural development. The present conclusion is that land reform is needed for the right of responsible access and community right to buy.

These shifting objectives make it hard for landowners to build a positive, integrated approach to access. As long as we remain unclear about what our objectives are we will continue to get newspaper headlines that portray the access debate as some kind of class war, where either ramblers are on the 'warpath' or landowners are on the 'warpath', clashing at the farm gate. The language is one of warfare, with 'battlelines being drawn' or with images of barbed wire and locked gates. Headlines from the late 1990s proclaim the same conflict as the headlines covering the Kinder Scout trespasses of the 1930s. Our boxed, stereotypical, and polarised thinking on access has not produced any real progress in the last 70 years or more.

The Access Forum (see Davison, this volume) has brought people together to identify real objectives for access. It has provided a unique opportunity to develop an integrated approach to access management. It is, however, easy to be lazy in this debate and revert to the comfort zone of stereotypes to introduce the deep-seated prejudices rather than to focus on real problems. Ask almost any landowner or manager about access problems and they will quote the 'unholy trinity' of dogs, litter and vandalism.

Dogs, litter and vandalism are not access problems; they are social problems. They are not uniquely countryside problems. Stray dogs roam around Perth and Pitlochry and may kill sheep if they find them. People leave litter in Wester Hailes and Wester Ross. Vandals smash things up in Easterhouses or East Linton. The common perception is that these are all access problems. Such a perception has prevented constructive discussions on real access issues. A way forward needs to be found.

6.4 Looking to the future

Perhaps if the debate was on good citizenship, dog welfare or the provision of leisure facilities, there may be some solutions to some of these social problems. Instead, they have been put into the box labelled 'access'. It has been forgotten that having them there has not solved the problems of the last 20 or more years, and it is unlikely to solve the problems in the next 20 years. There are real access issues for landowners, and real concerns about making a new approach to access work. But we need to be honest! The problem centres on taking a walk in the countryside. There are no real access problems for land managers, only perceived problems and these arise from the 'blinkered', boxed and stereotypical view of access.

There are genuine concerns about the provision of adequate resources to achieve the new view of access. In developing core path networks, will the money be there both to build and to maintain the routes? Current SNH work on pilot studies in Dumfries and Galloway, and elsewhere, give potential costs between tens of millions and hundreds of millions of pounds if applied to the whole of Scotland. If a modern, well managed path network is not delivered, who will be called to account? The chances are that the landowner will be blamed. This is a perception that gives landowners real problems in playing an active part in the access debate.

There are still many social and institutional barriers to integrated access. It is essential that a consultation process is developed which brings together all those people with an interest in the countryside. It will not be easy for busy farmers to find time to make their contribution. The communities who could benefit most from the process must not be excluded from the discussions. Local Access Forums should be created in towns and cities as well as the countryside, each with a diverse membership that reflects the nature of each community.

These Access Forums must avoid getting side-tracked away from the relevant debates. They will need clear, simple objectives. Responsibilities have to be both easy to understand and simple to implement. A right of responsible access will mean that land managers will have to develop or adapt some working practices, but this is not a big task, fading into insignificance in comparison with changes required for pollution control, for planning, for health (see Allison, this volume) and safety, etc. Real access, which meets the needs of real people, will not come cheaply, but it will come inevitably. But there will have to be a change in attitudes, moving away from stereotypes, and progressing the business of achieving a multi-benefit countryside.

Reference

Brown, J. (1891). *The History of Sanquhar, 2nd. edn.* J. Anderson & Son, Dumfries.

7 NATURE CODES: TOWARDS A COMMON VISUAL LANGUAGE

Bob Jones

Summary

1.   The various countryside codes contain so many head points that many countryside visitors fail to remember them.

2.   Forest Enterprise (FE) proposed to combine the various codes into a single visual 'alphabet', of which other countryside managers could also make use.

3   Scottish Natural Heritage (SNH) pioneered some work in conveying information and engaging with the visitor by a simplified sign language.

4.   Forest Enterprise has developed this approach, and has trialed it and surveyed a sample of about 300 visitors in two locations.

5.   The results were disappointing, as there appeared to be a considerable degree of 'sign blindness'.

6.   What does this signify for the future of the FE proposal? Although the concept appears sound, in practice the more traditional signage and other interpretative techniques may be more effective. More research and evaluation is needed.

7.1 Introduction

How many head points of the Country Code (Table 7.1) can you recall? Equally, how many head points from the other countryside-related codes can you recall? Taking the six codes listed in Table 7.2 there are 80 head points. In interpretation we expect people to assimilate between three and five new facts during a typical visit. For many people with an average memory, they can just about accommodate a seven-digit telephone number! And then only

Table 7.1. The 12 head points in the Country Code (from Anon., 1998).

1.	Enjoy the countryside and respect its life and work
2.	Guard against all risk of fire
3.	Leave all gates as you find them
4.	Keep your dogs under close control
5.	Keep to paths across farmland
6.	Use gates and stiles to cross fences, hedges and walls
7.	Leave livestock, crops and machinery alone
8.	Take your litter home
9.	Help keep all water clean
10.	Protect wildlife, plants and trees
11.	Take special care on country roads
12.	Make no unnecessary noise

Table 7.2. A comparison of the number of head points in six countryside codes.

Code	Number of head points
The Country Code	12
The Forest Code	12
The Mountain Code	16
The Water Code	24
The Forest Cycling Code	8
The Forest Horse Riding Code	8
Total	80

by frequent and repetitive use. How many such numbers can you remember? If we expect the visitor to the countryside to take on board a whole raft of behavioural messages – and we do – as well as other site or topic-based interpretation, then we need to simplify how these messages are delivered. We also need to deliver such messages in a positive and 'engaging' manner, not in a negative 'Do not ...!' tone, as exemplified by the sign in the Back O'Bennachie car park (see Plate 1a).

The purpose of this chapter is to explore the potential for the development of a single code using a visual vocabulary that cuts across a lot of 'wheel re-invention' and agencies having to 'do their own thing'. A single multi-image alphabet, to be used by managers as a mix-and-match menu of behavioural icons or pictograms, which can be drawn down as appropriate, could be a useful management tool. Obviously any selection would need to be particularly relevant or tailored to suit a given site or resource.

For the visitor, the primary audience, there could be a 'drip-feed' exposure to a consistent visual vocabulary that can become instantly, almost sub-consciously, recognisable. This could be analogous to the way that the road sign symbols or tourist information symbols work. These can be classified as primary level and secondary level visual alphabets respectively in terms of influencing how people behave in public areas. The proposed visual alphabet on access – or behavioural code - would be at a tertiary level, and would become equally familiar over time, providing reassurance and 'comfort'. It should be a language that transcends the written word, yet it would be unambiguous in meaning and positive in demeanour.

For the manager, a subsidiary but important audience, a single, visual behavioural code provides a uniform approach. It could be an off-the-shelf system of approved and tested images, even available as a word-processing font. The new and forthcoming access legislation in England, Wales and Scotland brings with it an obligation to interpret the Country Code (or its successor) and associated codes to the visitor, as well as to educate visitors in their meaning. Why develop separate programmes across the various agencies? Why 'teach' visitors different 'languages'? Surely it makes sense to mount a joint initiative, because of the potential accumulated costs to agencies doing their own thing, and the benefits of sharing of resources. This would be a strong demonstration of truly 'joined-up thinking'. But possibly more importantly, in a world of information overload, it would be a more responsible approach to communicating with visitors.

7.2 The background

Work by Scottish Natural Heritage (SNH) (H. Muschamp, pers. comm.) looked at the use of pictograms (graphic depictions of the subject matter) as a way of influencing visitor behaviour across Scotland's National Nature Reserves. This project gave rise to the sort of images shown in Figure 7.1. The declared aim of the project was to "address management

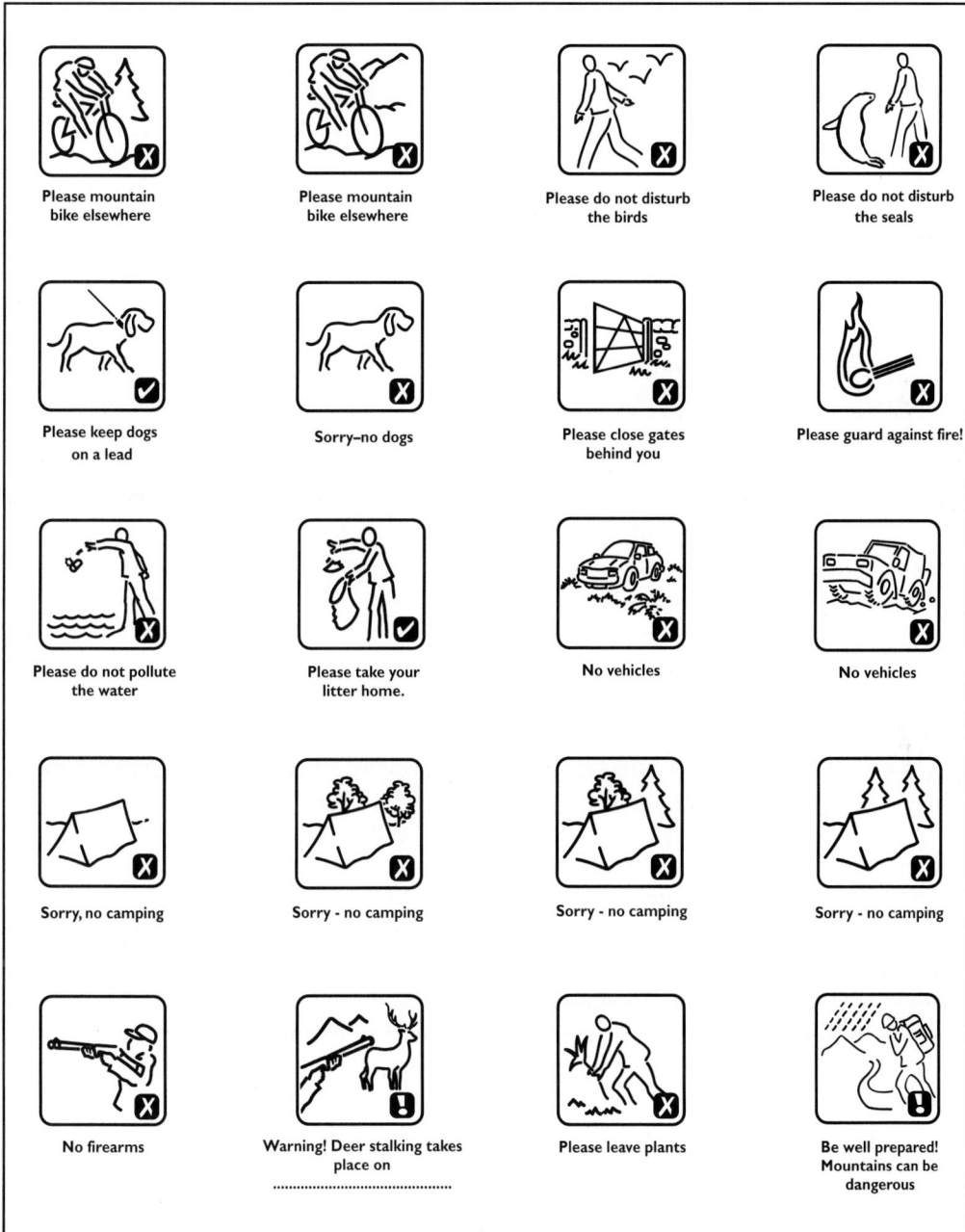

Figure 7.1. The original Scottish Natural Heritage pictograms developed between 1994 and 1998.

issues by promoting responsible access". In particular, seven objectives were to be encompassed by the pictograms. They should

- address public access and liability issues for site managers,
- be clearly understood and accessible by the majority of the recreational access audience,
- be effective in the short (mind engaging) time available,
- create links between people and their actions,
- promote understanding and responsibility,
- be appropriate for (reproduction in) signage and literature, and
- provide the basis for a single visual language.

An example of their use, at the Muir of Dinnet National Nature Reserve, is shown in Plate 1b.

These seven aims clearly fitted with those of Forest Enterprise (FE) which, co-incidentally as the SNH work matured in 1998, was beginning to look at a new programme of work driven by the increasing focus on managing access, safety and liabilities. FE's solicitors had begun to agitate for the development and application of a standard signing programme to be applied throughout the forest estate. The solicitors reasoned that if they were to defend against liability claims in an increasingly litigious society, FE should post the woodland and forest entrances with signs and notices which would clearly establish what visitors could and could not do. Also, the signs would need to indicate what visitors could expect to encounter by way of hazards and conditions (for example, exposed terrain or muddy paths underfoot). Initially this approach found favour within FE ranks, where the immediate reaction of managers was to 'watch your back'. Others in FE, however, began to feel this was a little excessive and potentially more damaging in the long term and costly in generating a backlash against officialdom and bureaucracy. It was clearly at odds with the 'visitors are welcome' ethos which FE had been building up over a number of years.

Additionally, because the Forestry Commission (FC) covers the whole of Great Britain, FE (the forest management arm of the FC) was acutely conscious of its responsibilities towards bilingualism, a statutory requirement in Wales. It has endeavoured to be pro-active in acknowledging Gaelic as a living language in the north and west of Scotland. Throughout Great Britain we live in an increasingly multicultural society with varied levels of literacy or familiarity with the nuances of the English language (let alone the local variations and nuances of the Welsh and Gaelic languages). In Scotland, in particular, the business of tourism, and hence the need for multilingual translation for overseas visitors, has become a central pillar of the rural economy.

However, bilingual media mean twice the text where words are used to convey a message. Multilingualism can mean text four, five, or six times the length of the original, which becomes confusing and visually inaccessible, as evidenced by one prominent example of a seven-language panel programme imposed upon one of Scotland's best known landscapes. All of this directly conflicts with the principles of good communication design.

If nature (behavioural) codes are to work, the primary factor in their presentation is that they should communicate with the intended audience. It is therefore fundamental that they should be simple, and that extraneous or irrelevant information is omitted.

The countryside codes, in their current form and number, have become over-prolific and complicated as far as the intended consumer is concerned. Indeed at times they appear to be more to do with functioning as a surrogate byelaws display. As a result there is a rapidly growing and widely held view that these codes – mostly originating from the 1970s and 1980s - may have become counter-productive and largely ineffective. The desirable goals of 'intervention in visitor behaviour' and 'engaging the mind' have become obscured.

7.3 The development of a common visual language

From the management of access and liabilities remit, a brief was set to evolve imagery which dealt with three critical areas, namely permitted activities, prohibited activities, and potential hazards and conflicts (for example, forestry operations or the presence of other forest users such as cyclists or horse riders). Within these three categories there should be a set of symbols, using an easily understood graphic form, which could be included on all media. In addition to the obvious images surrounding fire prevention, fishing, swimming, etc., there was a need to consider some more complex depictions (Table 7.3).

Table 7.3. Some examples of the more complex messages for which graphic symbols were required.

Message
This is a working forest
Conditions underfoot can change rapidly away from established paths
Forests are used for a wide range of purpose and activities
This is a challenging area for mountain bikers – experts only

As FE was aware of the SNH nature code work and the research undertaken by H. Muschamp (pers. comm.), it was most logical to build on that formative work. The basic design principles, which underpinned the SNH pictograms, contain six important points, namely

- the images should be readable by as many people as possible, including the colour blind;
- the images used should be simple with clear contrasts for those with impaired vision;
- the images should achieve near instant recognition;
- all images should be easily routable in timber;
- all images should appear positive by using a cross or tick rather than a red slash; and
- the number of images should be limited in any given location (three would be ideal, but five was a recommended maximum).

The SNH research also suggested the inclusion of words in certain situations, for example where a 'No Camping' pictogram was to be used. This would be accompanied by a message as to where the nearest public campsite could be found.

Consequently, FE borrowed the pictograms developed by SNH, adjusted some to fit its specific messages, and added new subject images in a similar illustrative style. These were then further divided into 'core' and 'non-core' messages, based on pilot work requested by the FE's Access Management Working Group at the time. The initial proposals were checked by a broad cross-section of FE's forest managers and rangers at three workshops, held across Great Britain, which focussed on access and liability issues. This sample of about 100 informed staff was broadly supportive of the concept, but had a more subjective opinion of the actual image design (for example, liking one rather than another, but with no rational explanation of why, nor being able to offer an alternative). Constructive amendments did result, in particular to the tick, cross and exclamation mark boxes incorporated in the pictograms. These elements were enhanced to become bolder and were imbued with colour - red for prohibition, green for permission, yellow for caution (a standard signage colour-coding convention) (see Plate 2 for the core pictograms, and Plate 3 for the non-core pictograms).

During 1999 FE piloted these symbols at several sites across Great Britain, and undertook surveys of visitor reactions in two locations – at Mallards Pike in the Forest of Dean (Ordnance Survey grid reference SO638094) with 175 interviews, and at Glencoe Lochan in the Scottish Highlands (grid reference NN104595) with 125 interviews (see Plate 1c).

FE sought to determine whether visitors actually saw the signs, and whether they understood the messages conveyed. The four main points relating to the visitors' reactions are shown in Table 7.4. The forest managers' reactions were generally supportive and significantly in favour of simple wordless symbols. Their main concerns centred on production and maintenance costs, due to the perceived level of complex detail and the use of colour. There was also some concern that the images were too small.

Table 7.4. Initial results of a survey of the Forest Enterprise's new signage in the Forest of Dean and at Glencoe Lochan.

Result	*Comment*	*Conclusion*
Between 48% and 70% had not seen one, some, or all of the signs	Does this suggest a level of sign-blindness?	Worrying
The simpler messages were easily and consistently understood: no cycling, no fishing, or swimming permitted were 98% correct		Predictable
Complex messages were not well or consistently understood, e.g. 'working forest' correctly perceived by 57%	However, 30% thought it meant 'do not cut down trees', ostensibly the exact opposite message!	Understandable
Many interviewees expected to find what we were telling them about in the forest environment	94% realised that conditions underfoot off the path would be different and probably rough	Reassuring

7.4 Looking to the future

As a result of this work there are four recommendations and conclusions. First, complex issues should be dealt with through more traditional interpretative programmes and media. It appears that such complexity cannot be reduced to simple pictorial images. Second, site specific issues (for example forest operations) should be dealt with through a standardised and more rigorously applied health and safety sign programme. This has now been implemented as a working instruction within FE. Third, FE should seek to work with other agencies in evolving a 'combination code' for countryside access, but this would not necessarily be based on the nature codes pilot work. Finally, reluctance was expressed with regard to continuing with the complex SNH symbols, with many in FE favouring a return to simpler symbols (for example, with a red bar across for prohibition).

If this final point is accepted then FE would limit its communication effort in developing a single behavioural code to basic 'do' or 'don't' issues. In the latter instance this would be a regressive step towards overtly negative messaging. It would abandon the original premise, which those closely involved with the project believe still holds good, i.e. to engage with the visitor. The maxim (with minor adjustment) at the heart of Tilden's (1957) seminal text on environmental and heritage interpretation remains pertinent, i.e. that

- through interpretation - education;
- through education - understanding; and
- through understanding – engagement.

(Tilden's original concluding line actually reads "through understanding – enlightenment").

The actual imagery to be used on signs and in other media is a design problem, and not a fundamental barrier to development of the concept. The principle of wordless communication, via a visual alphabet, to convey country code issues is a valid and appropriate solution in seeking to change the way in which visitors behave when in the countryside. However, as is often the case with a new approach, it may take a little time to get past the initial resistance to change on the part of countryside managers. Also, it may take some time for the countryside visitor to become acquainted with this new approach to signage.

Acknowledgement

The author is indebted to Hugh Muschamp, formerly of Scottish Natural Heritage, for access to his earlier work and research on this subject of a visual language, and for his support in taking it forward.

References

Anonymous (1998). *Care for Scotland's Countryside: follow the Country Code.* Scottish Natural Heritage, Perth.

Tilden, F. (1957). *Interpreting our Heritage.* University of North Carolina Press, Chapel Hill.

Postscript

As this book goes to press, a cross-agency working group has been established to take the idea of a common behavioural code forward. This initiative has come about as a direct result of interest expressed by those who attended the SNH conference in autumn 2000 and who took part in the Nature Codes Workshop. For further details, refer to the author — bob.jones@forestry.gsi.gov.uk — or to Scottish Natural Heritage, Awareness and Involvement Unit, Battleby, Perth — www.snh.org.uk.

PART TWO

Promoting Responsibility

8   Development of the United States 'Leave No Trace' Programme: A Historical Perspective*

Jeffrey L. Marion and Scott E. Reid

Summary
1.   The United States Forest Service created 'Leave No Trace' (LNT) in 1990.
2.   The mission of LNT is to promote and inspire responsible outdoor recreation through education, research and partnerships.
3.   LNT has grown into a national interagency educational programme with a full complement of educational materials, training courses, and over 200 agency, organisational and corporate partners.

8.1   Introduction

The goal of the United States 'Leave No Trace' (LNT) educational programme is to avoid or minimize impacts to protected area resources and to help ensure a positive recreational experience for all visitors. America's public lands are a finite resource with social and ecological values linked to the integrity of their natural conditions and processes. Land managers face a perennial struggle in their efforts to achieve an appropriate balance between the competing mandates to preserve natural and cultural resources and to provide high quality recreational use. Visitor education designed to instil low-impact ethics and skills is a critical management component and is seen as a light-handed approach that can reduce the need for more direct and regulatory forms of management.

"Wilderness management is 80-90 per cent education and information and 10 per cent regulation" (Max Peterson, former Chief of the US Forest Service, 1985).

"Education ... is a preemptive strike ... to teach the American people how to enjoy the wilderness without destroying it. All other methods merely try to repair the damage after it is done. Stronger wilderness education programs would dramatically decrease the need for law enforcement and cleanup" (James Bradley, former staff member, Subcommittee on National) Parks and Public Lands, US House of Representatives, undated).

This chapter describes the historical development of the LNT educational programme. It begins with a review of the need for the programme and traces its conception and early development in the 1970s, revitalization in 1991, creation of Leave No Trace, Inc., and the current status. The chapter concludes with a discussion of the elements of the programme that have made it successful and recommendations for the development of similar educational programmes.

---

*Plates 4 to 9 inclusive relate to this chapter.

8.2 The need

America's recreation lands, including private, local, state and federal holdings, are being used and enjoyed by more and more people. The most dramatic increases in outdoor recreation occurred in the 1960s when hiking, camping and backpacking first became popular. For example, use of National Forest primitive areas and wilderness tripled during the 1960s and public land visitation continues to increase. Recreation visits to National Forest lands have jumped from 4.6 million in 1924 to 900 million in 1999. Similarly, recreation visits to National Park Service areas were 33 million in 1950, increasing more than five-fold to 172 million in 1970, with more modest increases to 258 million in 1990, and 287 million in 1999.

This magnitude of recreation visitation periodically raises the issue in the popular media of whether Americans are 'loving their parks to death.' One hiker venturing off the trail or one group creating a new campsite may seem of little significance, but the combined effects of millions of such instances leave a substantial and cumulative mark on the land. Trampling by foot and horse traffic causes loss of vegetation cover and change in species composition, as well as compaction and erosion of soil. Other problems of recreation include damage to trees, campfire scars, litter, and improperly disposed human or dog waste (Hammitt and Cole, 1998; Leung and Marion, 2000). Such changes can also degrade the quality of outdoor experiences because they are most evident along trails and at recreation or camping sites where visitors spend the majority of their time. The expansion and proliferation of visitor-created campsites and trails also increase the aggregate area of human disturbance and lead to the fragmentation of wildlife habitat. Disturbance of native fauna can cause displacement from critical foraging or nesting habitats while individuals that obtain human food become beggars or nuisance animals that must be relocated or killed (Knight and Temple, 1995). Archaeological and cultural resources are also at risk from visitors who climb around to explore ruins or take artefacts like pottery shards as souvenirs. Increasing recreational visitation also causes crowding along trails and at campsites, which diminishes solitude. Incompatible activities or encounters with discourteous visitors can lead to conflicts between groups.

Unfortunately, research has shown that the majority of recreation-associated resource impacts occur with initial or low levels of use. For example, on campsites in the Boundary Waters Canoe Area Wilderness, 95 per cent of the total loss of tree seedlings and 61 per cent of the increase in soil compaction occurred on sites receiving just 12 nights of use per year (Marion and Merriam, 1985). Experimental trampling studies have consistently documented asymptotic responses between the amount of trampling and the severity of damage to vegetation and soils (Cole, 1993, 1995). Impacts occur rapidly at initial or low use levels but the rate of loss diminishes as maximum change approaches 100 per cent. These studies also demonstrate substantial differences in the ability of different vegetation and soil types to resist trampling damage and in their ability to recover from disturbance (Cole, 1987; Leung and Marion, 2000). Some important implications of these findings are that impacts can be effectively minimized by concentrating recreational traffic on the most resistant surfaces, including rock, sand, bare soil, snow, and grassy groundcovers.

Sustaining outstanding natural resource conditions and recreational opportunities are primary goals for public land managers, most of whom operate under dual legal mandates to protect natural resources and processes while providing for appropriate recreational uses. Research has demonstrated that resource degradation is an inevitable consequence of recreation visitation, even at low use levels. Similarly, as visitor use expands, so too will visitor encounters, jeopardizing opportunities for solitude. The challenge for managers is to eliminate avoidable impacts and to minimize those impacts that are unavoidable. For example, visitors who substitute camping stoves for campfires avoid a host of resource impacts related to the gathering and burning of firewood. Managers can achieve such ends through regulations, i.e. prohibiting campfires, or through education, i.e. highlighting campfire-related resource impacts and the advantages of using stoves.

Effective educational interventions can encourage visitors, individually and collectively, to think more deeply about the environmental and social consequences of their actions. In doing so, it is hoped that the visitors will gain a greater insight into outdoor ethics and will be encouraged to modify their own behaviour through the adoption of low-impact practices. For example, rock climbers who previously used pitons recognised the collective impact that these had on their favourite routes. The climbers surmised that piton use was not sustainable, and they modified their behaviour to adopt replacements (cams, stoppers and even fixed anchors) that had a lesser impact. This is an example of where ethical norms have changed (and indeed it could be argued that they have been elevated). Such approaches, often indirect, preserve visitor freedom from regulations and can also delay or forego the need to limit visitor use.

Educational programmes such as LNT provide a vehicle for promoting awareness of recreation impacts and encouraging visitors to become knowledgeable about how to reduce them. To halt and reverse current trends of recreation-caused resource degradation, visitors must become aware of their responsibility to reduce their impact on the land and to the experiences of other visitors. Low-impact ethics and skills need to become a standard code of conduct that promotes the stewardship practices necessary to protect the ecological and social health of recreation lands.

8.3 Programme conception and early development

As wildland use continued to expand in the 1960s, 1970s and 1980s, visitors to public lands began to witness the degradation of their favourite trails and campsites. The development of low-impact hiking and camping practices occurred incrementally over this period. The federal agencies, notably the Forest Service (FS) but also the Bureau of Land Management (BLM) and the National Park Service (NPS), developed numerous brochures during these years variously called *Wilderness Manners, Wilderness Ethics, Minimum-impact Camping*, and *No-Trace Camping*. In the late 1960s and early 1970s wilderness managers had initially applied regulations to address visitor impact problems but found them to be largely ineffective. In 1979, Jim Bradley, a FS wilderness specialist in the Pacific Northwest, wrote about the need for an educational approach for managing recreation impacts (Bradley, 1979). He noted that a purely regulatory approach is inappropriate because

- regulations antagonize the public rather than win their support,
- most impacts are not from malicious acts, but result from an insensitivity to the consequences of one's actions and from a lack of knowledge regarding appropriate low-impact practices, and
- enforcement of regulations is difficult in wildlands due to their large and remote nature.

FS wilderness managers developed an educational programme in the mid-1970s that emphasized personal communication at busy wilderness accesses. Wilderness information specialists sought out visitors using a friendly and hospitable approach to provide information that included no-trace travel and camping tips. These programmes evolved in the early 1980s into a more formal 'No-Trace' programme that relied on a humanistic approach, emphasizing the cultivation of new wilderness ethics and more sustainable no-trace travel and camping practices. The success of this programme led to interagency coordination and in 1987 the FS, NPS and BLM cooperatively developed and distributed a pamphlet entitled *Leave 'No Trace' Land Ethics*.

During this period a number of books and papers were also written about wildland ethics and minimum-impact camping practices. Books include *The Wilderness Handbook* (Petzoldt, 1974), the Sierra Club's *Walking Softly in the Wilderness* (Hart, 1977), *Backwoods Ethics: Environmental Concerns for Hikers and Campers* (Waterman and Waterman, 1979) and *Soft Paths* (Hampton and Cole, 1988). These books highlighted the advantages of low-impact camping and actively promoted a 'clean camping' crusade. They also provided 'how to' advice on travel and camping practices that would help recreationists lessen their individual impact. Similarly, the scientific community contributed a number of papers in conference proceedings and journals on 'information and education techniques to improve minimum impact use knowledge in wilderness areas' (Fazio, 1979), on 'managing campfire impacts in the backcountry' (Cole and Dalle-Molle, 1982), on 'wilderness campsite selection' (Cole and Benedict, 1983), and on 'low-impact recreational practices for wilderness and backcountry' (Cole, 1989).

8.4 Development of a national programme

A lack of national leadership, funding and training had limited the effectiveness of early minimum-impact educational efforts in the 1970s and 1980s. By 1990 the clear need for visitor education, coupled with increasing knowledge about visitor impacts from research, prompted the FS to convene a committee to discuss the potential for a national programme. The committee agreed that a single message should take the place of the various permutations that had developed over the years. After deliberating on several options, the 'Leave No Trace' phrase was selected as the new name for minimum-impact messages targeted to non-motorized recreational activities.

The FS also extended a partnership offer to the National Outdoor Leadership School (NOLS) to develop an LNT educational curriculum for wildland visitors. NOLS agreed to this offer in 1990 and a Memorandum of Understanding was signed with the FS in 1991. NOLS is a non-profit school founded in 1965 to teach leadership and outdoor skills that protect the user and the environment. The school has long been a recognized leader in developing and teaching minimum-impact hiking and camping practices. This knowledge was compiled and published in the book *Soft Paths* by Hampton and Cole (1987, revised 1995).

NOLS's involvement in the LNT programme marked the beginning of the partnership model that continues to the present day. NOLS was instrumental in working with the FS to make the programme science-based by collecting relevant scientific literature and consulting with scientists in the review and development of low-impact hiking and camping skills. NOLS also developed the ethics and experiential training aspects of the LNT programme, the capstone of which is a five-day Master Educator course for land managers, staff of organisations that lead trips, outdoor educators, and others.

> *"We have long recognized education as the best strategy for reversing the trend of damage to wilderness and undeveloped areas caused by recreation visitors ... Accordingly, the Forest Service developed and has actively sponsored Leave No Trace as our outdoor ethics program for non-motorized users..."* (F. Dale Robertson, former Chief of the US Forest Service, letter to regional foresters, April 1992).

As land managers learned of the successful educational partnership between the FS and NOLS, other federal agencies became interested in participating in the emerging national programme. The BLM joined the partnership in 1993, followed by the NPS and Fish and Wildlife Service (FWS) in 1994. A new Memorandum was signed in 1994 to formalize the LNT programme partnership between FS, NOLS, BLM, NPS and the FWS. This agreement committed the federal agencies to provide overall steering and direction for the national programme, with NOLS supplying curricula, training, and the development and distribution of LNT information. NOLS continued to manage the programme by producing and selling brochures, videos, posters and other educational materials via a toll-free number and a website.

NOLS also worked with the agencies and scientists to develop a mission statement, strategic goals, and eight principles of LNT (providing a focus for more specific educational practices). The mission statement called for the development of a nationally recognized minimum-impact backcountry educational system that would educate wildland user groups, federal land management agencies and the public through training and educational materials. Strategic goals focused on the development of high quality, science-based educational materials and courses for selected target regions and recreational activities, and networking to disseminate educational ideas and programmes nationwide.

For each target region and activity, NOLS has also developed comprehensive Master course curricula and a series of LNT outdoor skills and ethics booklets. The first 14-page booklet was produced in 1992, complementing and eventually replacing an LNT pamphlet and booklet set created by the FS in 1992 in cooperation with the BLM, NPS and the Izaak Walton League. Each year additional volumes have been added to the series, which currently numbers 16. Each booklet is developed through a comprehensive process involving the integration of research findings, backcountry travel and camping expertise from the target region and activities, and consultations with land managers from different agencies in each area. The booklets are written to convey the most effective LNT travel and camping practices while instilling an abiding respect and appreciation for wild places and their inhabitants. The rationale for each practice and the need to temper their application with good judgment is emphasized, along with the need for visitors to assume the responsibility to educate themselves and apply the learned skills.

8.5 Creation of Leave No Trace, Inc.
Although NOLS provided successful leadership in guiding development of the interagency LNT programme, partnerships with other educational organisations and adequate funding from the outdoor industry remained critical constraints on programme growth. Direct

federal funding of the LNT programme has always been quite limited and is often tied to specific projects. Land management agencies and NOLS recognized a need to involve outdoor product manufacturers, retail stores and other outdoor education organisations in the LNT programme. Accordingly, in 1993, an outdoor recreation summit was convened involving NOLS, the Outdoor Recreation Coalition of America (ORCA), the Sporting Goods Manufacturing Association (SGMA) and other outdoor manufacturing representatives. At the summit, these groups assessed their support of the LNT programme's partnership concept and the creation of a non-profit organisation.

Leave No Trace, Inc. was registered as a non-profit educational programme in 1994 and rapidly gained momentum with the support of 24 agency, commercial and non-profit partners. Fund-raising dominated the organisation's agenda during the initial years. Seed money to start Leave No Trace, Inc. came from NOLS, SGMA and ORCA. By 1996, the organisation had two full-time staff and a budget of $108,425 supported largely from 35 outdoor recreation manufacturers and retailers. The organisation's structure includes a Board of Directors, LNT Partners and LNT Members. The bylaws established a Board of Directors as the policy-setting arm of the programme. The Board numbered eight individuals in 1995, representing the federal agencies (non-voting), NOLS, science, and other non-profit organisations. LNT Partners are corporations and organisations interested in supporting the LNT programme through visible participation, sponsorship and support of LNT information dissemination. LNT Members are private individuals who use public lands. Members are asked to ensure that their personal outdoor recreation practices are consistent with LNT skills and ethics and to assist in training others.

The LNT educational model emphasizes the development and dissemination of effective and accurate LNT skills and ethics. The knowledge and expertise for this model is gleaned from the federal agencies involved in LNT, scientific research, industry, NOLS and other outdoor educators. Core LNT literature includes the skills and ethics booklet series and LNT plastic reference tags that list the principles and core statements describing low-impact travel and camping practices. Training opportunities include a five-day Master course, a two-day Trainer course, LNT workshops and public contacts (Table 8.1).

Table 8.1. The four main types of LNT training opportunities.

Opportunity	Description
Master course	Provides comprehensive coverage of LNT skills, ethics and teaching practices, including four days of experiential learning in a backcountry setting. Intended for agency staff and outdoor educators who will train others to train the public
Trainer course	An abbreviated version of the Master course for individuals who will be training the public directly, including agency staff, youth group leaders and outdoor adventure programme staff
Workshops	Formal but shorter duration LNT instruction, such as an afternoon session for Boy Scouts or an evening campfire presentation
Public contacts	Informal LNT instruction in visitor centers, at trail heads, and in the backcountry

8.6 Current status

Since its creation, the national LNT programme has grown steadily in both staffing, funding, educational materials and national visibility. Leave No Trace, Inc. currently has nine full time staff, with the continuing strong participation of the federal agencies and partners such as NOLS (four Outreach Office staff) and the Appalachian Mountain Club (one Education Office staff), a new training partner in 1999. Leave No Trace, Inc.'s budget has grown from $108,425 in 1995 to $630,000 in 2000. The LNT principles, revised twice since the programme's creation, now number seven (Table 8.2).

Table 8.2. The seven revised and current 'Leave No Trace' principles and practices.

Principles and Core Practices

Plan Ahead and Prepare
- Know the regulations and special concerns for the area you'll visit
- Schedule your trip to avoid times of high use
- Visit in small groups, split larger parties into groups of 4-6
- Repackage food to minimize waste
- Use a map and compass to eliminate the use of marking paint, rock cairns or flagging

Travel and Camp on Durable Surfaces
- Durable surfaces include established trails and campsites, rock, gravel, dry grasses or snow
- Protect riparian areas by camping at least 200 feet (60 m) from water
- In popular areas, concentrate use on existing trails and campsites, walk single file in the middle of the trail, even when wet or muddy, and keep campsites small (focus activities in areas where vegetation is absent)
- In pristine areas disperse use to prevent the creation of campsites and trails, and avoid places where impacts are just beginning

Dispose of Waste Properly
- Pack it in, pack it out. Inspect your campsite and rest areas for trash and spilled foods. Pack out all trash, leftover food, and litter
- Deposit solid human waste in catholes dug 6 to 8 inches (15 to 20 cm) deep at least 200 feet (60 m) from water, camp and trails. Cover and disguise the hole when finished
- Pack out toilet paper and hygiene products
- To wash yourself or dishes, carry water 200 feet (60 m) away from streams or lakes and use small amounts of biodegradable soap. Scatter strained dish water

Leave What You Find
- Preserve the past: examine, but do not touch cultural or historic structures or artefacts
- Leave rocks, plants and other natural objects as you find them
- Avoid introducing or transporting non-native species
- Do not build structures or furniture, or dig trenches

Minimize Campfire Impacts
- Campfires can cause lasting impacts to the backcountry. Use a lightweight stove for cooking and a candle lantern for light
- Where fires are permitted, use established fire rings, fire pans, or mound fires
- Keep fires small. Use sticks from the ground that can be broken by hand
- Burn all wood and coals to ash, put out campfires completely, then scatter cool ashes

---

Table 8.2. continued

Principles and Core Practices

Respect Wildlife
• Observe wildlife from a distance. Do not follow or approach them
• Never feed animals. Feeding wildlife damages their health, alters natural behaviors, and exposes them to predators and other dangers
• Protect wildlife and your food by storing rations and trash securely
• Control pets at all times, or leave them at home
• Avoid wildlife during sensitive times: mating, nesting, raising young, or winter

Be Considerate of Other Visitors
• Respect other visitors and protect the quality of their experience
• Be courteous. Yield to other users on the trail
• Step to the downhill side of the trail when encountering pack stock
• Take breaks and camp away from trails and other visitors
• Let nature's sounds prevail. Avoid loud voices and noises

Educational materials include a series of 16 skills and ethics booklets on environments ranging from tropical forests to deserts and canyons to the Alaskan tundra, and for recreational activities as diverse as caving, rock climbing and backcountry horse use. One booklet, several pamphlets, and a video have been prepared in Spanish for use in Central and South American countries. The programme's national visibility and success are addressed later in this chapter.

The current mission of Leave No Trace, Inc. is 'to promote and inspire responsible outdoor recreation through education, research and partnerships'. This mission has evolved from the programme's genesis, with its focus on wilderness and backcountry visitation, but also to address recreation use in more accessible 'frontcountry' settings, e.g. car campgrounds, day-use areas and urban parks. This shift was made to address growing problems with resource and social impacts such as dogs and dog waste management, litter, graffiti and visitor crowding and conflict in more developed recreation settings. Human-powered recreational activities remain the target audience for LNT, however, complementing parallel educational efforts by the Tread Lightly programme for motorized recreational activities.

The current composition of the Leave No Trace, Inc. Board of Directors reflects the changing nature of the programme. Corporate representatives have now joined the members from the federal agencies, non-profit organisations and outdoor educators. Current bylaws allow up to 12 voting Board members who may serve for two consecutive three-year terms. The Executive Director of Leave No Trace, Inc. is elected by a majority vote of the Board.

There are three designated standing committees including an Executive Committee, Advisory Committee and Education Review Committee. The Executive Committee consists of the Board officers (Chair, Treasurer and Secretary) and the Executive Director. The Advisory Committee consists of federal land managers and other members who assist the Corporation and its Board in developing an operating plan for the LNT programme, and both implementing and promoting LNT. The Education Review Committee is comprised of outdoor educators, land managers and scientists, and oversees LNT training efforts, curriculum development and educational material production.

As a non-profit organisation, Leave No Trace, Inc. seeks funding from private donors. The majority of Leave No Trace, Inc.'s funding is generated from grants and corporate sponsors. Grants are applied for and received throughout each fiscal year. Commercial partners are asked to contribute each year based on the company's total annual sales (e.g. a company with sales of $25-49 million is asked to contribute $5,000). In return, corporate sponsors are highlighted in LNT newsletters and publicity materials. Sponsors are permitted to use LNT educational materials, the LNT logo and other promotional items. Financial support demonstrates an organisation's commitment to preserving the condition of public lands and the quality of recreational experiences to be found there. Leave No Trace, Inc. is currently planning an initiative to increase personal membership, which has not previously provided significant programme funding.

Although the financial donations of partners are essential to the LNT programme's success, so too are the temporal donations of thousands of volunteers. Individuals who have completed the Master and Trainer courses (see Table 8.1) commonly volunteer their time to present LNT information to interested groups. Targeted audiences include youth groups, retail store employees, guides and school classes. Federal agency staff also devote considerable time conveying LNT information to area visitors, user groups and schools, and provide numerous LNT messages in forest and park literature and on trailhead bulletin boards.

The LNT website has become an important conduit for LNT information as the Internet has become more publicly accessible. The website (www.LNT.org) provides current information on courses, educational skills and ethics literature, research, LNT partners, and more. Application forms for LNT courses, scholarships and material donations are also accessible. The content of all LNT materials, including the skills and ethics booklets and succinct reference tags, is posted on the website and can be downloaded for printing and distribution. This broad access to all of the LNT educational material underscores the overall intent of the LNT programme - namely, to provide accurate, science-based information for all outdoor recreationists.

Material sales and distribution of printed literature has increased steadily since LNT, Inc.'s inception. As of September 2000, materials sales are at an all-time high. Approximately 50,000 skills and ethics booklets and 250,000 plastic reference tags have been distributed; over 100,000 people have been formally trained in LNT skills and ethics; and the LNT website has registered more than 100,000 visits. Additionally, an estimated 10.5 million people have received a LNT 'impression' (defined as an exposure to a logo, sign, booklet or training). Partnership numbers are also at an all time high, with 239 corporate partners and four federal agency partners actively involved in the LNT programme. In 1999, the Boy Scouts of America developed a patch (badge) recognition programme for Scouts that complete a standard level of LNT education. Since initiation of the programme, over 11,000 patches have been distributed. Statistics and trends such as these provide one measure of the programme's success.

To date 1,122 individuals have received LNT Master course training, including staff from the FS (254), BLM (121), NPS (107), FWS (4) and from many other organisations such as the Boy Scouts, Girl Scouts, Backcountry Horsemen, Outward Bound, YMCA and university outdoor educators. Individuals from a number of other countries - Canada, Mexico, Chile, Columbia, Argentina, Venezuela, Brazil, Finland, The Netherlands, Kenya and Australia - have also completed the course.

Another measure of LNT's effectiveness is increased visitor knowledge of LNT skills and ethics and a *per capita* reduction in impacts to resource conditions and to the experiences of other visitors. A pilot research effort is currently underway to begin empirical evaluations of the programme's effectiveness. An LNT laboratory project was initiated in the San Juan Mountains of southwest Colorado in 1999. The goal of this project is to measure the effect of LNT educational efforts on both visitor behaviour and recreation site resource conditions. Besides focusing LNT research on several sites in Colorado, the LNT laboratory will also supplement area LNT training and outreach efforts. Plans are underway to replicate the LNT laboratory model in a different region of the country beginning next year. Limited empirical research on the effectiveness of educational programmes has been conducted in the United States. However, administrators and scientists have highlighted the need for such efforts and methods for their evaluation have been described (Matthews and Riley, 1995; Passineau *et al.*, 1994).

Finally, LNT literature continues to be developed by the scientific community, agencies and other authors. Three texts on recreation impacts have been written (Hammit and Cole, 1998; Knight and Gutzwiller, 1995; Liddle, 1997), along with a paper summarizing visitor impact studies in wilderness (Leung and Marion, 2000). Doucette and Cole (1993) provided a comprehensive guide to alternative techniques for visitor education and Parker (1995) offered a guide to outdoor ethics-related programmes. Agencies contributed *Teach Leave No Trace: Activities to Teach Responsible Backcountry Skills* (BLM, 1996) and *Low Impact Food Hoists* (Vachowski, 1994). A number of new books on low-impact hiking and camping techniques have been published, including a revision of *Soft Paths* (Hampton and Cole, 1995), *The Basic Essentials of Minimizing Impact on the Wilderness* (Hodgson, 1991), *Wild Country Companion* (Harmon, 1994), *Leave No Trace: Minimum Impact Outdoor Recreation* (Harmon, 1997) and *Leave No Trace: A Guide to the New Wilderness Etiquette* (McGivney, 1998).

8.7 The future

The partnership triangle between the federal land agencies, NOLS and Leave No Trace, Inc., with its corporate and retail supporters, has been an exceptionally successful model that continues to serve the programme well. Future success requires expanded training, literature dissemination and publicity to reach a greater proportion of the public with consistent educational messages. As agency participation, corporate activities and publicity expand further, visitor awareness of LNT educational skills and ethics are expected to increase. Consistency, repetition and unified support are critical to the long-term success of the programme.

Other countries have also begun adopting or adapting the LNT programme or have developed their own educational counterparts. For example, NOLS staff have worked with managers and organisations in Mexico and other Central and South American countries to initiate 'No Deje Rastro' (Leave No Trace) programmes. Many of the educational materials have been translated into Spanish and a number of LNT Master courses in Spanish have been offered.

This chapter has traced the development of the LNT educational programme in the United States and offers some insights into what factors have contributed to the programme's expansion and success. Such information may assist other countries in developing their own programmes or initiating ties and adaptations of the United States LNT model.

References

Bradley, J.A. (1979). A human approach to reducing wildland impacts. In *Proceedings: Recreational Impact on Wildlands,* ed. by R. Ittner, D.R. Potter, J.K. Agee and S. Anschell. USDA Forest Service, Pacific Northwest Region, Portland, Oregon. pp. 222-226.

Bureau of Land Management. (1996). *Teach Leave No Trace: activities to teach responsible backcountry skills.* USDI Bureau of Land Management, Utah State Office, Salt Lake City, Utah.

Cole, D.N. (1987). Research on soil and vegetation in wilderness: a state-of-knowledge review. In *Proceedings: National Wilderness Research Conference - Issues, State-of-Knowledge, Future Directions*, comp. by R.C. Lucas. USDA Forest Service, Intermountain Research Station, General Technical Report INT-220, Ogden, Utah. pp. 135-177.

Cole, D.N. (1989). Low-impact recreational practices for wilderness and backcountry. USDA Forest Service, Intermountain Forest and Range Experiment Station, General Technical Report INT-265, Ogden, Utah.

Cole, D.N. (1993). Trampling effects on mountain vegetation in Washington, Colorado, New Hampshire, and North Carolina. USDA Forest Service, Intermountain Research Station, Research Paper INT-464, Ogden, Utah.

Cole, D.N. (1995). Experimental trampling of vegetation. I. Relationship between trampling intensity and vegetation response. *Journal of Applied Ecology*, **32**, 203-214.

Cole, D.N. and Benedict, J. (1983). Wilderness campsite selection: what should users be told. *Park Science*, **3**, 5-7.

Cole, D.N. and Dalle-Molle, J. (1982). Managing campfire impacts in the backcountry. USDA Forest Service, Intermountain Forest and Range Experiment Station, Research Paper INT-135, Ogden, Utah.

Doucette, J.E. and Cole, D.N. (1993). Wilderness visitor education: information about alternative techniques. USDA Forest Service, Intermountain Forest and Range Experiment Station, General Technical Report INT-295, Ogden, Utah.

Fazio, J.R. (1979). Information and education techniques to improve minimum impact use knowledge in wilderness areas. In *Proceedings: Recreational Impact on Wildlands,* ed. by R. Ittner, D.R. Potter, J.K. Agee and S. Anschell. USDA Forest Service, Pacific Northwest Region, Portland, Oregon. pp. 227-233.

Hammitt, W.E. and Cole, D.N. (1998). *Wildland Recreation: Ecology and Management.* John Wiley, New York.

Hampton, B. and Cole, D.N. (1988). *Soft Paths.* Stackpole Books, Harrisburg, Pennsylvania.

Hampton, B. and Cole, D.N. (1995). *Soft Paths, 2nd edition.* Stackpole Books, Harrisburg, Pennsylvania.

Harmon, W. (1994). *Wild Country Companion.* Falcon Publishing, Helena, Montana.

Harmon, W. (1997). *Leave No Trace: Minimum Impact Outdoor Recreation.* Falcon Publishing, Helena, Montana.

Hodgson, M. (1991). *The Basic Essentials of Minimizing Impact on the Wilderness.* ICS Books, Merrillville, Indiana.

Hart, J. (1977). *Walking Softly in the Wilderness.* Sierra Club Books, San Francisco, California.

Knight, R.L. and Gutzwiller, K.J. (eds.). (1995). *Wildlife and Recreationists: Coexistence through Management and Research.* Island Press, Washington, D.C.

Knight, R.L. and Temple, S.A. (1995). Origin of wildlife responses to recreationists. In *Wildlife and Recreationists: Coexistence through Management and Research,* ed. by R.L. Knight and K.J. Gutzwiller, Island Press, Washington, D.C. pp. 81-91.

Leung, Y.F. and Marion, J.L. (2000). Recreation impacts and management in wilderness: a state-of-knowledge review. In *Proceedings: Wilderness Science in a Time of Change,* Volume 5, comp. by D.N. Cole, S.F. McCool, W.T. Borrie and J. O'Loughlin. USDA Forest Service, Rocky Mountain Research Station, Ogden, Utah.

Liddle, M. (1997). *Recreation Ecology: the Ecological Impact of Outdoor Recreation and Ecotourism.* Chapman & Hall, London.

Marion, J.L. and Merriam, L.C. (1985). Recreational impacts on well-established campsites in the Boundary Waters Canoe Area Wilderness. University of Minnesota, Agricultural Experiment Station, Technical Bulletin AD-SB-2502, St. Paul, Minnesota.

Matthews, B.E. and Riley, C.K. (1995). *Teaching and Evaluating Outdoor Ethics Education Programs.* National Wildlife Federation, Educational Outreach Department, Vienna, Virginia.

McGivney, A. (1998). *Leave No Trace: A Guide to the New Wilderness Etiquette.* The Mountaineers, Seattle, Washington.

Parker, M. (1995). *Promoting Responsible Behavior: a Resource Guide To Outdoor Ethics-related Programs.* Izaak Walton League of America, Gaithersburg, Maryland.

Passineau, J., Roggenbuck, J.W. and Stubbs, C.J. (1994). Wilderness education in the United States: do we teach low-impact knowledge, behavior, or a wilderness ethic? In *International Wilderness Allocation, Management, and Research,* ed. by J.C. Hendee and V.G. Martin. International Wilderness Leadership (WILD) Foundation, Fort Collins, Colorado. pp. 276-83.

Petzoldt, P. (1974). *The Wilderness Handbook.* W.W. Norton and Company, New York.

Vachowski, B. (1994). Low impact food hoists. USDA Forest Service, Technology and Development Program, Technical Report, Missoula, Montana.

Waterman, L. and Waterman, G. (1979). *Backwoods Ethics: Environmental Concerns for Hikers and Campers.* Stone Wall Press, Boston, Massachusetts.

9 A REVIEW OF RESEARCH ON CHANGING RECREATIONAL BEHAVIOUR THROUGH COMMUNICATION

James Carter

Summary

1.   The theory of reasoned action, which suggests that peoples' behaviour is influenced by their intentions, attitudes, and socially determined norms, is supported as a model for how behaviour is determined.

2.   Using this model, communication initiatives can influence people's attitudes towards a given issue, and their intention to behave in a certain way, by presenting recipients with information about the consequences of their actions.

3.   Where recipients are not able to attend closely to, understand or respond to the message presented, its content is less important in determining its effect than 'peripheral' factors such as the perceived credibility of the source of the message.

4.   Effective communication initiatives should use multiple communication channels or media to be most effective.

5.   Strategies to encourage desired recreational behaviour patterns must include a wide range of management interventions in addition to communication initiatives.

9.1 Introduction

This chapter is based on a review of literature focusing on how communication might be used to influence recreational behaviour (Carter, 2000). The review concentrates largely on material in journals and books published since 1992. Drawing on this literature, the discussion draws out the theoretical foundations for influencing behaviour through communication, as well as reviewing some empirical research that has been conducted to establish their validity. Finally, the chapter presents a series of summary recommendations that can guide future communication initiatives.

Of course, communication is just one tool in efforts to influence recreational behaviour. Site and visitor management policies, as well as judicious use of surveillance and sanctions, must also play a part. These other techniques, and their relationship to communication, are discussed below, but the main emphasis of the paper is on the role of communication. A recurring theme of the chapters in this book is an assumption that better communication will achieve the desired result in campaigns to change recreationists' behaviour. Another theme is the need for better research into whether management initiatives are working. These two strands are drawn together in this chapter.

All attempts to influence people's behaviour through communication need to be based on a model of how behaviour is determined, and how people might process persuasive communication. The Theory of Reasoned Action, which *"rests on the assumption that humans are reasoning animals who systematically utilize or process the information available to them"* (Fishbein and Manfredo, 1992, p. 30) has underpinned much research in the field.

The theory suggests that an individual's behaviour is influenced by his or her intentions, which in turn are influenced by personal attitudes and by socially determined norms. Underlying these is a system of behavioural and normative beliefs (Figure 9.1). For example, if I believe that I shall drive more safely if I keep to the speed limit (behavioural belief), I will probably feel that keeping to the speed limit is a good thing (personal attitude). I may also think that the people travelling with me feel that keeping to the speed limit is a good thing (socially determined norm). If either or both of these conditions are met, I may plan to keep to the limit (intention) and may actually do so (behaviour).

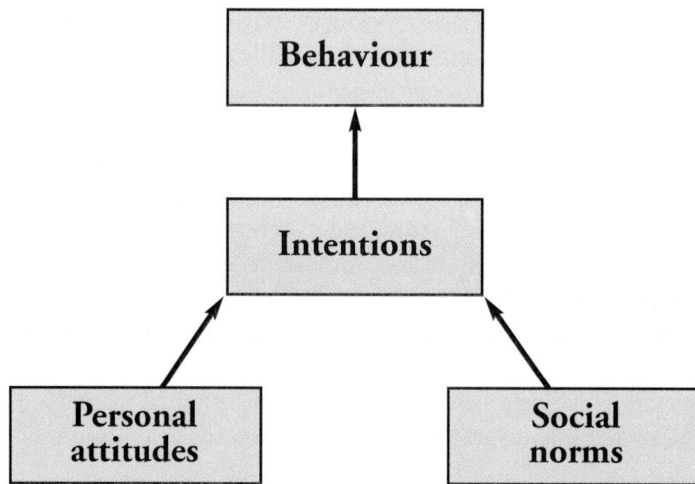

Figure 9.1. The relationship between behaviour, intentions, attitudes and norms.

The Theory of Reasoned Action suggests that communications designed to influence behaviour must therefore attempt to influence either personal beliefs and attitudes, or the social norms that influence a particular behaviour. This apparently simple proposition is fraught with complexities. The relative importance of personal and socially determined factors varies from individual to individual, and from behaviour to behaviour. It is therefore important that interventions designed to influence behaviour are based on a clear definition of what they are designed to affect, whether this is a personal belief, an attitude, or a social norm.

Decisions about what beliefs, attitudes and social norms are important in any given situation need to be based on research with the target audience group, though this research has often been lacking in communication programmes designed to influence behaviour in the countryside.

"… most messages and interventions are constructed somewhat arbitrarily based on intuition and on what too often turn out to be false assumptions about the determinants of the behavior one wishes to change" (Fishbein and Manfredo, 1992, p. 37).

Negra and Manning (1997), in a study seeking to identify the range of ethics and values among park visitors in Vermont, suggested that there is a degree of commonality in these factors across the majority of park visitors that would allow communication programmes to address a common set of values and thus reach a wider audience. Although this may be true, and may also be a necessary assumption in practical terms, it is still necessary to define those points of commonality through research rather than base them on assumptions. In addition, such research needs to be repeated at periodic intervals to detect changes in the visitors' characteristics over time.

Another complexity is in the nature of behaviour itself. Fishbein and Manfredo (1992) described four elements, variation in any one of which may mean that different forms of intervention may be more effective. They suggested that behaviour varies according to its

- **action**, for example camping or climbing in the Trossachs;
- **target**, for example camping in the Trossachs or camping on Nairn seafront;
- **context,** for example camping with friends or camping with family; and
- **time**, for example climbing in winter or climbing in summer.

The lesson for those wishing to influence recreationists' behaviour is that communication programmes must be designed for a clear combination of behavioural elements, and develop strategies appropriate to that combination.

9.2 Theory in action

Research findings generally support the broad principles of the Theory of Reasoned Action. When attitudes and norms that are directly relevant to the precise behaviour in question are targeted by communication, there is evidence that attitudes and beliefs are affected and that stated intentions to behave in a particular way are also influenced (Bright *et al.*, 1993; Gramman *et al.*, 1995; Petty *et al.*, 1992).

Much of the research reviewed is based on 'laboratory' studies which examine changes in participants' attitudes or intentions, often in response to hypothetical situations. However, the relatively small number of published field-based trials that are based on observation of actual behaviour also show that carefully designed communication which increases recreationists' awareness of their impact on the environment can also influence actual behaviour. Examples of two of these studies are discussed below.

9.2.1 Environmental briefings to divers

Medio *et al.* (1997) gave briefings to groups of boat-based scuba divers on an organised holiday for novice divers in the Ras Mohammed National Park. The briefings included information about coral reef ecology, covering issues such as the differences between living and dead coral, and explained which parts of the reef might be damaged if touched. Divers' behaviour was then observed underwater, unknown to the subjects, both in groups which had received the briefing and control groups with no briefing.

Divers who had received the briefings made significantly less contact with the reef, and the pattern of contacts they did make was different, with more reduction in their contacts with live coral than in contacts with non-living substrate. The rate of voluntary contact with rock, which has no damaging effect on the reef, increased markedly. Medio *et al.* (1997) noted that it would be difficult to give such briefings to dispersed users, such as divers using snorkels and reaching the reef from the shore.

Although this study was not designed to follow a particular model of persuasive communication or behavioural change, it gave strong support to the theory of reasoned action as a predictive model of how behaviour might be influenced. However, the high response rate may have been partly due to the divers' relative lack of experience; other research suggests persuasive communication is more effective among recreationists with little experience in an activity or geographical area (Roggenbuck, 1992; Roggenbuck and Berrier, 1982).

9.2.2 Different signs: different effects

Johnson and Swearingen (1992) concentrated on the effects of different trail side texts designed to discourage hikers from using trails liable to damage from over use. Their study compared the effectiveness of various sign texts and design options (Table 9.1).

Table 9.1 Examples of sign texts used in the experiment by Johnson and Swearingen (1992).

Sign number	Sign type	Sign content
1	Standard signs used in the past at the site	'No hiking, meadow repairs'
2	Newly designed signs giving a less cryptic explanation of the desired behaviour	'Stay on the paved trails and preserve the meadow'
3	A symbolic message showing an international prohibition sign	A red circle with a cross hatch over a hiker's profile
4	A hybrid sign	The symbol in number 3 combined with the text 'No off-trail hiking'
5	A sanction sign	'Off-trail hikers may be fined'
6	A humorous message	'Do not - tread, mosey, hop, trample, step, plod, tip-toe, trot, traipse, meander, creep, prance, amble, jog, trudge, march, stomp, toddle, jump, stumble, trod, sprint, or walk on the plants'

The results might seem rather depressing for those committed to a liberal management ethic. The sanction sign was significantly more effective than any other type, reducing off-trail hiking from 6.9 per cent in the control situation (no sign) to 1.7 per cent. Of the others, signs 2, 4 and 6 were about equally effective, reducing off-trail hiking to around 3.5 per cent. All of these three were more effective than the standard sign (sign 1). The symbol-only sign was not effective, although previous research had suggested symbol only signs were useful; the authors were unable to suggest clear conclusions to explain this.

The authors pointed out that these results should not lead to an uncritical use of sanction signs. Such signs can only be effective if the threatened sanction is credible: sanctions must be enforced and people must feel there is a reasonable chance they may be caught if they transgress. Sanction signs may also have unintended and adverse effects on the quality of visitors' leisure experience. The authors suggested that such signs should be viewed as a solution that is appropriate where sanctions can be enforced, and where the consequences of undesired behaviour are more serious.

An extension to this study looked at the effect of stationing uniformed employees near to the trail junctions concerned. The presence of uniformed staff seemed to have a positive effect on visitors' compliance with regulations, with visitors seeing the presence of such staff as a neutral or positive aspect of their leisure experience.

The results of this work may need some caution in the extent to which they can be applied in a UK context. National and Forest Parks in the UK are in general less regulated than in the United States, and have a less centralised management and patrolling system.

9.2.3 Unexpected responses

Although these two studies give encouraging results, it is not always possible to predict the exact effect of a message. Bright *et al.* (1993) attempted to influence attitudes towards the US National Park Service's Controlled Burn policy on bush fires, which is to let them burn themselves out where possible. Participants who were found to have an initially favourable attitude to this were exposed to a message that argued for a more negative position, while those with an initially negative attitude were exposed to a positive message.

The effects of these messages were not entirely as expected. Whereas those exposed to the message seeking to undermine their support for the policy changed their attitudes in the intended way, people exposed to a message designed to increase support for the policy did not.

Bright *et al.* (1993) suggested four possible explanations for this. First, they cited other research suggesting that messages are more likely to be effective if they are novel or unexpected. In this context, the National Park Service would not be expected to present arguments attacking controlled burn. Second, they discussed the concept that it is easier to change things that people believe to be true than things they believe not to be true. For example, negative attitudes towards the controlled burn policy might be based on beliefs that it is not beneficial to wildlife. This 'disbelief system' may be more resistant to change than a 'belief system' that supports the policy. Third, they considered the possibility that those with negative attitudes towards the policy actually hardened those attitudes in the face of arguments to the contrary. Lastly, there is the possibility that aspects of the experimental procedure, such as sample size and response rate, or subtle differences in the content of the two sets of messages, affected the results.

9.3 Beyond conscious reason

Many studies supporting the Theory of Reasoned Action as a predictive model for how attitudes and behaviour might be influenced are based on situations in which the recipients of the message have a high level of attention to the message and are highly motivated to attend to and process it. But it is often impossible to guarantee that recipients will be motivated to attend to a message, or that they will be able to understand and process it. This is particularly true of many situations in which recreation managers might seek to influence behaviour in the countryside.

An extension of the Theory of Reasoned Action, the Elaboration Likelihood Model, tries to explain how attitudes may be influenced when recipients are not motivated to pay close attention to a message or are unable to process it fully (Petty *et al.*, 1992). The model proposes that there are two main routes to persuasion - central and peripheral.

In the central route, recipients are able or motivated to pay close attention to a message: the situation is exemplified in the study by Medio *et al.* (1997) and by most laboratory experiments. In these circumstances people are likely to be persuaded by good arguments that support a particular position. Attitude change via this route seems to be relatively persistent, predictive of behaviour, and resistant to change unless subjects are exposed to counter arguments that persuade them to hold other attitudes (Petty *et al.*, 1992).

When people are not motivated to attend closely to a message, or are unable to process it in detail, it may still influence their attitudes, but so called 'peripheral cues' become more important as determinants of the effect of the communication. These cues include the credibility or attractiveness of the message source, or the simple number of arguments advanced in support of a position. In this peripheral route the relative strength of the arguments presented has little effect, whereas for recipients who are attending closely to a message strong arguments lead to greater attitudinal change and weak arguments to less. In addition, attitude changes brought about via this peripheral route seem to be less persistent (Petty *et al.*, 1992).

Petty *et al.* (1992) also suggested that the qualitative difference between the effects of the central and peripheral routes makes them appropriate for different situations. For example, if the goal is to instil a positive attitude towards safety in the mountains, techniques should be developed that use the central route to persuasion. If the goal is more immediate and short term, for example encouraging visitors to use one trail rather than another, the peripheral route may be sufficient.

A further area of difficulty is that people do not always behave in accordance with their stated attitudes or intentions. Again, this is particularly relevant to countryside management, where people may hold that picking wildflowers is wrong, yet still do so when they come across a patch of bluebells. Another example would be that of a mountain bike user who knows that he or she should ride slowly down a loose surfaced slope, but yields to the temptation of a fast run downhill (Carter, unpublished).

In situations like these, where people are either not motivated consciously to consider their behaviour, or do not have the opportunity to do so, the degree to which their attitudes towards a situation are accessible may be a significant determinant of their behaviour (Vincent and Fazio, 1992). Highly accessible attitudes are defined as those that are recalled automatically in response to a stimulus.

Two principles emerge from research on this idea that may help in designing attempts to establish new attitudes or strengthen existing ones. Direct experience makes attitudes more accessible, so intervention programmes should seek directly to involve as many participants from the intended recipients of the persuasion as possible. Attitudes can also be made more accessible through repeated expression, so opportunities should be sought to present the desired message in many different situations (Vincent and Fazio, 1992).

9.4 Wider programmes of influence

The efforts to refine the Theory of Reasoned Action are all based on trying to understand how behaviour is determined and might be influenced when it is not under any clear logical control. This has been a particular concern in the field of health education, where major campaigns are mounted to influence behaviour, for example to persuade people to change their eating habits, stop smoking, or practise safe sex (Cole, 1995a, b).

All of these behaviours are the product not just of logical processing, but of a mixture of deeply ingrained social norms and sometimes of physical need or addiction. This combination of factors is similar to that affecting many outdoor pursuits where countryside managers might want to encourage a particular code of behaviour. It has been addressed in the health sector through a wider approach to influencing behaviour (Carter, unpublished; Winett, 1992; Allison, this volume).

Current thinking in health promotion suggests that people must be supported in the desired behaviour through other means than relying purely on communication with the target group. This leads to integrated campaigns operating at a variety of levels and in different ways, but all planned to a defined model of how behaviour might be influenced and with clearly defined goals. In 'safe sex' promotion work, for example, these might include wider policy development to address issues of social and economic deprivation; publicity campaigns to encourage people to see condoms as more erotic (thus influencing social norms); and initiatives to make the desired choices easier, for example by making condoms freely available (Tones, 1995).

Recently representatives from the health sector have met representatives from the fashion industry to discuss how the industry might change its obsession with unhealthily thin models, an example of how communication initiatives may have to be developed in partnership with others if they are to target the socially determined attitudes that really matter (Gillan, 2000; Ward, 2000).

In countryside management, such partnerships could be with outdoor equipment manufacturers to discuss the imagery used in their advertising, and to develop initiatives through which codes of behaviour can be attached to merchandise at the point of sale. In the USA and Australia programmes operated by not-for-profit organisations seek to develop such partnerships and also provide training in a set of environmental behaviour ethics to people such as outdoor pursuits instructors and others who might have an influence on recreationists' behaviour. Examples of these approaches are the Leave No Trace and the Tread Lightly programmes (Marion and Reid, this volume).

A further area of partnership would be for conservation agencies to build closer relationships with organisations concerned with offering instruction in outdoor pursuits, so as to encourage instructors to include in their programmes messages about the nature of the environment and about appropriate behaviour (Hanna, 1995, Medio *et al.*, 1997). This form of intervention may be particularly useful since research suggests that people with little experience of an activity, who are more likely to take part in courses of instruction, are more receptive to persuasive communication designed to influence their behaviour (Roggenbuck, 1992).

Applying the integrated approach now being used in health promotion to countryside management, the range of work covered by an integrated campaign might include the seven elements listed in Table 9.2.

Table 9.2. Seven likely elements in an integrated campaign to influence behaviour (adapted from Carter, 1999).

Element	Comments
Information and education	For example, codes of conduct which give information about desired behaviour, together with reasons for it
Working with target groups	Planning information campaigns in consultation with representatives of the target group
Developing a consistent message among different agencies	Working with other organisations who have an interest in the recreation or the behaviour involved so as to ensure that all concerned are presenting the same messages
Signs	These are a special form of information to remind countryside users of desired behaviours, preferably at the points where they may be tempted to abandon them. Signs cannot be expected to work on their own: they should reinforce messages received through other media, or established through peer group influence
Physical interventions	Such as speed bumps or gates, or landscape design that aims to encourage use of one area rather than another
Surveillance and 'policing'	These may be the only options to address malicious behaviours
Strategic policy development	For example, working with government departments and commercial sector interests

9.5 Pointers for the future

A number of points emerge from the literature surveyed that can guide the development of future communication interventions. The points are divided into those affecting the overall design of communication campaigns and general policy, factors relevant to the context within which communication takes place, and guidelines to what makes the content of communication effective.

9.5.1 General

Decisions about the aims of any campaign, the techniques to be used, and the content of communication should be made on the basis of research with the target group, and be specific to the exact combination of behavioural factors concerned. Managers' intuitive assessments are not a sufficient basis for action (Bright, 1997; Bright *et al.*, 1993; Fishbein and Manfredo, 1992; Johnson and Vande Kamp, 1996; Petty *et al.*, 1992).

Techniques to encourage compliance with a particular behaviour must balance their deterrent effect on non-compliance, an acceptable level of non-compliance, and their potentially negative impact on visitor experiences. For example, visitors may find numerous signs about desired behaviour intrusive, and too many signs detailing possible sanctions may be seen as unacceptable (Johnson and Swearingen, 1992; Johnson and Vande Kamp, 1996; Roggenbuck, 1992). Most campaigns will need to use multiple techniques to influence behaviour, since no one technique addresses all forms of non-compliance, nor all motives for non-compliance with desired behaviour. Direct communication with countryside users is only one of these possible techniques (Cole, 1995a, b; Johnson and Vande Kamp, 1996; Tones, 1995).

Whatever other influences are at work, people will only behave in a way consistent with a new belief or attitude if they know how to perform the necessary actions and feel confident to do so. Research must establish the extent of capability and confidence in a target group to perform a given behaviour. If this is found to be lacking, campaigns must address this issue as well as trying to persuade people to behave in the desired way (Cottrell and Graefe, 1997; Tones, 1995).

9.5.2 The context of communication

In general, messages or reminders about a specific desired behaviour should be presented as close as possible in time and place to where that behaviour is relevant (Johnson and Swearingen, 1992; Johnson and Vande Kamp, 1996). There are, however, circumstances in which it may be better to give information in advance. For example, campers respond better to persuasion to use alternative camp sites if they are given information about those sites at the start of a trail rather than when they arrive at a crowded site (Roggenbuck and Berrier, 1982). Where campers are expected to sort their rubbish into recyclable and non-recyclable categories, they need to be told about this before arriving at the rubbish disposal point (Ham, 1983).

Field research shows that stationing uniformed employees of an organisation responsible for an area, for example a National Park, near fragile resources is effective in encouraging behaviour in accordance with previously established codes. It also seems that most visitors regard the presence of such staff as a positive or neutral intervention in their experience, whereas this is not necessarily the case with signs (Johnson and Vande Kamp, 1996).

If there is physical evidence of non-compliant behaviour it should be removed as soon as possible, otherwise it may act as a signal that the behaviour is acceptable. The example set by others is a strong determinant of subsequent behaviour (Johnson and Vande Kamp, 1996).

9.5.3 Message content

People are more likely to comply when they are told the reason for a rule, for example explaining the environmental consequences of undesirable behaviour (Gramman *et al.*, 1995; Johnson and Vande Kamp, 1996). However, this technique is more effective among those with an already high level of social responsibility (Gramman *et al.*, 1995).

Fear of personal harm seems to be more effective in influencing the intention to behave in a particular way than an awareness of environmental consequences. For example, people are less likely to feed squirrels if they believe they may catch a disease if they are bitten than if they are told how bad a diet of picnic leftovers is for the squirrels (Schwarzkopf (1984) cited in Gramman *et al.* (1995)).

It is important to emphasise people's freedom to choose between given parameters. If communication appears to present too many rules it may produce a 'boomerang' effect of deliberate non-compliance. For example, a regulation might state, 'You must camp within Zone A' but then continue, 'Within Zone A you may camp anywhere that is more than 200 yards from a trail or water source' (Johnson and Vande Kamp, 1996).

In presenting arguments to support an advocated position, it is more effective to use evidence that is likely to be new to the target audience (Ajzen, 1992; Bright *et al.*, 1993). Using people regarded as credible or attractive by the intended audience to deliver or support a message can increase the likelihood of recipients attending to and accepting that message (Ajzen, 1992; Petty *et al.*, 1992; Allison, this volume).

Where it is important to encourage recipients to process the message consciously, Petty *et al.* (1992) indicated that this could be done through

- making the message appear more personally relevant by using personal language (for example addressing the audience as 'you');
- making the message easy to understand; and
- summarising the major arguments as questions (for example 'Wouldn't this help to prevent forest fires?').

9.6 Conclusion

Although the research reviewed provides a good basis for future communication initiatives, it is important to recognise that behaviour is a complex subject. No single theoretical approach can be applied in all situations, and no one campaign can predict with certainty what its outcome will be (Johnson and Vande Kamp, 1996). The models on which persuasion theories are based are still largely conjectural, but it is important that campaigns are based on a clear theoretical framework so that they can be properly assessed, and their techniques refined in future work.

There is also a clear need for further research that examines actual behaviour 'in the field'. Though laboratory research can help both to refine theories and to suggest possible solutions, the real test is in watching what people actually do.

References

Ajzen, I. (1992). Persuasive communication theory in social psychology: a historical perspective. In *Influencing Human Behavior*, ed. by M. Manfredo. Sagamore, Champaign, Illinois. pp. 1-27.

Bright, A.D. (1997). Attitude strength and support of recreation management strategies. *Journal of Leisure Research*, **29**, 363-379.

Bright, A.D., Manfredo, M.J., Fishbein, M. and Bath, A. (1993). Application of the theory of reasoned action to the National Park Service's controlled burn policy. *Journal of Leisure Research*, **25**, 263-280.

Carter, J. (2000). Encouraging responsible behaviour related to the new public right of access: a review of literature and experience. Unpublished report.

Cole, A. (1995a). A model approach to health promotion. *Healthlines*, (October 1995), 14-16.

Cole, A. (1995b). The persuaders. *Healthlines*, (December 1995/January 1996), 17-19.

Cottrell, S.P. and Graefe, A.R. (1997). Testing a conceptual framework of responsible environmental behavior. *Journal of Environmental Education*, **29**, 17-27.

Fishbein, M. and Manfredo, M.J. (1992). A theory of behavior change. In *Influencing Human Behavior*, ed. by M. Manfredo. Sagamore, Champaign, Illinois. pp. 28-50.

Gillan, A. (2000). Skinny models 'send unhealthy message'. *The Guardian*, 31 May 2000.

Gramman, J.H., Bonifield, R.L. and Kim, Y. (1995). Effect of personality and situational factors on intentions to obey rules in outdoor recreation areas. *Journal of Leisure Research*, **27**, 326-343.

Ham, S.H. (1983). Communication and recycling in park campgrounds. *Journal of Environmental Education*, **15**,17-20.

Hanna, G. (1995). Wilderness-related outcomes of adventure and ecology education programming. *Journal of Environmental Education*, **27**, 21-32.

Johnson, D.R. and Swearingen, T.C. (1992). The effectiveness of selected trailside sign texts in deterring off-trail hiking at Paradise Meadow, Mount Rainier National Park. In *Vandalism: Research, Prevention and Social Policy* ed. by H. Christensen, D. Johnson and M. Brookes. USDA Forest Service Pacific Northwest Station, Portland, Oregon: General Technical Report PNW GTR 293. pp. 103-119.

Johnson, D.R. and Vande Kamp, M.E. (1996). Extent and control of resource damage due to non-compliant visitor behavior: a case study from the US National Parks. *Natural Areas Journal*, **16**, 134-141.

Medio, D., Ormond, R.F.G. and Mearson, M. (1997). Effects of briefings on rates of damage to corals by SCUBA divers. *Biological Conservation*, **79**, 91-95.

Negra, C. and Manning, R.E. (1997). Incorporating environmental behavior, ethics and values into nonformal environmental education programs. *Journal of Environmental Education*, **28**, 10-21.

Petty, R.E., McMichael, S. and Brannon, L. (1992). The elaboration likelihood model of persuasion: applications in recreation and tourism. In *Influencing Human Behavior*, ed. by M. Manfredo. Sagamore, Champaign, Illinois. pp. 77-101.

Roggenbuck, J.W. (1992). Use of persuasion to reduce resource impacts and visitor conflicts. In *Influencing Human Behavior*, ed. by M. Manfredo. Sagamore, Champaign, Illinois. pp. 149-208.

Roggenbuck, J.W. and Berrier, D.L. (1982). A comparison of the effectiveness of two communication strategies in dispersing wilderness campers. *Journal of Leisure Research*, **14**, 77-89.

Tones, K. (1995). Making a change for the better. *Healthlines*, (November 1995), 17-19.

Vincent, M.A. and Fazio, R.H. (1992). Attitude accessibility and its consequences for judgement and behavior. In *Influencing Human Behavior*, ed. by M. Manfredo. Sagamore, Champaign, Illinois. pp. 51-75.

Ward, L. (2000). Fashion magazines agree to ban use of unhealthily thin models. *The Guardian*, 22 June 2000.

Winett, R.A. (1992). Behavioral systems framework for media-based behavior change strategies. In *Influencing Human Behavior*, ed. by M. Manfredo. Sagamore, Champaign, Illinois. pp. 103-125.

10 INFLUENCING RECREATION BEHAVIOUR TO REDUCE IMPACTS

M. Foley, M. Frew and D. McGillivray

Summary

1.   This chapter focuses upon the dilemma of managing the increasing impacts of countryside recreation whilst influencing behaviour in harmony with an ethic of care. Having developed a conceptual framework and mapped the theoretical terrain, it examines behavioural practice using a series of UK-wide case studies.

2.   With the development and complexity of countryside recreation it is not feasible to influence all behaviours in all contexts. Impacts should be classified according to whether they affect habitats, land managers and their work, or other recreational users. This provides a basis with which to target mechanisms that will effectively influence behaviour.

3.   Aspects of current practice (i.e. socialisation, marketing communications, restrictions, rational economic, on-site approaches and experiential learning) are revealed. Behaviour could be disaggregated into a series of phases, namely decisions to go (whether to and where), travelling to, arrival at, on-site behaviour, departure, return and reflection.

4.   Strategically, an unequivocal message can access target markets via an integrated relationship-marketing brand. This brand should provide an image that is recognisable and should incorporate the twin objectives of education and promotion.

5.   Site managers should be enabled to provide site-specific measures, identifiable within the overall message. The relationship between the strategic and operational contexts is of key importance if influencing strategy is to be effective.

10.1 Introduction

This chapter is based upon research commissioned by Scottish Natural Heritage (Foley, 1997). The intention of this introductory section is to illustrate the motivation for the research, document its principal aims and then outline the approach taken (i.e. its conceptual framework and methodology). The chapter will then engage specifically with the issues raised by the research project.

SNH has a wide remit covering the conservation, enhancement, enjoyment and understanding of the natural heritage. Through the publication of its policy statements on access in 1994 and environmental education in 1995, SNH has been increasingly concerned with managing a reduction of recreational impacts on the natural heritage and developing an 'ethic of care' amongst recreational users. As a result, a need to identify the best ways of influencing recreation behaviour as a way of reducing impacts on the natural heritage and improving the management of sites has arisen. From this policy context, the four aims of the research were to identify and assess the components of recreation behaviour and their associated impacts on the natural heritage; to review the development of theory and practice in influencing recreation behaviour; to assess the effectiveness of the various methods by which recreation behaviour might be influenced; and to identify and evaluate the different approaches that might be adopted by SNH in order to meet its objectives in this field.

10.2 Conceptual development

The conceptual development of the research was based on the assertion of Urry (1995) that places can be consumed. This assertion allows the theories of consumer behaviour (Clarke and Schmidt, 1995) to be used in conceptualising and modelling the experience of use of the outdoors.

Figure 10.1 outlines the framework for investigation of the processes inherent in decisions to consume the outdoors, together with the range of possible influences that affect these. This model was derived from the arguments presented by Foley (1997), and recognises that any study of recreational behaviour must incorporate both rational economic factors as well as the psychological profile of the participants, the societies in which the behaviour takes place and the cultural background in which it arises. The incorporation of a decision-process model (Kotler, 1967; Engel *et al.*, 1968) provided the overall conceptual model with a tool for disaggregating the elements of decision and consumption processes which can then be applied to outdoor behaviour. A key element of the diagram is the feedback loop between evaluation and every other component.

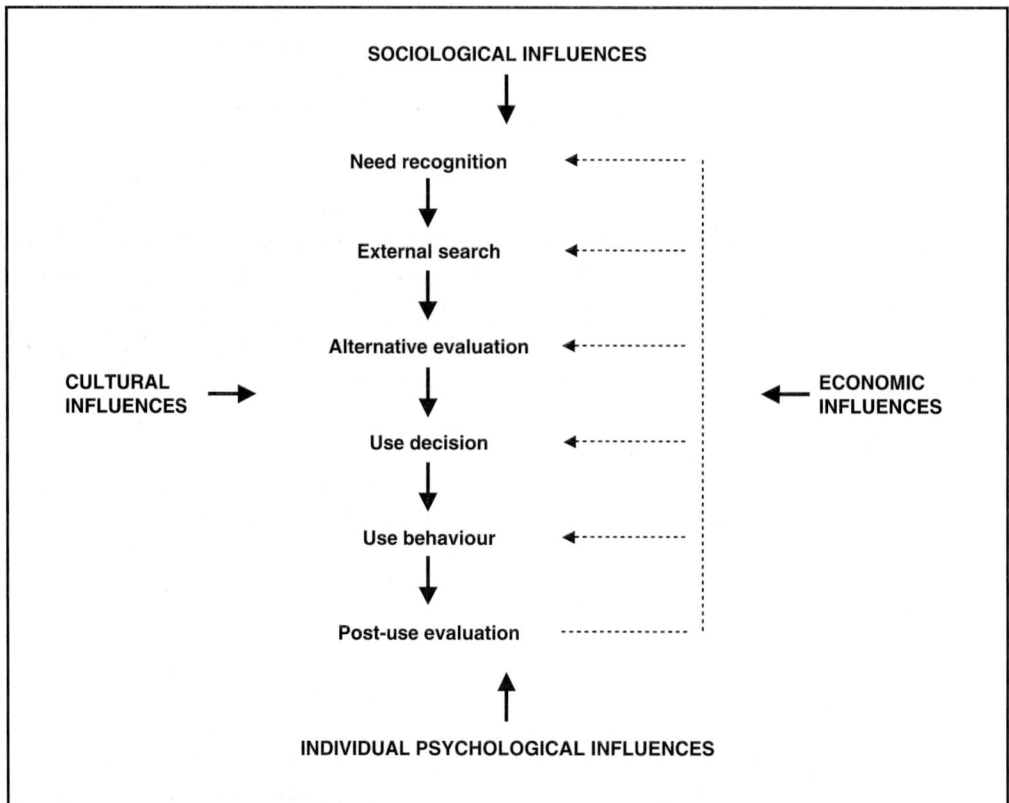

Figure 10.1. The processes and influences that affect outdoor recreation decisions.

While it was tempting to launch the investigation into isolating each of the points in Figure 10.1 (or 'moments of truth') in the user's metaphorical journey and investigating the optimum influence at each, it is unlikely that such disaggregation of a conceptual model will secure effective understandings of the real world. Rather, the model needs to be used to inform a more holistic approach that recognises that both the 'moments of truth' and the potential influences can be integrated within certain current practices. It is these practices, itemised in Table 10.1, which formed the critical issues for investigation. They were plotted on a conceptual 'map' of the user 'journey' containing measures designed both to encourage positive behaviour and to discourage negative behaviour, on a continuum between participants' origins and destinations.

Table 10.1. The four practices which formed the critical issues for the conceptual development

Practice	*Important aspects of practice*
socialisation processes	secondary socialisation at school and college and tertiary socialisation, via peer pressure, possibly during or after use, for particular behaviours
marketing communications	leaflets, advertisements and other forms of 'public relations' which are intended to foster a positive relationship between users (or potential users) and the outdoors
restrictions	formal rules and regulations and imposed codes of practice or other use restrictions such as bye-laws, designations, licensing and permits
rational economic	charging for services on-site, but also attempts to communicate the real cost of a visit to the countryside

On the basis of this analysis, there were four main areas for investigation. First, there were the contact personnel, expressed as the role and perception of rangers and other on-site human resources. Second, there were non-human interventions, such as the provision of signage, other user information and interpretative facilities. Third, there was the effect of other users on-site and their behaviours, whether positive or negative. Fourth, there was the use of the natural resources themselves to illustrate and modify behaviour, possibly through growth or incursion into 'busy' areas, and erosion or other natural processes providing 'dangerous' or 'hostile' environments.

The conceptual base suggested that post-use evaluation presents opportunities for behavioural change in the future. In fostering critical reflection and evaluation of use among visitors, there are opportunities to extend their ownership of sites used regularly and, concomitantly, their understanding of their impact upon sites not yet visited. Such evaluation will affect future expectations of the sites themselves and the individual's personal behaviour across all aspects of the user journey. Thus, the last area for investigation was the opportunity for experiential learning designed to affect future expectations at the current site and at other sites.

10.3 Components and key impacts of recreation behaviour

Recreation behaviour was modelled according to the user's experience of a 'journey' to the outdoors. Thus, the decision to go (including knowledge of the site), travelling to the chosen destination, the arrival on-site, behaviour during the main purpose of the visit, the return trip and subsequent reflection upon the overall experience, are the key headings used to disaggregate recreation behaviour. These can be seen as a continuum, as shown in Figure 10.2.

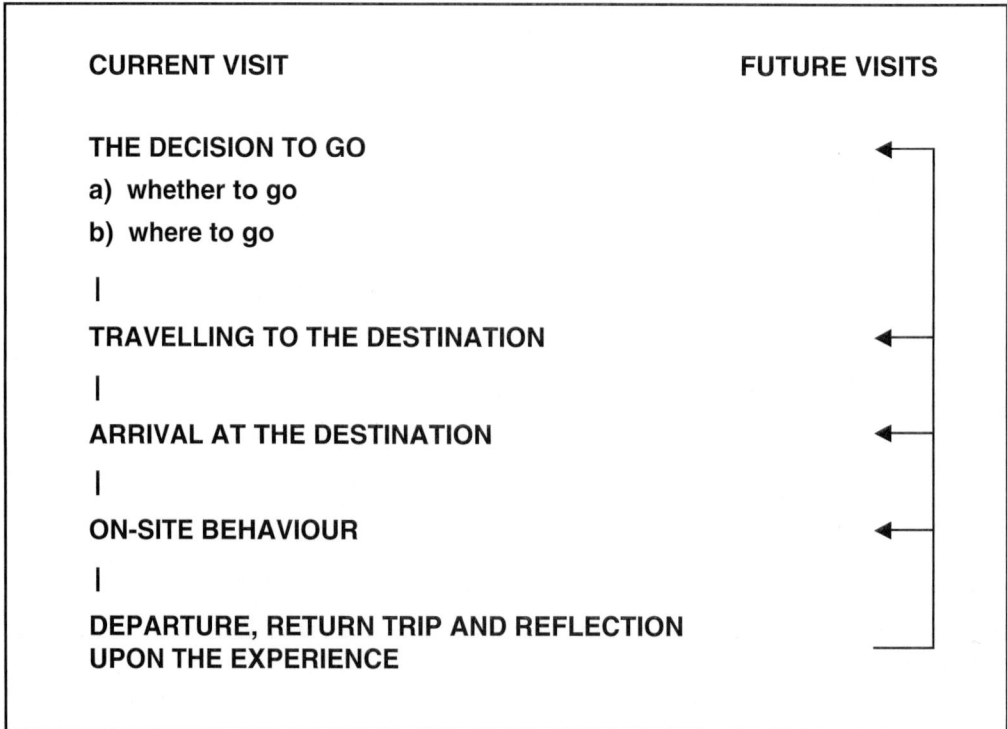

```
CURRENT VISIT                                    FUTURE VISITS


THE DECISION TO GO                                      ◄───┐
a)  whether to go                                           │
b)  where to go                                             │
                                                            │
   |                                                        │
                                                            │
TRAVELLING TO THE DESTINATION                           ◄───┤
                                                            │
   |                                                        │
                                                            │
ARRIVAL AT THE DESTINATION                              ◄───┤
                                                            │
   |                                                        │
                                                            │
ON-SITE BEHAVIOUR                                       ◄───┤
                                                            │
   |                                                        │
                                                            │
DEPARTURE, RETURN TRIP AND REFLECTION                   ────┘
UPON THE EXPERIENCE
```

Figure 10.2. Disaggregating the components of recreation behaviour.

This framework was explored within the context of the main preoccupations of land management, habitat destruction and impacts upon other users. In turn, this was informed by a review of theory and practice, and by the use of focus group interviews conducted with practitioners in Scotland. The review of theory and practice was conducted via a keyword search of various recreation sources, including *Recreation, Leisure and Tourism Abstracts*, The Natural History Bookshop and *The Applied Social Science Index & Abstract* (Foley, 1997). The key discussion points emerging from this search were then consolidated into a schedule for the focus groups, which were conducted with both users and providers of countryside recreation in Scotland.

10.3.1 *The decision to go*

There is considerable evidence to suggest that it is possible to affect behaviour at this stage of the process. This can be achieved in two ways: firstly, through long-term socialisation and, secondly, through influential marketing. Of the socialisation processes, it appears likely (Bromley, 1994) that primary schooling (i.e. secondary socialisation) and peer pressure in the teenage years (tertiary socialisation) will have the greatest influences among young people across the social spectrum. Although primary socialisation, within the family, may offer young people strong and positive role models, it seems that this is not universally the case for all socio-economic groups. Currently, the differential nature of background education about the environment among adults of different ages, and of different social, economic and cultural backgrounds, makes the preparation and presentation of common and integrated messages very difficult.

It appears that people have a repertoire or library of sites which they may visit under certain circumstances and that these sites will often be influenced by individual experiences (Bull, 1995). Whereas this may not hold for all social groups, it is sufficiently powerful to be included in a model of recreation behaviour.

A final opportunity at this stage is the prospect of using both marketing and demarketing techniques to influence decisions 'to go' and thus influence recreation behaviour. Marketing techniques attempt to match the needs of users and providers with a view to satisfactorily achieving both of their objectives. Much of the effectiveness of marketing techniques in recreation contexts is based upon the availability of information to users and potential users. Demarketing, on the other hand, limits the flow of information about crowded or sensitive sites (e.g. the location of nesting white-tailed eagles, *Haliaeetus albicilla*) with a view to minimising the influx of mass visitors.

10.3.2 Travelling to the site
A number of instances of influencing recreation decisions and subsequent behaviour arise from opportunities presented during journeys to outdoor sites. Moreover, there is also the possibility of encouraging reflection upon the decision to travel, the implication of this decision upon the environment and any potential alternatives that might have been more resource friendly. Identified instances of behaviour modification *en route* include local radio, signage, and liveware roadside information services. The first and last of these require that the visitor takes some action (i.e. switches on the radio or accesses these information services). Information services and signage are relatively indiscriminate, although local radio enables the targeting of a well-defined segment or group.

10.3.3 Arrival and reception
The review of theory and practice established that issues of arrival and reception tended to be seen in terms of two 'competing' approaches to interpretation, and thus competing opportunities for influencing behaviour. These approaches were either the use of human resources (e.g. ranger services) or the use of impersonal approaches (e.g. signage). Where the issue of affecting behaviour was considered at the point of arrival, there tended to be an assumption that a visitor centre of some sort was in use. However, there were no analyses found of the role played by integrated approaches that reinforce messages received earlier in the trip, or from previous visits to the countryside.

10.3.4 On-site behaviour
Attempts to influence behaviour varied between fairly crude examples of rationing approaches involving elements of pricing and more sophisticated approaches based upon information, interpretation, environmental education and ranger staff. It is clear from the information reviewed that each site, each issue, each impact and the predominant user

group or groups responsible for it should be analysed together. On-site approaches will need to be constructed from an understanding of local conditions and will have application only on that particular site.

According to some participants in the focus groups, some sites can take fairly substantial impacts associated with mass use and still be relatively non-problematical in terms of land management and habitat destruction. Other, more fragile, sites are unable to sustain high levels of use. To take this a stage further, some impacts at a local level are the result of deviant behaviour associated with male youth cultures, themselves intended to compromise the efforts of land managers or to destroy habitats (e.g. vandalism). Other impacts may be the result of ill-informed, or ignorant, behaviour, even by 'respectable' user groups who fail to understand the effect of their recreation behaviour (see Carter, chapter 13, this volume). The particular impacts that may be most effectively reduced, and particular perpetrators who may be most susceptible to attempts to influence their behaviour, were selected for analysis.

Alongside impacts upon habitats and landscapes are the ways in which one user group affects another user group. Much has been written about user conflict and there are a number of codes and conventions of conduct. However, the literature tends to concentrate simply upon practical consideration of securing a *modus operandi* between two groups rather than exploring the social and cultural significance of the impacts. In this regard, a number of relatively new pursuits were roundly condemned in the focus groups, particularly those which involved invasion of the space of 'traditional' recreation, e.g. by groups which had secured access to air, piste or water through relatively inexpensive new technologies (examples are snowboarding, mountain biking and jet-skiing).

10.3.5 *Departure, return and reflection*

Despite the growing acceptance of relationship marketing in recreation (Spink, 1994), there was little literature available that considered use of the countryside as anything but a single transaction. Thus, despite the intuitive feeling and objective evidence that users of the countryside return again and again, whether to one or to many sites, this did not feature in any modelling or marketing techniques used by previous studies.

10.4 Resultant actions and impacts

A key outcome of the focus groups was agreement that action at the general level (e.g. affecting overall participation or decisions to participate) could be introduced more easily than specific agents of behavioural influence at site level. Behaviour on-site is where impacts are most prevalent and where it is most possible to influence local policies. Nevertheless, it should be borne in mind that in all of the focus groups, participants opined that influencing decisions to travel and, especially, influencing choice of travel mode could make significant, positive environmental impacts, possibly greater in their effect than on-site measures.

It is essential to differentiate between purposive action, where users may deliberately impact upon the environment in full awareness of the consequences, and actions that arise from ignorance of the effects of particular behaviours. Some evidence from the focus groups suggested that there may be a third category which could be described as 'ambivalence': impacts arising from neither deliberate negative behaviour nor ignorance, but rather from a casual, but deliberate, disregard.

Although the final impact of all of these behaviours may be similar, it is important to distinguish between their origins where attempts to influence behaviour are to be introduced. Uncovering the origins of non-acceptable behaviour will expose the attitudes, motivations, beliefs, norms, knowledge and experiences that define the behaviours. Thus, it is most useful to conceive of actions on a continuum, stretching from malice at one end, via disregard, to ignorance at the other.

Any one action may be placed on the continuum according to the perspective of the interpreter of the behaviour. In some cases, there may be the possibility for differentiated perspectives based upon social, cultural and economic norms (e.g. destruction of saplings), but in others (e.g. almost any activity rooted in youth or popular culture) these external variables may lead to rather different interpretations of action along the continuum. The focus upon on-site impacts has, inevitably, given prominence to wholly on-site behaviours and actions as shown in the first two columns in Table 10.2.

Table 10.2. Behaviour, associated actions and resultant impacts

Recreation behaviour	Associated action	Resultant impacts	Examples
Malice			
Access to all groups	Vandalism by some groups	Damage to natural heritage	Habitat, vegetation, fauna, aesthetics
		Effects on land management	Opportunity costs of clear-up, disturbance, siege mentality
		Implications for other users	Spoils visit, fear
Visiting urban fringe	Threat of illegal actions perceived by land managers	Damage to natural heritage	Habitat, fauna
		Effects on land management	Restrictions, fear, unco-operative, livestock disturbance, fence destruction
		Implications for other users	Future users are discouraged
Disregard			
Need for refreshment on site	Litter	Damage to natural heritage	Eco-balance, visual detraction
		Effects on land management	Opportunity costs, problems of dispersal
		Implications for other users	Safety, may imitate behaviour, spoils visit
Toilet needs	'Pink paper syndrome'; latrine pits	Damage to natural heritage	Soil structure, habitat, aesthetic
		Effects on land management	Clear-up, safety
		Implications for other users	Safety, spoils visit, imitative behaviour

Table 10.2. continued

Recreation behaviour	Associated action	Resultant impacts	Examples
Exercising dogs	Dog fouling	Damage to natural heritage	Soil structure, habitat, aesthetic
		Effects on land management	Clear-up, disturb fauna and livestock
		Implications for other users	Health, aesthetic
Ignorance Not socialised into positive values	Failure to recognise consequences of some actions	Damage to natural heritage	Potentially entire ecosystem
		Effects on land management	Prohibition of access, opportunity costs of repair
		Implications for other users	Frustration, anger, compromise current and future enjoyment
Car borne visitation	Parking problems	Damage to natural heritage	Ground cover, habitat, revegetation problems, aesthetic
		Effects on land management	Affects working access, stock driving problems, prohibition
		Implications for other users	Imitative behaviour, spoils visit
Participation in 'new' recreations	User conflicts over space and values	Damage to natural heritage	Due to increased or unforeseen use
		Effects on land management	Resultant need to reconcile conflicts
		Implications for other users	Rage, misunderstandings, conflicts, demonisation
Visiting 'honey-pot' sites	Pressure on all resources and infrastructures	Damage to natural heritage	Vegetation, habitat, ground cover, soil erosion
		Effects on land management	Compromises access for work, opportunity costs of repair
		Implications for other users	Aesthetic, noise, compromises solitude, imitative behaviour

On the basis of discussions at the focus group interviews, these behaviours and actions can be taken a stage further towards their resultant impacts. The third and fourth columns of Table 10.2 attempt to present, for the series of key recreation behaviours, their associated actions and examples of the resultant impacts.

10.5 Direct and indirect influences

It was agreed in the focus group discussions that a number of techniques had utility in more than one context of what has been called the 'user journey'. The reconciled feelings of participants, shown in Table 10.3, take account of the belief that some techniques could be either direct or indirect influences within each context. It is not claimed that the list is exhaustive even within the narrow parameters of the techniques explored. Consideration of influencing agents beyond these factors (see Burgess *et al.*, 1988a,b; Harrison, 1981, 1991) suggests that there could have been many other possibilities, e.g. personal experience, but when these were explored at the focus group interviews they were discarded as being of low feasibility within the aims of the research.

Table 10.3. Direct and indirect behavioural influences on the user journey

Components of recreation behaviour	Direct influence	Indirect influence
Whether to go	Media-based strategies	Media-based strategies
Travelling	Rationing	Media-based strategies
Arrival	Visible presence; rationing	Media-based strategies; integration strategies
On-site behaviour	Visible presence; rationing; community experience	Media-based strategies
Departure and reflection	Media-based strategies	Media-based strategies

This typology places a heavy emphasis upon the media-based approaches that enjoyed considerable support in the focus group discussions. Media are a range of approaches that could extend from simple signage to TV and cinema advertising campaigns. The prevalence of these approaches is indicative of the range available for use. Table 10.3 informed the selection of case studies for the next stage of the research and reassured the team that opportunities for influence were being considered across the spectrum of options.

10.6 Case studies

Case studies were chosen as a means of exemplifying current practice at a number of sites in the United Kingdom. In particular, the criteria for selection of case study venues were, first, the presence of actions, behaviours or impacts which corresponded to those present in Scotland, and, second, evidence or belief that these had had some form of success.

10.6.1 Codes of conduct and other 'educative approaches'

It was clear from correspondence received and from the focus group interviews that codes of conduct have a significant role to play in influencing behaviour. Key theoretical references are Clark *et al.* (1971), Christiansen and Clark (1979), Lucas (1982, 1983), Oliver *et al.* (1985), and Dwyer *et al.* (1989). The use of codes in other contexts presents some interesting possibilities. System Three (Scotland) (1996) conducted an evaluation of public awareness of the Country Code for SNH. Similar issues arise in industrial heritage tourism and may provide a good basis for initiating evaluation. Essentially, what was needed was a site in which a number of codes have been promulgated and evaluated. This would allow both a review of the general approach and an opportunity to develop a critique of approaches to evaluating effectiveness.

Projected over-supply in the used car market for four-wheel-drive vehicles up to 2001, together with rising insurance premiums for this type of vehicle, have led to beliefs that it will be possible to buy an off-road vehicle for little more than the price of a second-hand family car in the near future. It is widely accepted that many four-wheel-drive vehicles bought new in the last five years are unlikely to be taken off-road by their original owners, but this is expected to change when these vehicles reach the second-hand market where they may be used as recreational vehicles only. These forecasts, taken together with the growth of a commercial sector of entrepreneurs offering off-road safari experiences, led to concerns, especially in the Lake District National Park, that increases in the level of use of tracks and paths can be expected. One of the results was the development of a code of conduct.

The five key issues for the research arising from this case study were the importance of consultation in the development of any restraints upon behaviour; the targeting of the responsible user or club member and the importance of creating an incentive to be responsible; promulgation of the code via club networks; significance of peer group pressure; and communication mechanisms and channels that need to take account of the type of users.

10.6.2 *Visible presence*

There is a considerable body of work upon visibility, whether of personnel or remote techniques, and the reduction of deviant behaviour (Muchmore, 1975; Anderson, 1980; Christiansen, 1983; van der Stoep and Gramann, 1987). There are some suggestions that this visibility can extend further towards encouraging positive behaviour as well as reducing negative behaviour and a growing body of literature on the use of close circuit television (CCTV) in the outdoors. Opportunities for these techniques are both personal (uniformed staff; attitude and ethos of staff) and impersonal (surveillance from a remote point; CCTV). It seems likely that any successful use of this approach would combine elements of both of these but would retain the key feature of being overt (i.e. visible) rather than covert. Most focus group participants agreed that this could make the site 'look managed'.

The CCTV introduced at Chatelherault Country Park in Scotland was predominantly to monitor the car park, which had been subject to a large number of thefts. As this issue was developed in the focus groups, there was some disagreement over the 'ideological' and practical implications of CCTV. However, most participants felt strongly that verbal appeals, powerful role models and a series of integrated marketing messages delivered via appropriate media were useful in influencing behaviour.

The four key issues for research arising from this case study were that existing facilities may be able to be redeveloped to secure solutions; surveillance requires both personal and impersonal approaches to secure deterrence and persuasion together; the site must look as if it is being managed; and this was not a useful approach for remote or large sites.

10.6.3 *Community-based approaches*

Once again, this issue received considerable airing in the focus groups and, indeed, arose from a group itself rather than from the facilitator's agenda. Its introduction came after a discussion about voluntarism and the potential role of 'active citizenship' in promoting positive behaviours. There is a body of literature upon volunteering, voluntarism and volunteerism (see Hoggett and Bishop, 1986). Woodley (1993) pointed to a number of examples in Canada and others have examined community involvement in other contexts.

Of particular interest in the use of this type of approach is the Parish Paths Partnership that was initiated in England and Wales. This was designed as a local-based scheme to tackle the minor problems that make the rights of way network difficult to use and to promote and publicise the network. It was launched by the Countryside Commission in 1992 as part of their strategy to achieve targets laid down in *Enjoying the Countryside: Priorities for Action.*

The six key issues for the research arising from this case study were that voluntary involvement can increase awareness and use (potentially better quality use); better quality environments may engender better quality use (especially where a link can be made to personal interest); the use of this technique may be best applied to particular socio-economic conditions and user groups; transferability of new attitudes and behaviours is theoretically possible but under-researched in the outdoors; there is evidence of proprietorial values creeping into such initiatives; and publicity is not a universal panacea.

10.6.4 Integrating 'new' with existing activities

All participants in the focus groups felt that there was an issue of behaviour where newly introduced activities, such as mountain-biking, snowboarding, micro-light flying and jet-skiing, co-existed with current users of the outdoors. Although there were wide differences in the analysis of the problem (some saw the behaviour as depreciative, others as a simple manifestation of popular culture), there is little doubt of the importance of the issue. Several publications and websites were reviewed and the most obvious feature is the concentration upon speed, altitude and technology in the 'new ' activities. Many of the images evoke a sense of daring and danger. Essentially, the issue here is to consider strategies that have been used to secure effective integration or, alternatively, segregation of traditional users and new pastimes or pursuits.

The five key issues for the research arising from this case study were that maps and messages need to be integrated, otherwise the message is most likely to be lost; traditional users of a natural environment will become proprietorial, which can bring both positive, monitoring consequences and negative, exclusivity value-sets; it may be useful to segregate participants in recently introduced activities, especially where these are associated with youth and popular cultures; some users see the environment as a natural gymnasium which provides a challenge in athleticism; and land managers will need to be part of any attempt to introduce new marketing activities.

10.6.5 Media-based approaches

All participants in the focus groups felt strongly that a media and publications strategy had a vital role to play in reaching users and defining what amounts to 'appropriate' behaviour. It is also notable that participants in the System Three (Scotland) (1996) study of public awareness of the Country Code cited media as the most likely approach to increasing awareness.

Media campaigns in the public and voluntary sectors have attempted to socialise populations into changed behaviours. Of particular interest have been the campaigns run by the Health Education Board for Scotland (HEBS) relating to smoking, alcohol consumption and eating in Central Scotland (see Allison, this volume), the Department of Health campaigns intended to influence behaviour associated with the risks of contracting AIDS, and the Scottish Home and Health Department campaigns designed to reduce drinking and driving. The area of health education offers some of the most direct parallels in terms of type of influence, socio-economic status of groups targeted and geographical location. HEBS has evaluated its work regularly and a body of literature is available.

Six key issues for research arise from this case study. First, campaigns designed to influence behaviour need to be integrated to ensure recall and recognition between the communication mechanism (e.g. an advertisement) and the point of behaviour (e.g. reaching for a cigarette). This would suggest that a recognisable approach and simple statement of values could be branded across all aspects of outdoor recreation. Second, targeting, based upon understanding of the users who are most in need of influence, is critical to success. This means targeting both user segments and associated media. Third, events can raise awareness and can be operated inexpensively using PR techniques. Fourth, inter-agency co-operation can be a factor in securing success. Users seldom share the sensitivity that agency staff possess regarding boundary lines of responsibility and locus. One clear message will be the most effective. Fifth, role models are fraught with hazard as a means of suggesting behavioural change, although they may have some uses in imparting information and securing attention and awareness. Finally, a World Wide Web site is a useful means of reaching young people through schools, libraries and colleges and, increasingly, in the home.

10.6.6 Conclusions from case studies

Opportunities for influencing behaviour offer both a positive and a negative dimension (Table 10.4). Behaviour can either be encouraged or be discouraged. The means of achieving either of these can be through reward or punishment.

The complexity of securing targeted influence is well-illustrated by the ranges of typologies and potential interventions. While it is conceded that not all of these dimensions may be operational in any one context of influence, it is fairly apparent from the case studies that this may be possible and, indeed, that each may encroach upon and interact with others. Under these circumstances, it seems appropriate to consider an integrated framework for action and to attempt to produce guidelines for where actions may best be targeted.

Table 10.4. A framework for understanding behaviour and sanctions

Behaviour	Reward	Punishment
Positive	'Do it this way and you'll be rewarded'	'Do it this way, or you'll be punished'
Negative	'Don't do it that way and you'll be rewarded'	'Don't do it that way, or you'll be punished'

10.7 Conclusions

10.7.1 Strategic level

It is obvious from all of the data collected that it will not be feasible to influence all behaviours in all contexts. Thus it is imperative to identify priorities for minimising the effects by the most susceptible groups of users at the most likely sites where improvement can be achieved using messages and techniques targeted for this purpose. Essentially, this argues for an approach that adopts an overall framework, or strategy, within which a wide range of initiatives may operate, sharing a common set of goals and preoccupations. These would need to be led by a statement of the impacts to be targeted by the strategy, the groups at which the influences are aimed, the type of site or sites at which it is expected to 'improve' behaviour, and the specific techniques to be used for this purpose.

Strategic information needs to be imparted at the national level with an agreed set of priorities and parameters. Of crucial importance is the simplicity of the message in terms of what it wants the receiver to do, when to do it, how it can be made easier to do it, and who can help with more information now.

Strategic campaigns with an unequivocal message are not uncommon in the sphere of recreation. Slogans such as *Sport for All*, *Over 50 and All to Play For* in sport encouragement, *Walk About a Bit* in health education, and *Tread Softly* or *Cruisin without Bruisin* in the outdoors make their message clear to the recipient. *Sport for All* is a good example because the slogan is still used as a statement of values by practitioners outwith the Sports Council and by users themselves long after the campaign itself had ended. However, a great deal of the success has also depended upon the message reaching the target audience and the impact of that message when received. Moreover, there has been a strong dependence upon an integrated hierarchy of core, recognisable materials designed to be recognised by different types of user, at different levels of use and at the points of use themselves. This would argue for an integrated 'relationship marketing' approach based upon branding and user recognition as a key factor in establishing design criteria.

As this type of approach is most likely to have its primary focus upon the decisions 'whether to go' and 'where to go', messages should be aimed within this context. The messages should allow for reinforcement and minor modification while travelling, upon arrival, and during the visit itself. Later reflection could be encouraged either by the message itself or by site-based communications. The strategic approach adopted should accept the likelihood of changing behaviour incrementally over time, rather than just for one site on any one occasion.

10.7.2 Operational level

At the operational level, individual site managers will make decisions that correspond to their precise needs, priorities and user profiles. In terms of the strategic response outlined above, there is a need for site-level action to be identified within an overall message as well as to fulfil its own, local requirements. A weakness of current approaches is the absence of an apparent integrative focus between strategic and operational messages from the perspective of the user (or, at least, the non-expert user).

The idea of a visible presence, exemplified by the cameras and site assistant patrols at Chatelherault, offers opportunities for both positive and negative influences to be brought to bear upon user behaviours. What is clear from the situation as it has arisen at Chatelherault is that in combination, the possibility of encouraging positive behaviour and discouraging negative behaviour can be achieved using both positive and negative sanctions within the flexibility offered by both a human and a 'non-human' presence. It is also clear that these approaches are best utilised in reception and 'honey-pot' sites where large numbers of visitors congregate and the potential for influencing large numbers is high.

During use itself, there are possibilities for formal restrictions as well as voluntary restraint and associated peer-group pressure. There is a need for explanation to accompany any attempts to introduce or impose rules, regulations, zones, bye-laws and codes of behaviour. Again, this seems to be likely to be achieved within an integrated framework of messages already assimilated by users via strategic approaches but reinforced and contextualised, possibly using personal interventions or through recognisable, sensitive interpretative signage (see Jones, this volume). There was an oft-quoted desire to be 'realistic' in expectations of users. Many in the focus groups were sceptical about the scale of impact upon the outdoors attributable to recreation compared to the impact of modern agriculture or Mediterranean-scale tourism. It is vital, then, to maintain an understanding about what it is both within the activity being pursued and its geographical context that attracts the user and to demonstrate a sensitivity and sympathy to these needs, but to express this in terms of a trade-off for 'acceptable' behaviour that secures sustainability and biodiversity.

The socialisation process involved in operationalising voluntary codes of conduct, and the importance of peer pressure in gaining compliance, are also worthy of further examination. Codes work best among those who commit themselves to ownership of the image of their activities, rather than, say, a particular piece of land as a resource to be used solely and in perpetuity for one activity. Change in use, users and activity seems to represent the greatest challenge to those for whom it is a threat, rather than as an opportunity for compromise and integration.

The community-based project (section 10.6.3) seemed to offer the greatest possibilities for post-use reflection and for allowing users to address the implications of their use upon the natural resource and other users, both now and in the future. This too needs to be achieved within a strategic framework that encourages a mindset associated with reflection. Almost certainly, this should include initiatives where local communities take responsibility for redressing their own use and that of others. The economic benefits may, at least, be felt locally.

The key analytical point made is the importance of the relationship between the strategic and operational contexts of influencing behaviour. Much of the evidence suggests that there are opportunities for incremental and sustainable changes in behaviour where local policies are pursued and supported within a wider strategic framework. In turn, that framework should take account of the dimensions of recreation, the behaviour that is giving cause for concern, the resultant actions and impacts, and the variables affecting all of these.

Acknowledgements

The authors gratefully acknowledge the contribution of Bridget Dales and Richard Davison of Scottish Natural Heritage in the development of this research.

References

Anderson, G. (1980). Vandalism reward programme. *Park Maintenance*, **33**, 24.

Bromley, P. (1994). *Countryside Management*. Spon, London.

Bull, A. (1995). *The Economics of Travel and Tourism, 2nd Edn.* Longman, Melbourne.

Burgess, J., Harrison, C.M. and Limb, M. (1988a). Exploring environmental values through the medium of small groups. Part one: theory and practice. *Environment and Planning*, **20**, 309-326.

Burgess, J., Harrison, C.M. and Limb, M. (1988b). Exploring environmental values through the medium of small groups. Part two: illustrations of a group at work. *Environment and Planning*, **20**, 457-476.

Christiansen, H.H. and Clark, R.N. (1979). Understanding and controlling vandalism and other rule violations in urban recreation areas. State University of New York, College of Environmental Sciences and Forestry *Publication* **80-003**, 63-84.

Christiansen, M.L. (1983). *Vandalism Control Management for Parks and Recreation Areas.* Spon/Venture, London.

Clark, R.N., Hendee, J.C. and Campbell, F.L. (1971*).* Values, behaviour and conflict in modern camping culture. *Journal of Leisure Research*, **3**, 143-159.

Clarke, I. and Schmidt, R.A. (1995). Beyond the servicescape: the experience of place. *Journal of Retailing and Consumer Services*, **2**, 149-162.

Countryside Commission (1989). *Enjoying the Countryside: priorities for action.* CCP235. Countryside Commission, Cheltenham.

Dwyer, W.O., Huffman, M.G. and Jarratt, L.H. (1989). A comparison of strategies for gaining compliance. *The Journal of Park and Recreation Administration*, **7**, 21-30.

Engel, J.F., Kollat, D.J. and Blackwell, R.D. (1968). *Consumer Behaviour.* Holt, Rinehart and Wilson, Chicago.

Foley, M. (1997). Influencing recreation behaviour to reduce impacts. Unpublished report.

Harrison, C. (1981). A playground for whom? Informal recreation in London's green belt. *Area*, **13**, 109-114.

Harrison, C. (1991). *Countryside Recreation in a Changing Society.* TMS Partnership Ltd, London.

Hoggett, I. and Bishop, J. (1986). *Organising around Enthusiasms.* SSRC, London.

Kotler, P. (1967). *Marketing Management: Analysis, Planning and Control.* Prentice-Hall, Englewood Cliffs, New Jersey.

Lucas, R.C. (1982). Recreation regulations - when are they needed? *Journal of Forestry*, **80**, 148-151.

Lucas, R.C. (1983). The role of regulations in recreation management. *Western Wildlands*, **2**, 6-10.

Muchmore, J.M. (1975). The uniform, its effect. *The Police Chief*, **42**, 70-71.

Oliver, S.S., Roggenbuck, J.W. and Watson, A.E. (1985). Education to reduce impact on forest campgrounds. *Journal of Forestry*, **83**, 234-236.

Spink, J. (1994). *Leisure and the Environment.* Butterworth Heinemann, London.

System Three Scotland (1996). *Public Awareness of the Country Code.* Scottish Natural Heritage, Perth.

Urry, J. (1995). *Consuming Places.* Routledge, London.

van der Stoep, G.A. and Gramann, J.H. (1987). The effect of verbal appeal and incentives on depreciative behaviour among youthful park visitors. *Journal of Leisure Research*, **19**, 69-83.

Woodley, A. (1993). Tourism and sustainable development: the community perspective. In *Tourism and Sustainable Development: Monitoring, Planning*, ed. by J.G. Nelson, R. Butler, and G. Wall. Department of Geography, Waterloo. University of Waterloo. pp. 135-147.

11   PROMOTING HEALTHY BEHAVIOUR

Mary Allison

Summary

1.   The Health Education Board for Scotland (HEBS) works at three levels to improve health and tackle health inequalities by influencing culture and individual know-how, by capacity building, and by strategic development across settings and sectors.

2.   This chapter considers the development and evaluation of a mass media campaign to influence culture and know-how with respect to walking as a healthy activity.

3.   The campaign included a TV advertisement, press and PR activity and a free phoneline. Its impact was assessed in terms of pre- and post-campaign changes in knowledge, beliefs, motivations, intentions and behaviours.

4.   The campaign had significant positive impacts on changes in knowledge and beliefs about walking, but limited impacts on changes in walking behaviour.

11.1 Background

This chapter is a case study of a mass media campaign to promote behaviour change in health-related physical activity and, in particular, walking as a healthy form of exercise. The campaign was based on the premise that changing the behaviour of individuals is supported by a much broader cultural change in attitudes towards healthy behaviour in the population as a whole. In this context, influencing changes in knowledge and attitudes that surround walking was as important as changing individual behaviour. This approach, although focussing on a very different aspect of behaviour, has many potential parallels with changing behaviour in relation to outdoor access.

The Health Education Board for Scotland (HEBS) was established in 1991 as the national agency for health education in Scotland. The health education remit of HEBS is interpreted within the broader role of health promotion defined by the World Health Organisation (WHO) as the process of enabling people to increase control over, and to improve, their health. HEBS works at three levels (Figure 11.1) to improve health and tackle health inequalities: influencing culture and individual know-how, capacity building, and strategic development across settings and sectors.

Evidence of the contribution of HEBS to developing a more pro-health culture derives mainly from the evaluation of its mass media activities which, for adults, focus on Scotland's 'Big Three' causes of premature death – coronary heart disease, cancer and stroke. Thus, media campaigns (for adults) have a focus on diet, alcohol, smoking and physical activity.

In the recent health White Paper (Scottish Office, 1999), physical activity is identified as a target area for action. The promotion of physical activity is emphasised primarily because of its role in the prevention of coronary heart disease, stroke and vascular disease

HEBS' responsibilities

Influence culture and individual know-how

- pro-health culture
- provide information
- promote choices

Capacity building

- strengthen skills
- enhance confidence
- national and local

Strategic development

- develop structures
- support processes

The public

Partners/professionals

Settings/sectors

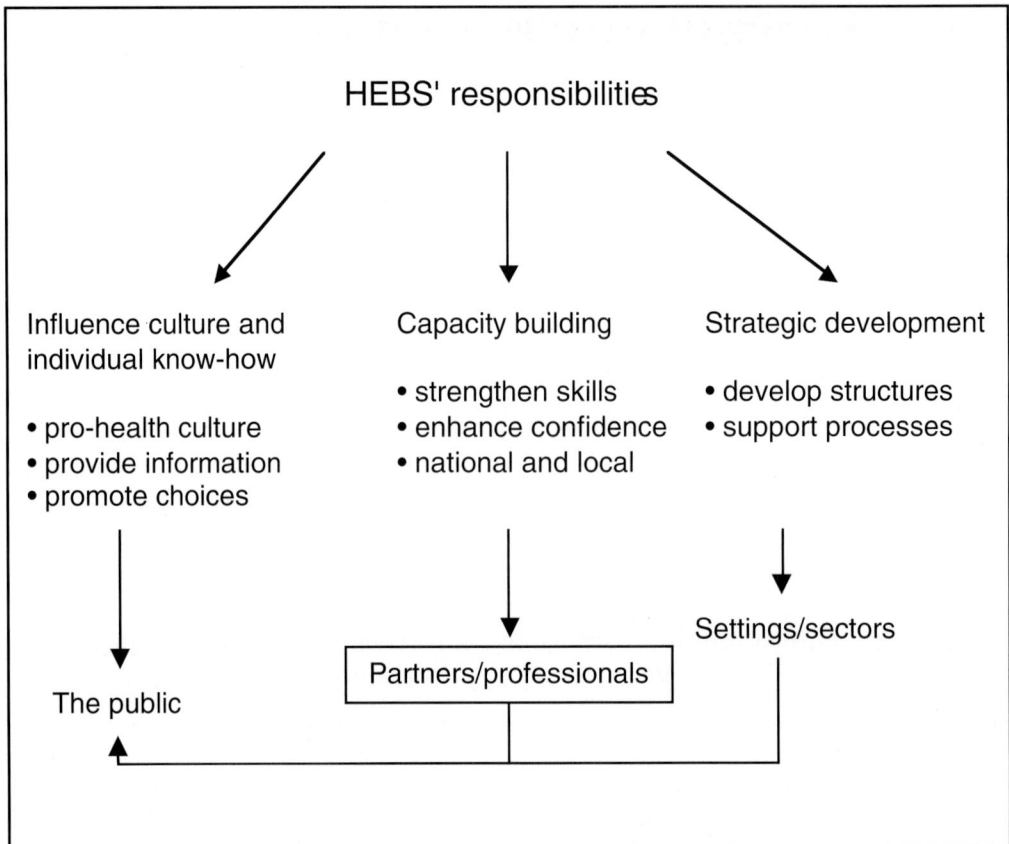

Figure 11.1. Responsibilities of the Health Education Board for Scotland (HEBS).

through modifying some of the risk factors for these diseases, including obesity, hypertension and raised blood cholesterol (Blair *et al.*, 1992; Bouchard *et al.*, 1993; Wimbush, 1995).

In June 1995, HEBS published a policy statement on *The Promotion of Physical Activity in Scotland* (HEBS, 1995) to inform its strategic development of work in the area of physical activity. It was intended that the policy statement would encourage co-ordination and consistency of action by the many agencies in Scotland contributing to the promotion of physical activity.

This policy statement recommended the adoption of an 'active living' approach which emphasises the health benefits of daily moderate intensity exercise, such as brisk walking, stair use and cycling. This approach reflected the revised recommendation "*to accumulate 30 minutes or more of moderate intensity physical activity over the course of most days of the week*" (Pate *et al.*, 1995). This was distinguished from the previous and more ambitious fitness-related guideline of regular vigorous intensity exercise at least three times a week (the traditional three times 20 minutes exercise prescription).

The HEBS' policy statement recommended that the moderate 'active living' approach should become the dominant message in Scotland, as the greatest gains in health would result from getting the sedentary population to be moderately active (Wimbush, 1995).

11.2 The development of the walking campaign

A mass media campaign to promote 'active living' was undertaken during 1995 and 1996. It focused on walking, the most popular active recreational pursuit across all age groups in Scotland and the most accessible form of everyday physical activity. The campaign was developed for women and men in the 30 to 55 year age range who are currently physically inactive and do not exercise on a regular basis. The campaign materials were developed with this group in mind, but with a bias toward C2, D and E socio-economic groups (skilled and unskilled manual workers).

11.2.1 Campaign objectives

The main aim of the walking campaign was to re-position walking as a healthy form of exercise. Within this broad aim, three objectives were defined to encourage the target audience to re-assess their attitude to walking (i.e. to regard walking as a form of exercise comparable to running, swimming, cycling), to motivate the target audience to increase both the quantity and quality of their walking, and to generate enquiries for further information about physical activity.

11.2.2 Developmental and pre-testing research

To guide the development of the mass media campaign on walking, HEBS commissioned developmental and pre-testing research. The research was carried out in three stages, an initial developmental stage and two stages of pre-testing, using a total of 16 focus groups. All focus group members were inactive but open to change and recruited according to age (30-45, 46-55, 56-65, 66-75), sex, social class (A, B and C1, C2, D and E groups) and lifestage (with/without dependants).

Four key findings and recommendations emerged. First, there was a credibility problem with walking - walking did not tend to be regarded as 'proper' exercise, particularly by men. It was clear that the campaign should challenge such beliefs by communicating concrete and surprising new information about walking as a form of exercise. Second, the campaign should be backed up with believable information on what levels/types of activity will achieve the desired ends, on safe levels of physical activity and by highlighting the credibility of HEBS as a source of reliable information. Third, to motivate people to walk more, the campaign should communicate the perceived benefits of regular walking - physical, mental, emotional and sensory - and create motivational images of walking. Thus, the campaign should create a strong visual appeal through advertising, emphasise the 'hassle-free' or ease factor of walking by comparison with other forms of exercise which are perceived as hard work, and emphasise walking as enjoyable exercise. Finally, to support behaviour change, the campaign should arouse sufficient curiosity to move people to want to test out the new ideas, adopt a provocative and challenging tone, provide general back-up information, and provide local information about suitable walks and organised events.

On the basis of the developmental research, a 'startling facts' approach was adopted, using the statement that 'walking a mile uses the same energy as running a mile'.

11.2.3 Campaign materials

A 40-second television advertisement was produced which featured Gavin Hastings, who was regarded as a credible spokesperson on physical activity as a previous captain of the

Scottish rugby team. He is seen walking briskly along a city street while asking the viewers *'Did you know that walking a mile uses exactly the same energy or calories as running a mile does? What's more, it's equivalent to swimming 15 lengths of a 25 metre pool, or playing 8 minutes of this* [squash] *non-stop! So if you want to be fit and healthy you don't have to* [shots of sweaty and energetic players of squash, rugby and weight-lifting], *you can do this'* [cut to the relative serenity of walking briskly in a city park]. The end-frame shows the HEBS' logo and super-imposed text: *'Walking. Take exercise in your stride'* and *'For your free exercise pack call 0500 023 024'*.

An information pack was produced for the campaign to tie in the supplementary information with the television commercial. The front cover featured a still of Gavin Hastings from the television advertisement and the inside of the pack provided facts about the energy expenditure involved in walking a mile compared with other more conventional forms of exercise and sport. The pack also contained copies of *Hassle Free Exercise* and a small booklet entitled *Walking: Where and When,* with contact names and telephone numbers for local walking groups. This was available to the public via a Freephone telephone line (*Fitline*).

Local radio stations highlighted local walking opportunities and interviews with local walkers and professionals such as health promotion officers and leisure and recreation staff of local authorities. Further, the campaign was launched on Scottish Television's (STV) programme *Scottish Action* on 12 September 1995, immediately before the first five week burst of television advertising (from 13 September to 17 October 1995). There was considerable local press coverage of the new campaign in the week after the launch which provided the Freephone telephone number and information about the local radio programmes on walking in the coming weeks. A second four week burst of television advertising followed in the spring (from 26 March to 21 April 1996).

11.3 Evaluation objectives and methods

The four objectives of the evaluation were to assess public awareness of the HEBS' campaign and campaign resources, to explore the role played by the walking campaign in the process of changing behaviour and post-test the campaign materials, and to monitor population changes in knowledge, attitudes and intentions about walking and walking behaviour.

A pre- and post-implementation appraisal of the campaign was conducted. There was no control group given that the mass media intervention extended to cover the whole population. Both qualitative and quantitative methods were used to assess the effectiveness of the campaign. The following methods of data collection were used.

11.3.1 Communications tracking survey

Public awareness of the walking campaign was assessed by asking questions about awareness of the campaign components (television advertisement, *Fitline* and booklet) in the ongoing Communications Tracking Survey carried out for HEBS three times a year. This survey consisted of personal interviews and used multi-stage cluster random probability sampling methods. This survey provided data on prompted awareness levels in the general population at the peak of the first burst of television advertising (October 1995) and then four months later (February 1996), before the second burst of advertising.

11.3.2 Baseline survey of Fitline callers
A baseline survey was conducted by the tele-marketing company that was commissioned by HEBS to operate the *Fitline* service. All those who actively responded to the campaign by phoning *Fitline* were asked by trained telephone operators to take part in a short questionnaire-based interview. The questionnaire included six questions about themselves and seven questions about their current level of walking and exercise, their knowledge about walking as a form of exercise, and their intentions with regard to walking more and being more physically active generally. This provided a baseline measure for assessing change in these variables.

The evaluation covered the contacts made with *Fitline* between 13 September and 25 October 1995. During this six week period, a total of 4,036 calls were received, and the response rate to different questions ranged from 62 to 86 per cent (the response rate declined steadily as callers progressed through the questionnaire).

11.3.3 Follow-up surveys of Fitline callers
The Centre for Leisure Research was commissioned to conduct two follow-up telephone surveys (10 weeks and 12 months) with a random sample of 700 of the 2,693 *Fitline* callers who consented to be followed up for research purposes. The response rate was 70 per cent and 58 per cent at 10 weeks and one year respectively. This research sought to assess the impact of the campaign on individuals' knowledge, beliefs, motivations, intentions and behaviour with regard to exercise and walking. The follow-up samples were intended to be representative of *Fitline* callers, but those aged under 20 years are slightly under-represented in both follow up stages.

11.3.4 Population survey
The impact of the campaign on individuals' awareness and behaviours about exercise and walking was also assessed at a population level through placing five questions in System 3 Scotland's monthly omnibus population survey, the *Scottish Opinion Survey*, in June 1995 and June 1996.

11.3.5 Group discussions
As part of the contract to follow up *Fitline* callers at 10 weeks, the Centre for Leisure Research was also commissioned to convene six group discussions (six to eight persons per group). These groups post-tested the content and format of the campaign materials and explored the ways in which the campaign contributed to changes in awareness of exercise and exercise behaviour. The groups were recruited from the sample of *Fitline* callers who had been followed up at 10 weeks.

11.4 Evaluation results

11.4.1 Impact on awareness
Immediately following the first burst of television advertising, high levels of public awareness had been achieved. In October 1995, 70 per cent of adults recalled having seen the 'Gavin' television advertisement based on being shown a still photograph taken from the advertisement (see Figure 11.2). Four months later in February 1996, before the second phase of television advertising took place, 54 per cent of adults still recalled the

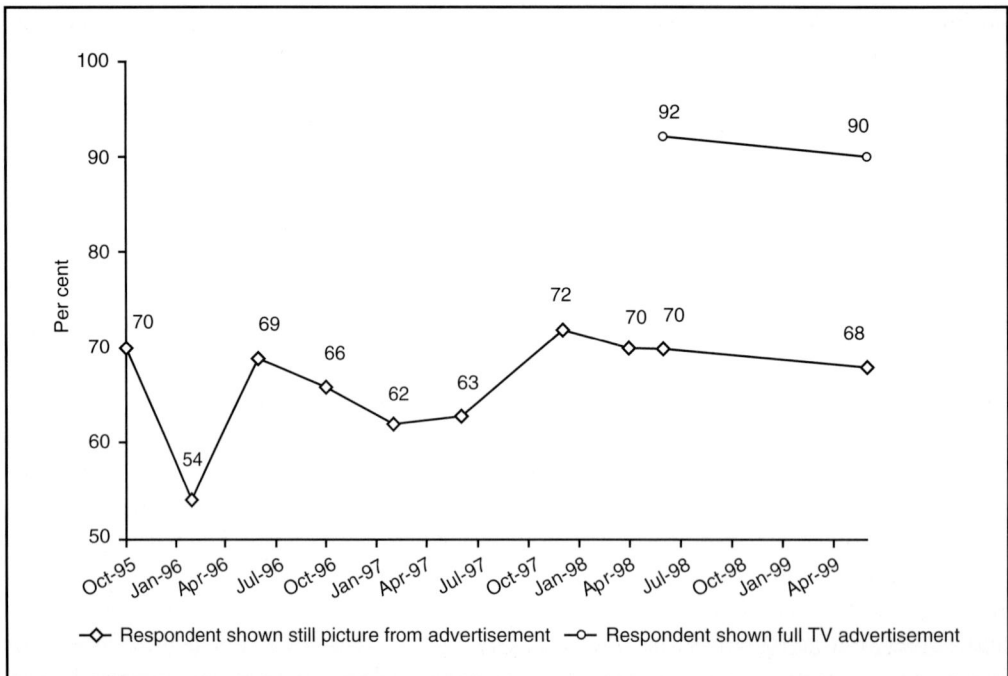

Figure 11.2. Awareness of the walking advertisement.

advertisement from its first broadcast phase. After the second phase of television advertising the percentage of adults recalling the advert had risen to 69 per cent.

Awareness levels have remained at similar levels over the past four years during periods when the advertisement has and has not been shown. The levels of awareness when respondents were shown the full advertisement during the interview (rather than the still picture) were tested in 1999, when around 90 per cent of the surveyed group said they recalled having seen the advertisement.

In October 1995, when the distribution of campaign materials was still at an early stage, only a small proportion (less than 5 per cent) of adults were aware of any other aspects of the campaign, but these awareness levels increased in the period between October 1995 and February 1996. By June 1996, 21 per cent of adults were aware of the radio advertising features which encouraged people to walk more.

Only a small proportion of respondents (5 per cent) were aware of the associated telephone helpline, *Fitline*, primarily through television advertising (75 per cent) but also through the local radio coverage of the campaign (26 per cent). Of those adults who were aware of *Fitline*, there was a small increase in the proportion who intended to use the service (from 6 to 10 per cent), although the majority (74 per cent) still had no intention of contacting *Fitline*.

11.4.2 Impact on knowledge and beliefs

The impact of the campaign on knowledge and beliefs about walking and exercise was assessed in both the *Fitline* caller surveys and the population surveys. These approaches asked respondents if they agreed or disagreed with four statements about exercise and walking. The first two of these were directly linked to the walking campaign. The four statements are

- walking a mile uses up the same energy as running a mile,
- walking is a good form of exercise,
- you need to get 30 minutes exercise a day to benefit your health, and
- exercise only does you good if it makes you sweaty and out of breath.

The data from both the population surveys and the surveys of *Fitline* callers show that the walking campaign had a positive impact on knowledge and beliefs about walking as a form of exercise (see Figure 11.3). The greatest shift was found in responses to the 'surprising fact' statement which was featured on the television advertisement that 'walking a mile uses up the same energy as running a mile'. The population survey showed a significant increase in those strongly agreeing with this statement, from only 1 per cent in June 1995 to 14 per cent in June 1996. Among *Fitline* callers, general agreement with this statement increased from 60 per cent at baseline to 68 per cent at the 10 week follow-up.

With the three other statements about walking and exercise, similar changes occurred in the strength of agreement. A significant increase was shown in those strongly agreeing with the statement 'walking is a good form of exercise', from 38 per cent in June 1995 to 57 per cent in June 1996. Similarly, significant changes were recorded in the proportion of respondents that strongly agreed with the other two statements.

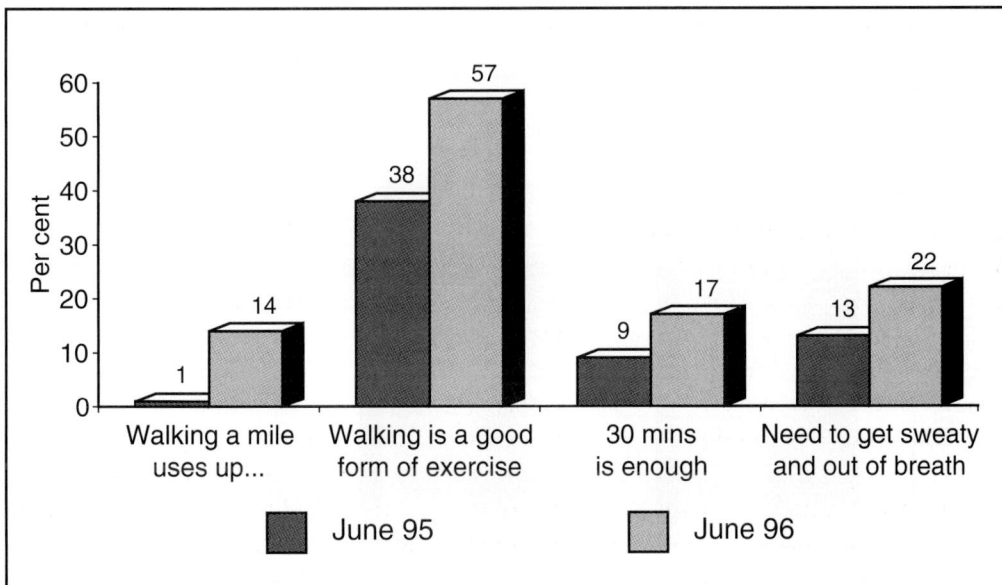

Figure 11.3. Changes in knowledge about walking in the general population.

11.4.3 Impact on exercise intentions

The impact of the campaign on exercise intentions was assessed in three ways. First, the number of active responses to the campaign in terms of calls to *Fitline* prompted by the walking campaign was counted. Second, changes in exercise intentions among *Fitline* callers at baseline and follow-up were assessed. Third, changes in exercise intentions with regard to walking among the population as a whole were measured.

According to the survey, 5 per cent of adults in Scotland actively responded to the HEBS' walking campaign and used the *Fitline* service. In total, 4,036 people called *Fitline* during the first five week period of television advertising, an average of 807 calls per week. From the baseline survey data of *Fitline* callers, it was found that only a small proportion of callers were sedentary (15 per cent) but most (66 per cent) were in the target age range for the campaign (see section 11.2) and around half (51 per cent) were not active on a regular basis.

Among those actively responding to the walking campaign and contacting *Fitline*, the campaign appears to have had a positive impact on exercise intentions. In the baseline survey, 59 per cent of callers reported that they would like to be more physically active, with the major motivational factor being the desire to feel healthier and fitter (61 per cent). This increased to 80 per cent of callers who intended to be more physically active at the 10 week follow-up survey.

Overall, there was no evidence of a significant change in exercise intention with regard to walking among the general population between June 1995 and June 1996. The proportion of adults who stated that they would like to walk more than they did at present changed from 55 per cent in June 1995 to 57 per cent in June 1997.

11.4.4 *Impact on behaviour*

The impact of the walking campaign on exercise behaviour was assessed by changes in self-reported physical activity for exercise and 'stages of change' in exercise behaviour among *Fitline* callers at baseline and follow-up, by *Fitline* callers' self-assessed change in physical

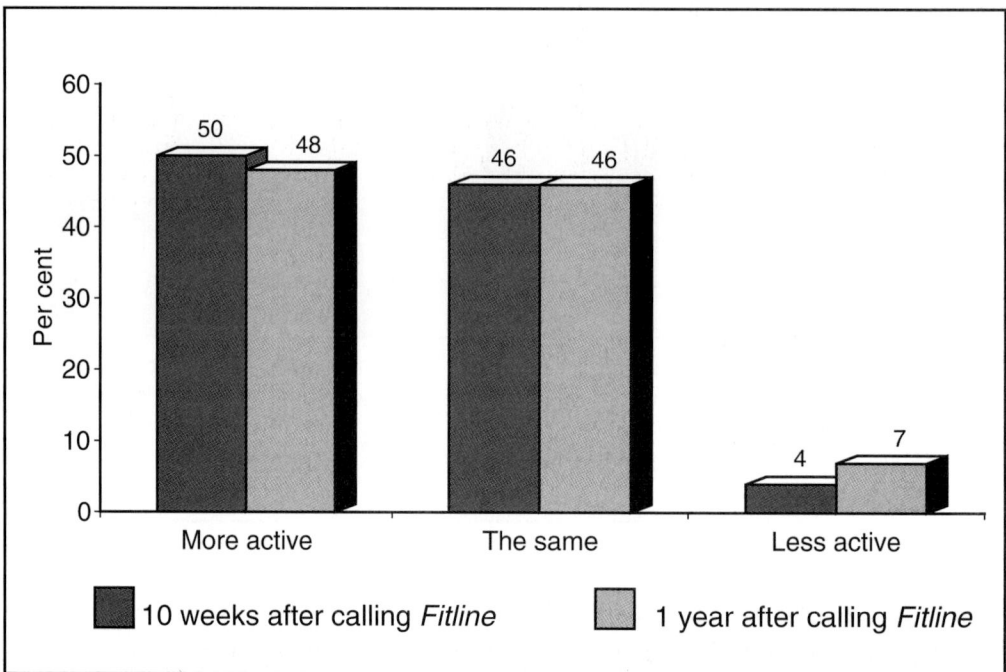

Figure 11.4. Changes in walking behaviour among callers to *Fitline*. Note that the percentages have been rounded to the nearest whole number.

activity level, and by changes in walking behaviour among the population as a whole. There was a slight increase in the self-reported physical activity levels of *Fitline* callers between baseline and follow-up surveys. The results of the 10 week follow-up survey of the sample of *Fitline* callers demonstrated that half of the respondents (50 per cent) claimed to be more physically active than they had been at the time of their initial call and one year later almost the same proportion (48 per cent) still claimed to be exercising more (see Figure 11.4).

Of those who had not been more active since contacting *Fitline,* over half (54 per cent) had not tried to increase their amount of exercise. The main difficulties cited included lack of time (48 per cent), lack of motivation (17 per cent) and illness (13 per cent).

By combining variables measuring current exercise behaviour and future exercise intention, a composite five level 'stage of change' variable was devised and used at baseline and follow-up. When assessed at an aggregate level, there was an overall shift from the 'contemplation' stage at baseline towards the 'action' stage at the 10 week follow-up and this largely was maintained in the follow up one year later (see Figure 11.5).

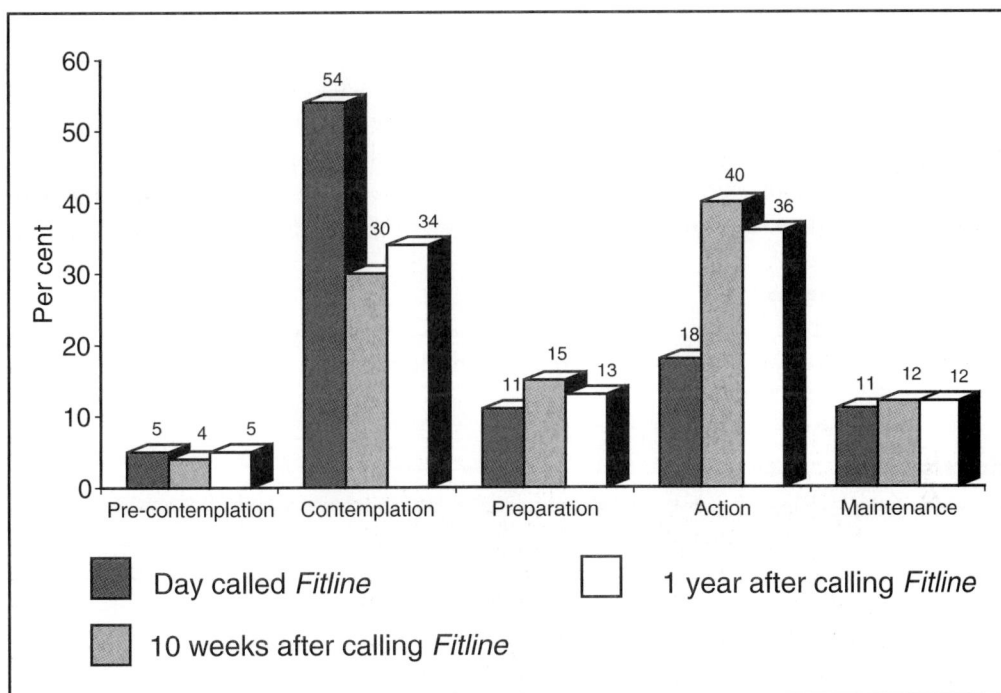

Figure 11.5. Changes in 'stage of behaviour change' among callers to *Fitline.* Note that the percentages have been rounded to the nearest whole number.

11.5 Conclusions

Initial evaluation of the HEBS' walking campaign suggested that it was successful in a number of ways, but especially with regard to the 'Gavin' television advertisement which achieved high levels of awareness. Moreover, there is evidence to suggest that the television advertisement campaign stimulated a significant change in knowledge and beliefs about the health-related benefits of walking as a form of exercise among adults in Scotland.

Among the *Fitline* callers, the campaign had a positive impact on knowledge, beliefs and exercise intentions with regard to walking. In terms of the campaign's impact on behaviour, half of the respondents reported at the 10 week and at the one year follow-up that they were more physically active than when they first contacted *Fitline*. Of this group, the majority had attempted to increase their exercise patterns in terms of frequency, duration and intensity, and 94 per cent reported increasing the levels of their walking. At the 10 week follow-up, 40 per cent of the sample were classified as in the 'action' stage of behaviour change, compared to 19 per cent at baseline.

During the first phase of television advertising over 4,000 people responded to the campaign and phoned *Fitline*. Around half of them were in the intended target group: of them 52 per cent of callers were in the target age range, and 51 per cent were irregular exercisers. However, there was a bias towards owner-occupier and employed groups, and thus the issue of how to reach the C2, D and E social classes (skilled and unskilled manual workers) and the least active people remains a responsibility for HEBS' work in influencing cultures and know-how, building capacity and developing strategic partnerships.

The results of this campaign suggest that a mass media programme for changing knowledge and awareness about new outdoor access codes may result in significant changes in the population. However, although greater awareness may be developed in the population as a whole, this does not necessarily translate, at least in the short term, into changed patterns of behaviour. It is likely that a much longer period of time is required before broader cultural shifts in beliefs at a population level are translated into large scale changes in individual behaviours.

Acknowledgements

This chapter is based on development and analysis undertaken in 1995/96 by Erica Wimbush (Research and Evaluation Manager) and Elizabeth Fraser (Data Analyst), Health Education Board for Scotland.

References

Blair, S.N., Kohl, H.W., Gordon, N.F. and Paffernbarger, R.S. (1992). How much physical activity is good for health? *Annual Review of Public Health*, **12**, 99-126.

Bouchard, C., Shepherd, R.J., Stephens, T., Sutton, J.R. and McPherson, B.D. (eds) (1993). *Exercise, Fitness and Health: A Consensus of Current Knowledge*. Human Kinetics, Champaign, Illinois.

Health Education Board for Scotland (1995). *The Promotion of Physical Activity in Scotland. A Policy Statement*. The Health Education Board for Scotland, Edinburgh.

Pate, R.R., Pratt, M. and Blair, S.N. (1995). Physical activity and public health: a recommendation from the Centre for Disease Control and Prevention and the American College of Sports Medicine, *Journal of the American Medical Association*, **273**, 402-407.

Scottish Office (1999). *Towards a Healthier Scotland – a White Paper on Health*. The Stationery Office, Edinburgh.

Wimbush, E.J. (1995). A moderate approach to promoting physical activity: evidence and implications. *Health Education Journal*, **53**, 322-336.

Plate 1

Three views of a visual sign language in use.

(a) A series of negative access notices in the Back O'Bennachie car park in October 1998.

(b) The sign for the Muir of Dinnet National Nature Reserve, with some of the newly-developed pictograms across the bottom, in February 1998.

(c) Experimental use of the new Forest Enterprise pictograms at Glencoe Lochan in September 1998. Photos: Bob Jones, Forest Enterprise.

SNH 'style' format

Please... have care
and consideration
for other forest users

Expect poorer conditions
under foot off
waymarked tracks

Be well prepared!
Mountains can be
dangerous

Please... take care,
this is a
working forest

Challenging area,
experts only

FE 'revised' format

Please... have care
and consideration
for other forest users

Please... have care
and consideration
for other forest users

Expect poorer conditions
under foot off
waymarked tracks

Be well prepared!
Mountains can be
dangerous

Please... take care,
this is a
working forest

Beware... area
suitable for expert
cyclists only

Do not.....

Caution / beware....

Suitable for....

Plate 2

The development of a series of core pictograms. Those to the left are in the original Scottish Natural Heritage format, whereas those to the right indicate the developments by Forest Enterprise.

SNH 'style' format	FE 'revised' format	'Negative' format

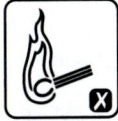

Please...
guard against fire!
It only takes one spark

Please...
guard against fire!
It only takes one spark

Please...
guard against fire!
It only takes one spark

Please...
keep dogs on a lead.
Even well trained dogs
can disturb wildlife

Sorry...no dogs.
Even well trained dogs
can disturb wildlife

Please...
keep dogs on a lead.
Even well trained dogs
can disturb wildlife

Sorry...no dogs.
Even well trained dogs
can disturb wildlife

Sorry...no dogs.
Even well trained dogs
can disturb wildlife

No vehicles please.
Authorised access only

No vehicles please.
Authorised access only

No vehicles please.
Authorised access only

Please...
ride with care
and consideration
for other forest users

Please...
ride with care
and consideration
for other forest users

Sorry...no horses.
OR
Please dismount

Sorry...no horses.
OR
Please dismount

Sorry, no camping.
Please use the nearby
site at
....

Sorry,
no overnight camping

Sorry, no camping.
Please use the nearby
site at
....

Sorry,
no overnight camping

Please mountain bike
elswhere.
There are better places

You may mountain bike
here, but please
remember you share
the forest with others

Please mountain bike
elswhere.
There are better places

You may mountain bike
here, but please
remember you share
the forest with others

Please mountain bike
elswhere.
There are better places

Key:

Do not.....	Caution.... Beware....	Suitable for....

Plate 3

The development of a series of non-core pictograms. Those to the left are in the original Scottish Natural Heritage format, those in the centre are in the revised Forest Enterprise format, whereas those to the right are in a negative, but more abrupt, format.

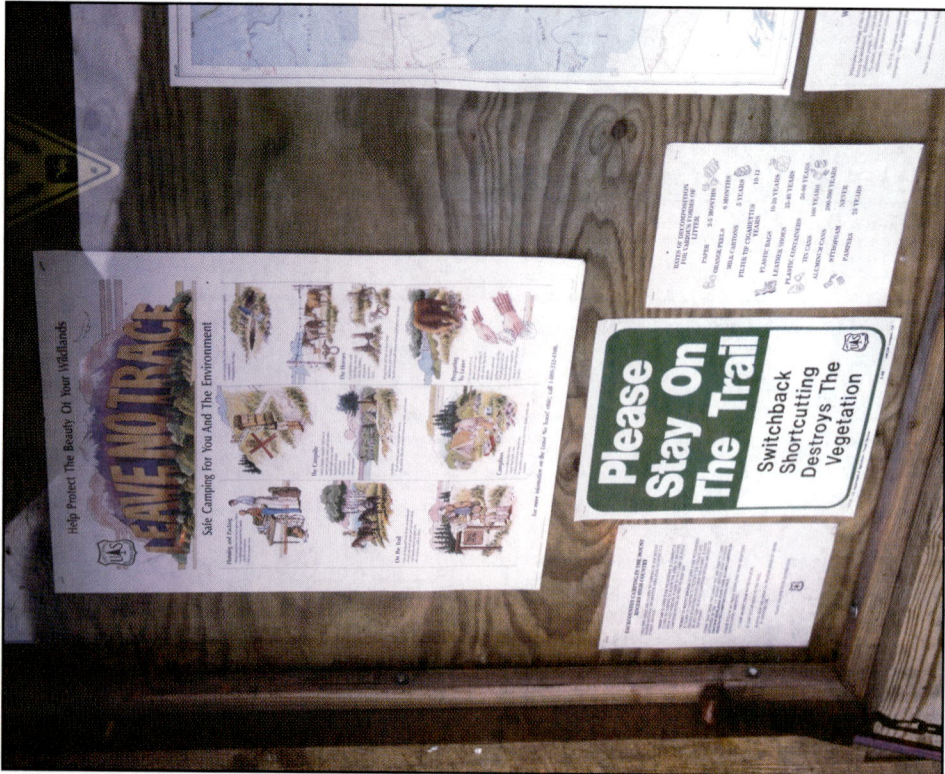

Plate 5

The extreme muddiness of this trail is predominantly due to poor location in wet, organic soils, but also to heavy use by horseback riders and hikers. The trail is located in the Bob Marshall Wilderness of Montana, managed by the US Forest Service. Photo: Jeff Marion.

Plate 4

Leave No Trace hiking and camping skills are communicated to visitors through training courses, printed literature, and trailhead posters (shown here). (Note: this was taken at a trailhead for the Mount Rogers High Country, Jefferson National Forest, Virginia). Photo: Jeff Marion.

Plate 6

The severe soil erosion on this trail in Patagonia, Chile, is due to many factors: a poor trail design that directly ascends the slope, lack of maintenance features that divert water off the tread, and poor guidance to visitors in travelling on a single tread. Photo: Jeff Marion.

Plate 7

The Leave No Trace principle "Minimize Campfire Impacts" targets campfire-related impacts by encouraging visitors to substitute cooking stoves. The people are US Forest Service staff on a 'Master of Leave No Trace' course on the George Washington National Forest in Virginia. Photo: Jeff Marion.

Plate 8

Research has found that grassy groundcover is substantially more resistant to trampling than forestland broadleaf herbs. The Leave No Trace principle "Travel and Camp on Durable Surfaces" encourages visitors to hike and travel on durable rock or gravel surfaces where possible, or on grassy vegetation such as shown here. The campsite for canoeists and fishermen is on the Delaware Water Gap National Recreation Area, National Park Service, Pennsylvania. Photo: Jeff Marion.

Plate 9

Recreation ecology is a field of study that documents the types and extent of resource impacts associated with recreation visitation to protected areas. An improved understanding of the relationships between amount of impact and use-related, environmental, and managerial factors can assist managers in selecting and applying effective strategies and actions. Photo shows Jeff Marion taking measurements on a trail in the Howler Monkey Preserve, Belize, investigating the environmental impacts of ecotourism visitation. Photo: Tracy Farrell.

Plate 10

The site is simple though well maintained.

Plate 11

Three stone and turf crescents are arranged to face each other.

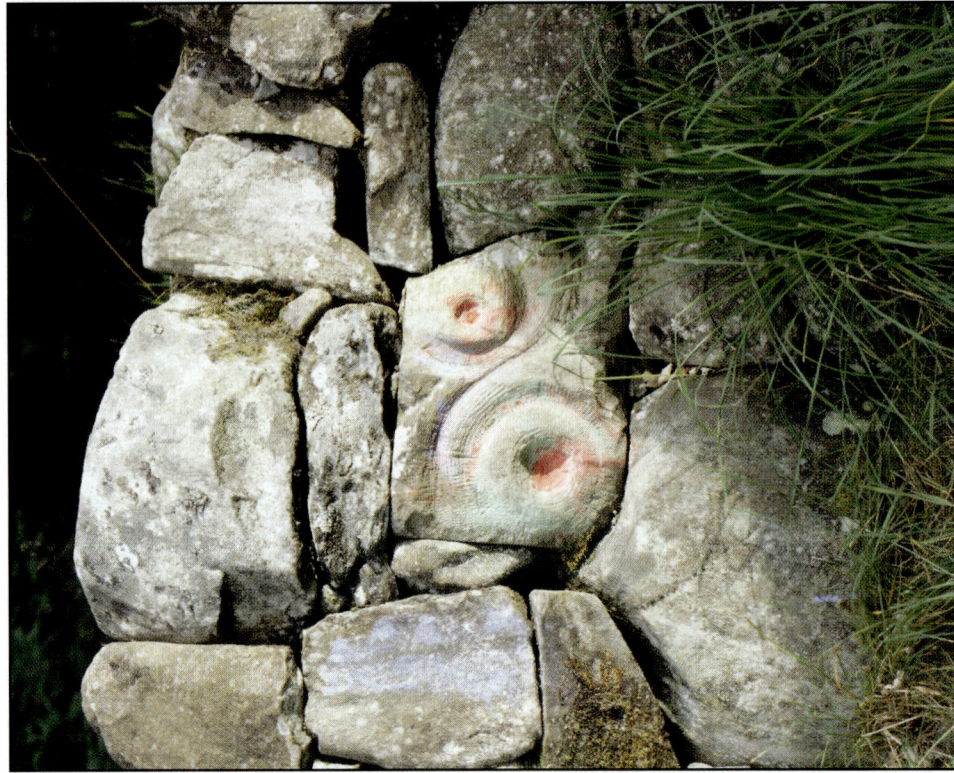

Plate 12

The back wall of each crescent is decorated. Judging by the chalk colouring, the walls are popular with visiting children.

Plate 13

Does this sign relate to the pipe in front of it, or to the site in general?

12 Rights and Responsibilities on the Road: A Case Study of Influencing Driving Behaviour

Stephen G. Stradling

Summary

1.   Exercising one's rights in a responsible manner often involves some apparent paradoxes, contradictions and tensions for the individual.

2.   Those promoting a balance between rights and responsibilities in the exercise of any activity should know their market ('Who is doing this?'), undertake a task analysis ('What are they doing?') and develop a research-based theoretical framework to understand departures from desired behaviour ('Why are they not doing what we want them to do?').

3.   There are proven techniques which are effective in changing behaviour.

4.   A common component of these techniques is that compliance with desired behaviour should be made as easy as possible.

12.1 Paradoxes, contradictions and tensions

The notion of enjoying the natural heritage in a responsible manner contains within it some paradoxes, apparent contradictions and thus, for the user, some tensions. On the one hand the message is 'Have fun!', while the strong caveat is 'But do so in an orderly manner, please!'. To enjoy nature in the raw invites you to 'Have an experience with an uplifting, spiritual dimension which elevates you out of your mundane, quotidian round' but, to enable others to also enjoy this experience, 'Be sure to tidy up after you' – what in the jargon of research design would be called 'sampling with replacement'.

This is well embodied in the estimable 'Leave No Trace' ethic (Marion and Reid, this volume) which urges an asymmetrical relationship between the individual and the natural environment - 'Leave no trace of you on the environment, but make sure the experience leaves a lasting trace on you!'.

This combination of 'Meet your needs whilst respecting the needs of others' is at the heart of establishing a balance between rights and responsibilities, and can probably be traced back at least as far as the tensions between Dionysian and Appollonian tendencies in human nature. Striking this balance is a process, not an outcome, requiring continual maintenance work.

Recent research in transport psychology (Stradling *et al.*, 1999) found a not dissimilar tension behind the wheel of a car. Table 12.1 shows from this research that drivers find the automobile attractive because it conveys autonomy as well as mobility, and does so in a variety of ways, but that many also report the experience of driving a car on today's highways as stressful, taxing and dangerous.

While almost all (95 per cent) of a sample of nearly 800 English drivers 'Agree' or 'Strongly Agree' that 'Driving a car gives me the freedom to go where I want, when I want',

Table 12.1. Proportion of car drivers agreeing and strongly agreeing with attitude statements (from Stradling *et al.*, 1999).

'Driving a car ...'	Per cent that either strongly agree or agree
Pleasures	
Gives me freedom to go where I want when I want	95
Gives me a feeling of independence	81
Gives me a spontaneous way of making a journey	77
Gives me the feeling of being in control	45
Gives me a feeling of self-confidence	40
Gives me a sense of personal safety	38
Provides the opportunity for me to practise my skills as a driver	35
Gives me the chance to express myself by driving the way I want to	18
Is a way of projecting a particular image of myself	15
Gives me a feeling of power	15
Perils	
Is stressful because of congestion on the roads	53
Is stressful because of the behaviour of other drivers	53
Is dangerous because of other drivers	42
Gives me a headache, back pain or car-sickness	14
Is uncomfortable because of the driving position	12
Gives me a feeling of guilt	6

half find it stressful because of congestion (53 per cent) or because of the behaviour of other drivers (53 per cent). We may have a right to use our cars, but we also have a responsibility to use them in a manner which minimises harm – harm to ourselves, harm to other road users and harm to the environment. Currently the United Kingdom (UK) Government is attempting to achieve more responsible car use by promoting reductions both in car use (though not reductions in car ownership!) and in speeding.

To understand how best to constrain, restrain or otherwise change a pattern of behaviour, it is necessary to understand why and how that behaviour comes to be performed in the first place. Here research can help.

12.2 Know your market

Data from the United Kingdom's National Travel Survey (DETR, 1997) shows how travel patterns are changing. For example from the mid-1970s to the mid-1990s the annual total number of trips made (journeys per person per year) increased by 14 per cent but the proportion of trips made by car increased by 47 per cent. The demographics are also changing. There are today around 17 million male driving licence holders and 13 million female driving licence holders in the UK. But while 80 per cent of eligible males are licenced, only 55 per cent of eligible females are. Whereas the figure for males has probably reached an asymptote, that for females has plenty of room for further growth. As the population of the UK, like most of the Western world, ages, there is likely to be a big increase in the number of elderly female drivers on the road. This will have consequences for congestion, for crashes and for trip types.

From recent research (Stradling *et al.*, 1999, 2000) we have identified seven different types of car uses. In likely decreasing order of the time pressure associated with each they are as follows.

- Driving as part of work - almost two-thirds of those in work (64 per cent: 75 per cent of males and 49 per cent of females) say they drive a car 'as part of their work' at least some of the time.
- Driving to and from work - 69 per cent of car drivers in employment (78 per cent of those in full-time employment) used their car to travel to and from work 'every working day'.
- Child escort duties - ferrying children around, both to school and to other places. Seventy-four per cent of rural mothers report they have others dependent on them for transport. Many motorists, when driving, are not just meeting their own transport needs.
- Life and network maintenance tasks, such as shopping, visiting friends and relations, and evenings out.
- Using the car as a load carrier.
- Driving for holidays and weekends away.
- Life enhancement activities, such as voluntary work, hobby support or just driving for pleasure.

This enumeration of activity types is relevant to both of the Department of the Environment, Transport and the Region's current goals. First, it leads us to ask which of these types of car use could be reduced, and how. Second, these are the obligations that motorists are meeting when they speed and when they have accidents.

12.3 Task analysis

So it is useful to 'know your market'. What are people doing? How many and what kinds of people are doing these things? But there is nothing more practical than a good theory, and a good theory here would address the question 'What, as a matter of fact, are people doing when they do the things you are interested in?'.

In the case of driving the first step is a task analysis. Our analysis of the driving task sees driving a car as being a skill-based, rule-governed, expressive activity. Thus learning to drive (or, better, learning to become a member of the driving community) has three components. First, mastering the technical skills of vehicle handling and positioning. Initial driver training and the practical driving test concentrate on this aspect of driving. Second, learning the rules, both formal and informal, in order to 'read the road' and anticipate hazards. The Driving Theory Test pays attention to this aspect of driving, though mostly to the formal rules of driving as contained in The Highway Code, whereas hazard perception increases with driving experience. Unfortunately, crashes may occur while this experience is being gained. Finally, resisting self-serving impulses that bring immediate gratification but might place others at risk through speeding and other unlawful activities. The choice of vehicle to drive and the manner in which you drive it make expressive statements on the theatre of the road.

12.4 Unlawful behaviour on the road

We know that speed kills. The laws of physics dictate that the higher the velocity at impact the more energy there is to be absorbed and thus the more damage will be done to hard metal, soft tissue and brittle bones. But research (Stradling *et al.*, 1999) has also shown that the kinds of drivers who commit speeding offences are over 50 per cent more likely to be involved in a crash. Of those with no speeding convictions in the previous three years, 22 per cent had been involved in an accident. But of those with one or more speeding convictions, 35 per cent had been involved in an accident, an elevation of crash-risk of 60 per cent.

Stradling *et al.* (1999) also examined differences between speeders and others on a range of demographic and vehicle variables. Drivers were asked at what speed they normally drove on four types of roads: motorways, other main roads, suburban roads, and rural roads. The differences in speeding behaviour are summarised in Table 12.2.

Table 12.2. Demographic, vehicle and vehicle use characteristics of car drivers reporting higher normal speeds (from Stradling *et al.*, 1999).

Driver and car characteristics	Group reporting higher speeds
Age band	17-24 year olds fastest; then 25-58; 58 years plus slowest
Sex	Males faster than females
Social class	A/B fastest; then C1 C2; then D/E and retired slowest
Household income	£30 k pa fastest; then £20-30 k pa; below £20 k pa slowest
Domicile	Group living out-of-town faster
Experience	Group with 1-3 years' driving experience faster
Engine size	Drivers of cars with engines sizes of 1.6 l and above faster
Age of car	Drivers of cars 1-7 years old faster
Annual mileage	Groups driving above 10 k miles pa fastest; then 5-10 k; group below 5 k slowest
Company car	Company car drivers faster
Drive as work	Driving as part of work faster

Those driving at higher speeds are more likely to be young, more likely to be male, from higher social classes and with higher household incomes. They also tend to live out of town, to be inexperienced drivers, to drive larger cars (60 per cent of those who had been penalised for speeding drove cars of 1.8 l engine size or above; such cars comprise 29 per cent of the UK car fleet), to drive newer cars, to drive a high annual mileage, to drive a company car and to drive as part of their work.

This pattern of results resolves into two main groups – young, inexperienced drivers and those who drive large cars for large distances as part of their work. Amongst the young drivers, young females (17-20) report normal speeds as fast as young males, but males then report faster normal speeds than age-equivalent females up until age group 50-59. Amongst those who drive as part of their work, males report higher speeds than females, and higher speeds than males in work who do not drive as part of their work.

12.5 Theory

So that is the phenomenon. It explains who is doing what in the domain of unlawful behaviour on the roads. Theory then plays a part here by locating speeding as part of a larger group of driving behaviours. Earlier research studies, summarised in Stradling and Meadows (2000a, 2000b), had shown aberrant driving behaviours resolving into three groups: violations, errors and lapses. Violations include speeding (easily the most common driving violation), close following, overtaking on the inside, showing hostility to other road users, racing from the lights, running through red lights, and drink-driving (thankfully the least common driving violation these days). Errors include failures of observation (not noticing a cyclist coming up on your nearside) and failures of judgement (misjudging an overtaking gap). Lapses include embarrassing but recoverable behaviours such as taking the wrong lane at a roundabout, or switching on the lights instead of the wipers.

From a number of studies, summarised in Stradling and Meadows (2000a, 2000b), a profile of high violating drivers was developed, because it is drivers who score high on violations, not those who score high on errors or lapses, who are more likely to have been involved in a crash in the past and more likely to be involved in a crash in the future. The profile is shown in Table 12.3.

Table 12.3. Characteristics of drivers who score high on driving violations (from Stradling and Meadows, 2000).

more likely to be young, to be male, and to be A/B, C1 social class

more likely to be high mileage drivers, and to drive as part of their work

more likely to consider themselves (even) better drivers than do others

more likely to report higher normal and preferred speeds on different road types

more likely to over-estimate the number of other drivers who violate

more likely to rate the potential adverse consequences of their actions (e.g. having an accident, being stopped by the police) as less likely, and as less bad

more likely to believe that their significant others are less likely to disapprove

more likely to think that other drivers will be less upset by the bad behaviour

more likely to experience immediate positive affect ('feel good') while violating

less likely to anticipate feeling regret after violating

more likely to think that refraining from their undesirable behaviours would be more difficult, and thus that they are less in control of their behaviour

more likely to show greater outward irritability (anger directed towards others)

12.6 Explaining violations

Why do drivers violate? One approach to an answer is to examine the conditions under which violations take place. Typically, there is a high likelihood of someone violating when it is inconvenient to comply, when there is no pressure to comply, when it is easy to violate, when there is little likelihood of detection, and when violating does not attract immediate adverse consequences.

As Battmann and Klumb (1993) noted, rules attempt to limit the behavioural space of the individual and "... *rules which do not support individuals' attempts to optimize their actions are likely to be violated. Seen from this perspective, rule violations are the result of a conflict between the individuals' optimization attempts and organizational prescriptions which try to keep these attempts within 'permissible' limits*" (p. 39).

Conversely there is typically a low likelihood of someone violating when it is socially unacceptable to violate, when there is no pressure to violate, when there is a high likelihood of detection, and when negative outcomes are likely.

12.7 Changing behaviour

How can drivers be prevented or discouraged from violating? To change a behaviour one can either change the person or change the conditions under which they are operating. Changing the person is not quite as draconian as it sounds. It typically involves changing their interpretation of the situation and their evaluation of the consequences that may ensue. Sometimes this can be done by the provision of information, if this contributes to changing the beliefs, attitudes or values informing the behaviour. On the road, changing the operating conditions to constrain speeding behaviour can involve changes to road engineering, car engineering, or enforcement. Such constraint can be expensive and entails continual maintenance work. Encouraging restraint, however, passes the responsibility from the provider to the user and although it, too, requires maintenance work, it is usually 'greener' – providing durable, self-sustaining change with low consumption of natural resource or physical energy.

So compliance should be made as easy as possible. If the aim is to get drivers to stick to the speed limit it should be made as easy as possible for them to discern 'How fast am I going?' and 'What's the speed limit here?'. Most driving takes place in populated areas where the speed limit is 30 mph. Few car speedometers show '30' on the dial. Many transitions into a 30 mph speed limit are signalled by one small, old, grubby, overhung, easily missed sign. While the speed and the limit are not clear, the message to the motorist, unfortunately, is all too clear: 'close observance of the 30 mph speed limit is not that important, or they would make more effort to provide me with the information I need for compliance'.

Stradling *et al.* (1999, 2000) reported that many drivers would like to reduce their car use, but feel themselves unlikely and unable to do so. Indeed one in three would like to reduce their car use, one in three would like to increase their use of public transport, and one in five would like to do both. But only three per cent feel they are likely to do both. They felt that there was no alternative. Their transport choices are constrained by current land-use patterns. "*Nice house on an estate, but the nearest shop is four miles away, the school is three-quarters of a mile away, the nearest pub is certainly a car drive*" (Mitchell and Lawson, 1998, p. 11).

Psychology has identified a number of effective behavioural change techniques, which have been shown to produce sustainable and enduring change. Therapy for emotional distress – 'the talking cure' - for example, is extremely effective when the following conditions apply. Current behaviour is causing problems in living for an individual and their significant others. The client accepts ownership of the problem and shows 'readiness for change'. The client receives regular and graded help from a qualified and experienced counsellor with whom he or she can form a therapeutic alliance involving mutual respect and regard in a non-threatening setting. Jointly the therapist and client can agree a series of small, manageable steps to bridge the gap between the start state and the desired end state. Akin to a sports coach or driving instructor the counsellor can monitor progress and give fast feedback to modify aspirations and techniques. Once change is achieved, mechanisms to assist maintenance and prevent relapse can be put in place.

Research on parenting suggests the following steps are efficacious. First, do not just say 'Stop it!' or smack, say 'Don't do that, because ... <set of plausible and compelling reasons involving upset and lack of equity>'. Second, suggest alternative behaviours, saying 'Why not do this instead, because ... <set of achievable, laudable and pleasant consequences for self and others ensue>'. Third, give procedural assistance, pointing out 'Here's how you can do <wished alternative>'. Finally, indicate that a competent authority will expend resource, time and effort in establishment and maintenance of new behaviour '<parent, teacher, probation officer, government, etc.> will help you', signalling that successful adoption of new behaviour is actually of concern to those in a position to facilitate its adoption.

Both, of course, involve fairly intense, face-to-face interactions. Those unable to engage so directly with their 'clientele', whose behaviour they wish to influence, may have to adopt 'one-to-many' rather than 'one-to-one' approaches, such as signage and publicity. They can estimate the likely effectiveness of their procedures by gauging to what extent, and in which particulars, they are able to approximate the efficient procedures above.

12.8 Making compliance easy

Wardman *et al.* (2001) tried out a new approach to understanding travel behaviour in order to influence it. They saw individuals as possessing a personal resource budget on which they draw when making a journey. This personal resource budget includes not only the familiar variables of time and money which have generally figured in attempts to model travel choice, but also the amounts of physical, cognitive and affective effort that must be expended in undertaking a journey. Most students of travel behaviour concur with the general opinion of motorists that using the car is just so much more convenient. But what, exactly, does this convenience consist of? Wardman *et al.* (2001) turned the question round and asked, instead, what makes a journey inconvenient?

They conjectured that a journey is inconvenient if it involves unanticipated and unwelcome expenditure of physical, cognitive or affective effort, as illustrated below. Physical effort includes things like walking (to a bus stop, at an interchange) and coping with burdens (luggage up the stairs, buggy on the escalator, shopping on the bus). Cognitive effort includes things like planning a journey (locating information or interpreting maps and timetables), monitoring progress (route compliance, hazard checking) and 'error correction' when things go wrong (a turning or connection missed, a route thus re-planned). Affective effort is primarily derived from 'worry'. New, or potential, mode users suffer 'procedural uncertainty' ('how do I do this' and 'if I do it wrong will I look stupid?') and regular users suffer frequent affective load (will I get there on time today, will it be safe, or is this money well spent?).

Wardman *et al.* (2001) suggested it is these psychological components of the travel mode decision that contribute to keeping people in their cars – and the research results bear this out. Those commuting to work by car rated their journey as involving low levels of physical effort, and medium levels of mental and emotional effort. And while they saw their alternative journey to work by bus as requiring less cognitive effort, they saw it as demanding more physical effort and much more affective effort. So they continue to commute by car, despite its demands and uncertainties.

Wardman *et al.* (2001) concluded that providers of alternatives to the car will have to make their services more psychologically attractive to potential users. For example, if the bus service is reliable you can put your trust in it. And trust is a core psychological component of any successful relationship.

12.9 Conclusion

In general, those who wish other people to behave in accordance with rules, regulations or codes of conduct should make compliance as easy as possible. This may be done in two ways. If retribution is sure and swift then high levels of compliance will be achieved. This, however, requires continual enforcement effort, and thus high maintenance costs, and the compliance may be cowed and surly. It is better is to provide the facilities that facilitate easy compliance.

The first requirement of the 'Leave No Trace' ethic (Marion and Reid, this volume) is to 'Plan Ahead and Prepare' and it gives as an example "Use a map or compass to eliminate the use of marking paint, rock cairns or flagging". This may be achieved by body-searching all arrivals and forcibly excluding from access all those without a map or compass. Alternatively, the same end may be served by providing a map and compass shop at entry with sale or loan-and-return facilities for those who have forgotten, plus readily available instruction on how to use maps and compasses for those lacking competence or confidence. Durable change and pleasurable, responsible use of the natural heritage is more likely to result from the second than from the first alternative.

Whilst somewhat implausible, this example makes a general point. In summary, there are clearly some analogies between natural heritage recreational activities and behaviour on the roads. Both provide opportunities while at the same time bringing obligations. Both require a delicate balance between rights of access and responsible action. The attempt to constrain behaviour on the roads, whether level of car use or incidence of speeding and other violations of the law, has been informed by research looking at who is exhibiting undesired behaviours, the conditions under which undesirable behaviours are performed, and the personal benefits that undesirable behaviours bring the perpetrators. Behavioural change techniques work by offering manageable and attractive alternative behaviours, help in achieving them, and mechanisms that support the new, more desirable, behaviours. Helping people to change is a more sustainable alternative than forcing people to change.

References

Battmann, W. and Klumb, P. (1993). Behavioural economics and compliance with safety regulations. *Safety Science*, **16**, 35-46.

Department of the Environment, Transport and the Regions (DETR) (1997). *National Travel Surveys.* The Stationery Office, London.

Mitchell, C.G.B. and Lawson, S. (1998). *The Great British Motorist 1998.* Automobile Association, Basingstoke.

Stradling, S.G. and Meadows, M.L. (2000a). Are women better drivers than men? Tools for measuring driver behaviour. In *The Applied Psychologist, 2nd Edition*, ed. by J. Hartley and A. Branthwaite. Open University Press, Buckingham. pp. 126-145.

Stradling, S.G. and Meadows, M.L. (2000b). Highway code and aggressive violations in UK drivers. Global Web Conference on Aggressive Driving Issues, at www.drivers.com.

Stradling, S.G., Meadows, M.L. and Beatty, S. (1999). *Factors Affecting Car Use Choices.* Transport Research Institute, Napier University, Edinburgh.

Stradling, S.G., Meadows, M.L. and Beatty, S. (2000). Helping drivers out of their cars: integrating transport policy and social psychology. *Transport Policy,* **7**, 207-215.

Wardman, M., Hine, J. and Stradling, S.G. (2001). *Interchange and Travel Choice.* Central Research Unit, Scottish Executive, Edinburgh.

13 PUTTING OUT FIRES WITH IMAGINATION: A CASE STUDY USING INTERPRETATION TO ENCOURAGE DESIRED BEHAVIOUR

James Carter

Summary

1.   Many of the most challenging behavioural issues facing countryside managers involve situations where recreationists are acting, not out of malice, but from ignorance, or are doing something they see as integral to their activity.

2.   Such behaviours may be determined largely by social norms and unconscious attitudes, rather than by rational decision patterns. Communication that aims simply to inform recreationists about desired behaviour may not be effective in these situations.

3.   Interpretation, as a specialised form of communication, offers a way to encourage particular behaviours through building links between recreationists' expectations and values, the desired behaviour, and the characteristics of a site. It must also be linked to careful site design and an integrated management regime.

13.1 Introduction

Perhaps the thorniest behavioural challenge to a countryside manager is when people do something the manager would rather they did not, but which they do without any malicious intent; indeed they may even see their actions as an integral part of their recreation. This chapter is an attempt to deal with this situation through interpretation.

What defines interpretation as a specialist type of communication? Most definitions of interpretation paraphrase or amplify Tilden's (1977) statement that it is

"an educational activity which aims to reveal meanings and relationships through the use of original objects, by firsthand experience, and by illustrative media, rather than simply to communicate factual information" (p. 8).

Whatever gloss is put on this, all definitions share a common element: interpretation is about encouraging visitors to appreciate and value the places they visit (Carter, 1997; Ham, 1992). This has usually entailed offering information that will help visitors to understand a place from the perspective of the specialists who have studied it. At a nature reserve this might involve explaining how a particular ecosystem works, or at an historic site telling the story of the events that happened there. Giving visitors facts about the place is an important part of interpretation, but its real essence lies elsewhere, as acknowledged by Tilden (1977) –

"Information, as such, is not Interpretation.   Interpretation is revelation based on information" (p. 9).

In other words, interpretation should help visitors to engage with the concepts that lie behind the facts, or with a wider story that is illustrated by the facts. I would go further than this. I believe interpretation is essentially about stimulating visitors' imaginations or emotions so that they engage positively with the places that they visit. This quality of imaginative engagement and stimulus underpins the role of arts work in interpretation, the focus of much recent interest, where the goal may not be to explain any particular facts at all but to allude to ideas and provoke new thoughts and associations (Carter and Masters, 1998; Carter, 1999).

Interpretation is often cited as a valuable management tool; indeed some authors suggest that interpretation needs to justify itself by the contribution it can make to management goals and ultimately to a financial bottom line (Sharpe and Gensler, 1978; Veverka, 1994). I cannot go along with this completely: I think that telling stories to each other about the places we think precious, and why we think them so, has a value far deeper than anything that can be described by economics or defined in management practicalities. I share the view first articulated by F. Tilden that interpretation has a spiritual role to play in connecting us with our environment, our heritage, and ultimately with each other (Tilden, 1977; Strang, 1999). Interpretation is not just about educating visitors so that they know more about a place, nor is it about persuading them to embrace the managerial goals of the organisation responsible for it. It is an essential part of how, as a species, we explore our surroundings and exchange experiences.

But interpretation does clearly have a role to play in the practicalities of site and visitor management. In the context of managing the natural environment this has usually involved explaining the reasons for regulations, or encouraging visitors' awareness of the environmental characteristics of a site so they understand better how to behave there without damaging it (Ham, 1992; Medio *et al.*, 1997; Sharpe and Gensler, 1978). The devices used to achieve these worthy goals have not always been entirely even-handed: as all parents know, attempts to influence behaviour must occasionally involve subterfuge. Interpretation is no exception. Examples of cunning in its use include providing a self-guided trail that uses a relatively robust area in the hope that visitors will be diverted away from more fragile parts of a site, or, more ingeniously, organising well-publicised guided walks that will attract crowds of people at times and places previously favoured by poachers (Sharpe and Gensler, 1978).

The difficulty is that all these initiatives rely on people being interested enough to attend to the interpretation fairly closely, and able to understand the information provided. There is good evidence that where this does happen, information can have an effect on people's attitudes, intentions and behaviour (Ajzen, 1992; Roggenbuck, 1992). But in managing informal recreation we cannot always rely on such levels of attention. Other research shows that audiences who are not motivated to attend to what is presented to them are not greatly influenced by fascinating facts and good arguments. Instead they are swayed more by things such as the attractiveness or perceived credibility of the message's source, or by social conditioning of which they may have no conscious awareness. Petty *et al.* (1992) described communication using these devices as using a 'peripheral' route to persuasion, in contrast to the 'central' route of reasoned argument supported by facts. It is in these circumstances of casual attention that both the imaginative appeal of interpretation, and a method of delivering a message that can suggest ideas without the need to digest much information, become important.

13.2 'Bad' behaviour: a case study

I want now to apply these ideas to an example of unwanted visitor behaviour that I know intimately, since I was one of the visitors involved. The site concerned is a campground in the Highlands of Scotland run by Forest Enterprise, the part of the state-run Forestry Commission that manages the nation's forest holdings. The campground is small and informal with simple facilities: a single building housing toilets and wash basins, with water stand pipes and rubbish disposal bins at several places around the site. There is no permanent member of staff on site: the warden visits in the evening or the morning to collect campers' fees. It offers a perfect getaway for people who want a relatively 'remote' camping spot (Plate 10).

I visited the site in May 2000 with a group of friends, all of whom brought children ranging in age from 2 to 14. Demographically I would estimate that we all fell into social class B, with a reasonably comfortable level of family income. I reckon that we would have achieved a high score for environmental awareness in any objective test: many of the group are members of conservation organisations, work on environmental schemes or cultivate allotments. Several had been boy scouts or girl guides, if that can be taken as an indicator of environmental awareness. And we had deliberately chosen a remote camp site with basic facilities. In other words, we were a typical group of middle class nature lovers looking for a 'back-to-basics' experience.

In the furthest corner of the campground we found an intriguing group of three crescent shaped structures made from stone and turf (Plate 11). The back wall of each was decorated with designs suggesting cup and ring marked carvings, a feature of many prehistoric sites in Scotland, or with hand silhouettes reminiscent of cave paintings (Plate 12). The crescents were arranged so that they faced inwards towards a central point, reinforcing the sense of a ritualistic space suggested by the carved decorations. In the centre of one of the crescents was a small circle of blackened earth where a fire had recently burned. We liked this corner of the site and set up camp there. But we were faced with a puzzle: what were the crescents for? There was no notice to explain them, and although the children loved running up and down them they clearly had some purpose other than as climbing ramps.

In circumstances like these, a powerful and often overlooked channel or medium of communication is the physical character of the site itself. We looked at the crescents and saw that their different orientations would provide shelter from the wind whatever its direction. The arrangement of the crescents suggested a communal gathering place; there were ashes in one of them. Our conclusion was unanimous: these were cleverly designed shelters in which the camp site's weekend nomads could gather around a camp fire.

Another overlooked aspect of communication is that people will insist, often very inconveniently, on making their own meanings from the messages offered to them, and these meanings can sometimes be entirely different to those intended. Near our chosen camp site was a water stand pipe and rubbish bin, and next to this was another enigmatic structure, this time with a sign behind it (Plate 13). It was a low pipe about 750 mm across, set into the ground with its open end uppermost and a metal grille laid across it. The sign read 'No Fires'. The pipe was fairly clearly a disposal point for waste water. We took the sign as a warning to those unused to camping that the whole structure was not a barbecue: an interpretation which would have been quite possible since the grille looked like a good place to spread charcoal.

Our reaction to this sign may seem naïve, and you can probably guess the end of this story! But there is an important point here: physical objects, and their relationship, communicate strong messages. The position of the 'No Fires' sign suggests that it relates to the water drain, even although the structure of the drain could be taken to be a barbecue. We had already decided that fires were allowed, indeed encouraged, in the crescents, and there was no list of rules posted anywhere on the campground that prohibited fires across the site as a whole. So we made our interpretation of the sign fit our perceptions of the situation, built a camp fire and had a very enjoyable evening singing songs around it.

The next evening, just as we were stoking another fire, the warden came by and gently told us that the crescents were intended as shelters to protect small tents from the wind. No fires were allowed on the site. We apologised profusely, and felt rather embarrassed.

13.3 'Bad' behaviour: a possible response

Our experience presents an interesting communication and management challenge. How could the managers of this site encourage people to see the crescents as tent shelters, a facility I have never seen on any other camp site, rather than fire pits? How could a set of desired behavioural conventions for the site be presented so that every visitor sees them? And how could this be done so that the essential character of the place as somewhere to experience a simple and relatively unregulated form of camping is preserved?

Campers cannot be expected to attend closely to conventional interpretation panels: they have come to relax, not to learn or to study lists of rules. Instead, any communication designed to influence their behaviour must use the 'peripheral' route to persuasion (Petty *et al.*, 1992). This involves appeals to conditioned responses, governed by social norms and intuition, rather than reasoned argument. It must also use easily accessible and attractive channels to get its message across.

I suggest that interpretation can offer a solution here by creating an imaginative association between the crescents and their intended use. There could be many possible ways to this: the device, or interpretive concept, I want to explore is to build on the similarity between camping and a nomadic lifestyle. In doing this I am making two assumptions about the target audience. First, that people who spend a holiday or a weekend in a tent enjoy the simple, temporary nature of this accommodation. Second, that campers have a higher than average level of interest in the environment, and see camping as a chance to live rather closer to nature than they do in their daily lives. I should emphasise that these assumptions about campers' attitudes are untested and based largely on the characteristics of our own group. They would need to be refined in any future application of the proposals that follow, and the proposals adapted accordingly (Bright, 1997; Bright *et al.*, 1993; Fishbein and Manfredo, 1992).

The imaginative link I want to make is to compare modern camping with the lifestyle of prehistoric people. In many ways camping is the closest we get in western civilisation to the lives of prehistoric people before there were established settlements. Given the decorations on the crescents, and their associations with prehistoric cultures, interpretation could suggest to campers that they have an affinity with the groups of hunter gatherers who may have passed through the area a few thousand years ago, and who would have needed a sheltered place for their temporary camps. This idea can then be associated with the crescents and their intended use.

This emotional link between outdoor recreation and a simpler, untrammelled way of life is not new. I have drawn it partly from a promotional poster for the French National Parks, which shows a view of a mountain landscape seen through the window of a mountain hut, with the caption 'La vraie liberté c'est le vagabondage' (true freedom lies in travelling). A similar concept lies behind many advertising campaigns for outdoor clothing or equipment, a powerful influence on the attitudes of many recreationists. For example, a recent campaign for waterproof clothing showed an eagle wearing a pinstripe suit, with mountains in the background. The emotional message is that the waterproofs facilitate an escape from city life and allow you to 'live with the eagles' while you wear them. Interpretation needs to borrow some of this promotional language and adapt it to serve management goals.

There remains the question of what medium would be appropriate to deliver this idea. One option would be to site a panel next to the crescents. But this is unattractive - much of the site's charm lies in its informality, and a panel would be an intrusion into this. A better option would be for all campers to be given a publication when the warden first meets them to collect their fees. It would need to be attractive enough for people to read it, if only briefly, rather than put it in their pocket as an irrelevant piece of official 'guff'. This could be achieved by printing it on stiff card rather than paper, and designing it so that it carried an attractive image of the crescents on one side, with the reverse carrying a short piece of text designed to communicate the intended idea. This text might read something like

'Thousands of years ago, groups of hunters wandered these hills, staying a few days before moving on. They may have built walls to protect them from the wind, like the tent shelters you'll find at the far end of the site. Enjoy your stay here, sharing the lifestyle of those early hunters and the rhythm of the seasons'.

This could be accompanied by a simple line drawing of a tent pitched within one of the crescents as a visual reinforcement of the message. As an added inducement to read the text, the whole card could be designed so that it could be used as a postcard.

In order to communicate the general regulations that apply at the site, the publication could be extended to consist of two cards, with perforations at the join so the 'postcard' can be easily detached. One side of the second card would carry a welcome to the site, together with a short statement asking people to observe rules such as the prohibition against fires. It would be important to give the reason for these rules: research suggests that people are more likely to respond positively to a regulation if they know the reason for it and that reason seems credible (Gramman *et al.*, 1995; Johnson and Vande Kamp, 1996). The other side of the second card could be used to promote the walks available from the site. These are currently listed on a panel on the toilet block, but without any information about the character of each route. This section of the card could also act as a receipt for camping fees.

13.4 Discussion

This example of a possible response to recreational behaviour illustrates how communication needs to be targeted at a precise set of behavioural characteristics (Fishbein and Manfredo, 1992). The messages presented, and the imaginative context within which they are set, are designed to fit the particular circumstances of the site and a set of behaviours. Different circumstances would need different solutions.

Whatever the circumstances, management interventions and policies need to be developed alongside communication initiatives. In this example, it would be important to ensure that campers received the postcards early on in their stay, and certainly before their first night. This might mean that the wardens had to adjust the hours at which they visit the site. It might be possible to distribute the postcard from a self-service dispenser, but this would need to be placed at the entrance to the site where campers would be more likely to pick it up as they arrived. It would also be necessary to clear away evidence of any fires that were lit, since evidence of previous behaviour is taken as a strong indication of what is acceptable (Johnson and Vande Kamp, 1996).

Of course, a camp fire would have been an integral part of the prehistoric nomads' lives, and it could be argued that it should also be possible for it to be an integral part of a modern camping trip. In other countries cooking food on an open fire is regarded as a standard part a visit to the countryside: in some Finnish National Parks, for example, communal fire pits and a supply of wood are provided for walkers (M.B. Usher, pers. comm.). A similar approach is taken to providing barbecue sites in Australia. The question of whether forbidding all fires is a desirable or even sustainable policy opens a separate, controversial area of countryside recreation management that is rather outside the scope of this chapter, but a more realistic approach at camp sites like this might be to provide set areas where fires are allowed, with a supply of suitable wood.

The focus of this case study, however, is on how to establish the idea that the crescents are intended as tent shelters, in a way that both adds to visitors' appreciation of the area's history and aims to build on a set of positive emotional associations. Communication lies at the heart of the approach described here, as it does in so many debates on the future needs of countryside recreation management. But communication needs to be seen as a wide ranging discipline, embracing the 'messages' conveyed by the physical characteristics of the site, as well as those carried by words and images. Any approach to influencing behaviour must also develop appropriate managerial policies and practices together with communication initiatives as an integrated whole.

The nature of communication also needs careful planning and a dash of creativity. It is here that the real challenge lies for future work, and here too that many of the discussions presented in this book find common ground. Many projects now aim to communicate a desired set of behaviours to recreationists (see, for example, Allison, this volume; Marion and Reid, this volume). Increasingly they use messages that are designed to be as clear and constructive as possible, in contrast to the stark prohibitions that might have been common 50 years ago (see Jones, this volume). They also use more sophisticated delivery mechanisms, designed to reach a clearly defined target audience in situations where the message presented will be relevant (see, for example, the 'Leave No Trace' programme, described by Marion and Reid, this volume).

But simply presenting visitors to the countryside with information is not enough. As discussed elsewhere (Carter, this volume, chapter 9), social norms are a powerful influence on personal attitudes, and are increasingly recognised as vital factors in the pattern of recreational behaviour in the countryside (Butterfield and Long, this volume; Fenn, this volume). Communication that has an emotional or imaginative appeal has the best chance of influencing these norms and through them, perhaps, behaviour. This has long been recognised in commercial advertising, which tries to make links between a product or service and a desirable set of values or associations. The idea has also been adopted to some extent by modern health awareness campaigns (Allison, this volume) and in safe driving campaigns (Stradling, this volume).

As new legislation brings new rights to recreationists in Scotland's countryside, a new or expanded set of responsibilities needs to be fostered to accompany them. I suggest that this can best be done through putting forward new ways for people to engage mentally and imaginatively with their environment, so that the social norms associated with the countryside can keep pace with its changing economic base and with the range of recreational activity that now takes place there. Interpretation offers the key to this. At its best it provides a link between visitors' interests and motivations and the essential characteristics of a place in a way that encourages visitors to see the countryside as a place for inspiration and fascination. It engenders a feeling that this is a place to respect.

References

Ajzen, I. (1992). Persuasive communication theory in social psychology: a historical perspective. In Influencing Human Behavior, ed. by M. Manfredo. Sagamore, Champaign, Illinois. pp. 1-27.

Bright, A.D. (1997). Attitude strength and support of recreation management strategies. Journal of Leisure Research, 29, 363-379.

Bright, A.D., Manfredo, M.J., Fishbein, M. and Bath, A. (1993). Application of the theory of reasoned action to the National Park Service's controlled burn policy. Journal of Leisure Research, **25**, 263-280.

Carter, J. (1997). A Sense of Place – an Interpretive Planning Handbook. Tourism and Environment Initiative, Inverness.

Carter, J. (1999). Where does this adventure go to? Interpretation Journal, **3** (3), 14-15.

Carter, J. and Masters, D. (1998). Arts and the natural heritage. Scottish Natural Heritage Review No. 109.

Fishbein, M. and Manfredo, M.J. (1992). A theory of behavior change. In Influencing Human Behavior, ed. by M. Manfredo. Sagamore, Champaign, Illinois. pp. 28-50.

Gramman, J.H., Bonifield, R.L. and Kim, Y. (1995). Effect of personality and situational factors on intentions to obey rules in outdoor recreation areas. Journal of Leisure Research, **27**, 326-343.

Ham, S.H. (1992). Environmental Interpretation: a Practical Guide for People with Big Ideas and Small Budgets. North American Press, Golden, Colorado.

Johnson, D.R. and Vande Kamp, M.E. (1996). Extent and control of resource damage due to non-compliant visitor behavior: a case study from the US National Parks. Natural Areas Journal, **16**, 134-141.

Medio, D., Ormond, R.F.G. and Mearson, M. (1997). Effects of briefings on rates of damage to corals by SCUBA divers. Biological Conservation, **79**, 91-95.

Petty, R.E., McMichael, S. and Brannon, L. (1992). The elaboration likelihood model of persuasion: applications in recreation and tourism. In Influencing Human Behavior, ed. by M. Manfredo. Sagamore, Champaign, Illinois. pp. 77-101.

Roggenbuck, J.W. (1992). Use of persuasion to reduce resource impacts and visitor conflicts. In Influencing Human Behavior, ed. by M. Manfredo. Sagamore, Champaign, Illinois. pp. 149-208.

Sharpe, G.W. and Gensler, D.L. (1978). Interpretation as a management tool. Journal of Interpretation, **3**, 3-9.

Strang, C.A. (1999). Interpretive Undercurrents. National Association for Interpretation, Fort Collins, Colorado.

Tilden, F. (1977). Interpreting our Heritage, third edition. University of North Carolina Press, Chapel Hill, North Carolina.

Veverka, J. (1994). Interpretive Master Planning. Falcon Press Publishing, Helena, Montana.

14 YOUNG PEOPLE AND THE NATURAL HERITAGE: KEY INFLUENCES AND OPPORTUNITIES

Adrian Fenn

Summary

1.   Much of the recent environmental education effort with young people has been focused on the 5-14 year age group. There has been relatively less focus on older teenagers.

2.   To help to address this imbalance, SNH has undertaken research into the attitudes of 15-16 year olds towards the natural heritage. Key findings are reported, and opportunities are identified for developing educational approaches appropriate to this age group.

14.1 Introduction

"Scotland in the future should be characterised by life lived in a country which safeguards its own and the global environment, which fosters enterprise and creativity, and which is concerned with social inclusion in all its aspects" (McGettrick, 1999).

This quotation highlights an issue which is recognised as being central to the sustainable development debate, namely that the pursuit of sustainable development, including the safeguarding of our environment, requires the active participation of all sectors of the community. Agenda 21, the blueprint for action for sustainable development which was a product of the Earth Summit in Rio de Janeiro in 1992, highlighted the need in particular to encourage participation from groups such as young people, who are often under-represented in decision-making processes. Such an emphasis on young people also accords with the UK Government's policies on social inclusion. From an environmental perspective, this emphasis makes timely an examination of how young people view the natural heritage, what influences their attitudes, and how they might best be engaged in contributing to its care.

Much of the recent investment in young people by Scottish Natural Heritage (SNH) and other environmental organisations has been through the formal education system. This investment has particularly benefited the 5-14 year age group, especially through the extensive development of curriculum resource materials to support the Scottish 5-14 curriculum, and in particular the Environmental Studies component of it. Much of the other environmental education work undertaken with schools has also been with this age group, and in particular with Primary Schools. This includes initiatives such as Grounds for Learning, a Scotland-wide project which aims to encourage schools to develop and use their grounds as environmental education resources.

In comparison, less focus has been placed on older teenagers of 15 and 16 years old. Reasons offered for this include the problems associated with integrating environmental education into a secondary school system which is subject-orientated and examination-orientated, and the well-documented difficulties of communicating in general with young people at this stage of their personal and social development. However, this age group represents an important audience for environmental education. This is the stage at which young people are beginning to make significant personal decisions, for example as consumers. They are also preparing to move on into further or higher education, training or employment, and adult life generally.

There has been a perceived gap in our current knowledge about the attitudes and needs of these older teenagers with regard to the natural heritage, both within and outwith school education. This chapter details the findings of research undertaken by SNH into these issues (Market Research Scotland, 1999).

14.2 Aims and methods

The aims of the research were

- to investigate the range of awareness of, attitudes to, and actions for the natural heritage shown pupils in their Senior Four (S4) school year (15-16 years old); and
- to identify key influences involved, and opportunities to work with young people resulting from these.

The research methodology comprised two phases. Phase 1 involved the use of 12 focus groups to map out the range of attitudes held and behaviour shown by young people towards the natural heritage. The results also provided guidance on the construction of a quantitative questionnaire, the use of which with 5,089 S4 pupils comprised Phase 2. In both phases, the key sample data gathered were gender, academic status (intention to leave or stay in the education system) and geographic location.

14.3 Key findings

The findings are presented in relation to four key questions posed by the research. A full account of the research is given in Market Research Scotland (1999). In thinking about these key questions, it should be borne in mind that the 15-16 year old group generally had a low level of concern about environmental issues.

14.3.1 *How do young people define the environment?*

Most young people defined the environment in terms of issues rather than areas, as Figure 14.1 illustrates. Awareness of environmental issues (Figure 14.2) tended to be focused on major environmental concerns such as the greenhouse effect, depletion of the ozone layer and pollution, mainly because these are the most heavily discussed issues in the media and at school. These issues were also perceived to be the most important, both because of the degree of media coverage they received and because of their scale.

In contrast, there was less awareness of the sort of issues which might be seen to be particularly pertinent to Scotland such as afforestation, access to the countryside, and endangered species. The environmental issues which impact most on young people's lives are litter, obvious local pollution, and traffic congestion with the resultant noise and air pollution.

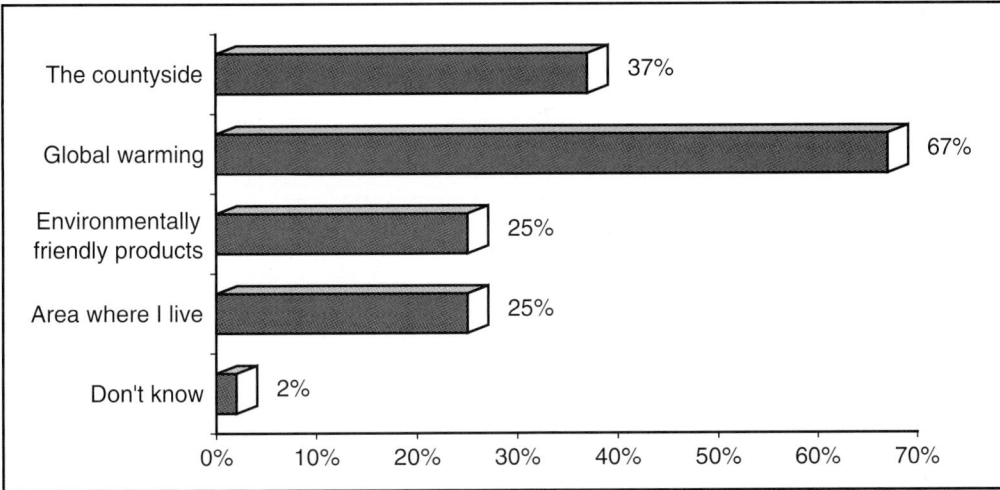

Figure 14.1. When someone mentions the 'environment', what do you think of? The data are based on 5,089 questionnaires. (Source: Market Research Scotland, 1999).

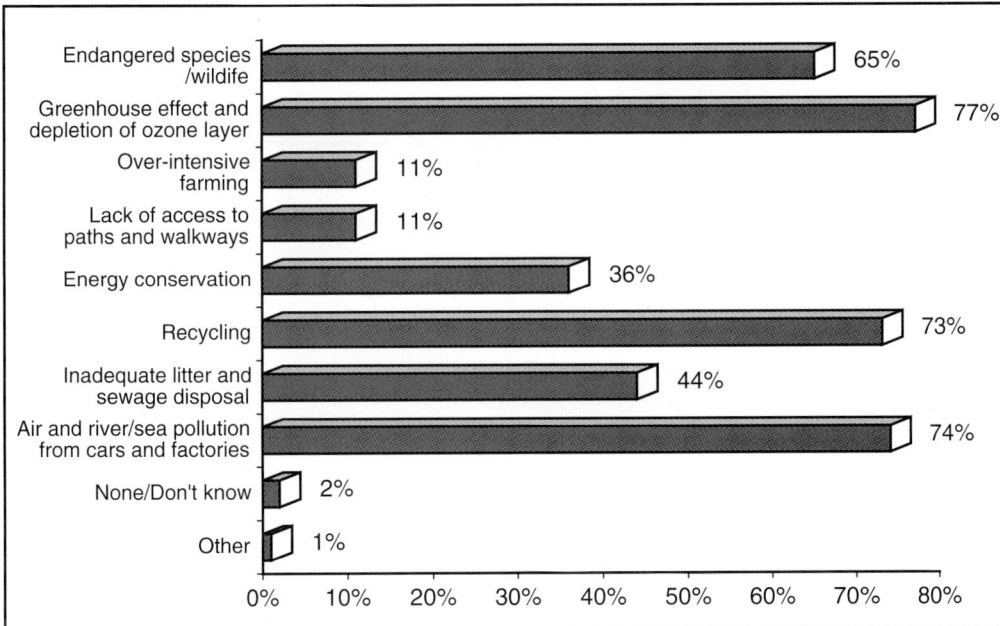

Figure 14.2. What issues do you think of when you think of the environment? The data are based on 5,089 questionnaires. (Source: Market Research Scotland, 1999).

14.3.2 What are young people's attitudes towards the natural heritage?

Scotland's natural heritage is most often identified by this age group as geographical features such as hills, rivers and coastlines (Figure 14.3). It is less likely to be seen as including flora and fauna and, in a third of cases, buildings were mistakenly included. Around half of the young people claimed to be interested to some degree in Scotland's natural heritage.

More young people claimed to be interested than disinterested in the natural heritage. However, most of such interest was expressed as 'slight', whereas around a third of

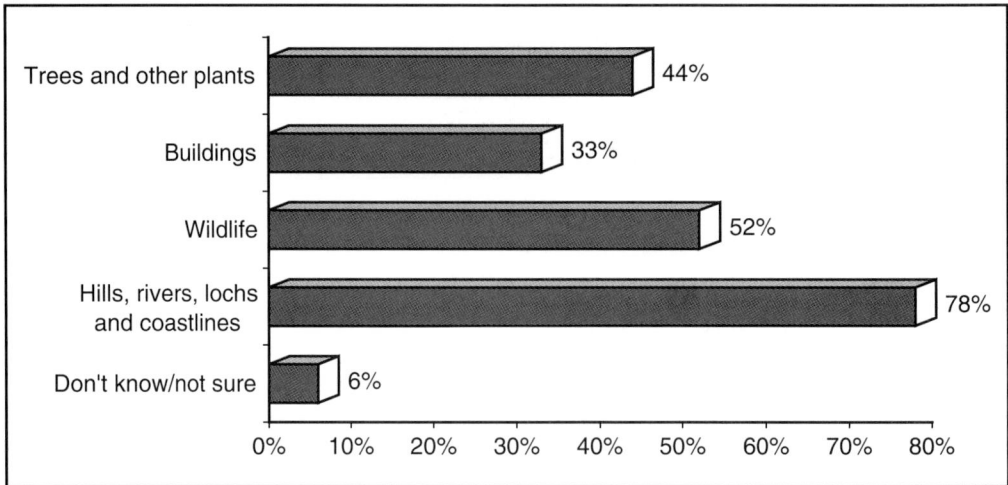

Figure 14.3. What do you think is meant by Scotland's natural heritage? The data are based on 5,089 questionnaires. (Source: Market Research Scotland, 1999).

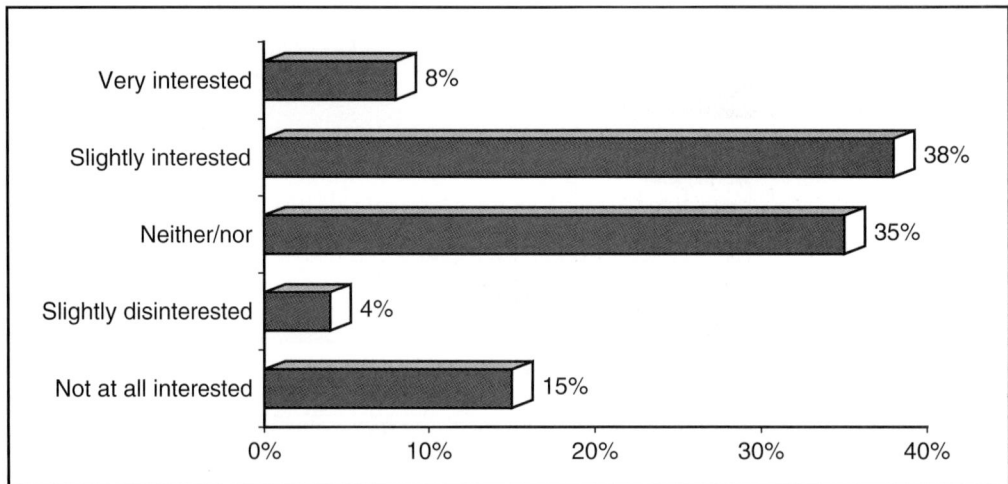

Figure 14.4. How interested are you in Scotland's natural heritage? The data are compiled from the responses to 5,089 questionnaires; note that the totals sum to 100% as only one category could be chosen. (Source: Market Research Scotland, 1999).

respondents were neither interested nor disinterested. The impression gained by the researchers was one of latent apathy (Figure 14.4).

However, the qualitative research suggested that young people found the natural heritage boring, largely because of a perceived lack of things to do. Most young people saw the countryside as a place to visit and enjoy only when they got old or had children of their own. They associated it with parents and tourists.

These results highlight an interesting general distinction, noted by the consultants, between the qualitative and quantitative findings. They suggest that the attitudes expressed by the young people tended to be more negative in the qualitative study, and that peer pressure was a significant factor in this.

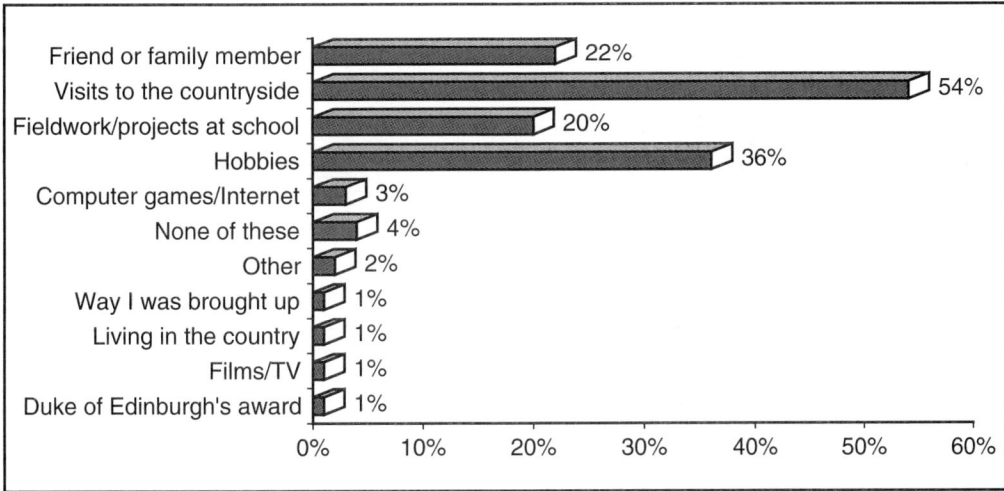

Figure 14.5. What got you interested in Scotland's natural heritage? The data are based on 2,368 questionnaires, i.e. those respondents in Figure 14.4 who said that they were either 'very interested' or 'slightly interested'. (Source: Market Research Scotland, 1999).

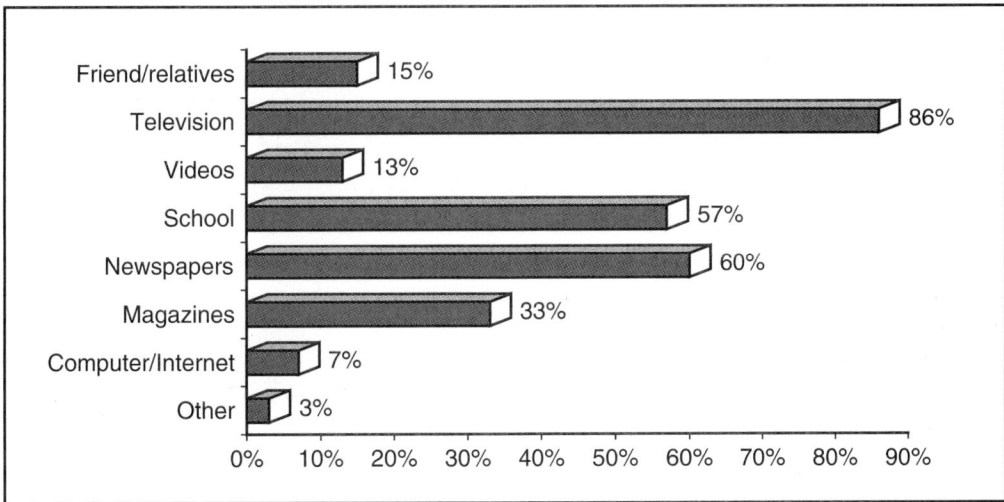

Figure 14.6. Where do you get most of your information about the environment from? The data are based on a set of 5,089 questionnaires. (Source: Market Research Scotland, 1999).

In summary, the research concluded that young people did not believe the natural heritage to be important in their lives. Scotland's natural heritage was seen as a stable, largely unthreatened and unchangeable object. Its future therefore was not a priority concern. Scotland's environment was considered by many as being not relevant to their age group, believing that they had more interesting and exciting things to do with their time.

14.3.3 What influences young people's attitudes to the natural heritage?
Figure 14.5 illustrates the range of influences which stimulated an interests in the natural heritage. First hand, outdoor experiences were felt to be important influencing factors. For

many, national pride in Scotland and its heritage was an important motivator. As suggested previously, contrasts between views expressed in the group discussions and the quantitative research suggest that peer group pressure encourages and reinforces a negative view of the countryside. Set against this, involvement with other young people is a substantial motivation, regardless of the subject matter.

Of current influences, television was identified as the source of information most favoured by young people (Figure 14.6). Schools also featured highly on this list. While only a quarter of those involved felt that the environment, as an issue, was boring, the lack of proactive interest was self-justified by the belief that the young people themselves have little power to effect change. A lack of appropriately presented information or opportunities was identified by many as a key reason for their lack of interest.

14.3.4 How might efforts be more positively targeted to engage young people with the natural heritage?

Many young people considered that they received too little information on their environment and are receptive to receiving more. The use of appropriate media and presentation style is important. Communication which has impact, which is stimulating, and which encourages participation or involvement was particularly favoured. School was identified as the favoured option for communication.

The social dimension of activities is important to this age group. However, many were no longer participants in youth organisations. Issues need to be relevant to the experience of young people; many favoured using local issues as a starting point.

14.4 Some opportunities

The research suggested an attitude of latent interest towards the environment generally, and the natural heritage in particular, amongst this age group. It appears to be an attitude of apathy rather than hostility. The research also identified six important lessons to be learned by those wishing to engage young people in environmental education and action. These are that

- any approach needs to build from identifying issues which young people consider to be relevant, especially those which they experience locally;
- communication should use methods favoured by young people, who should be involved as deliverers as well as receivers;
- involvement should be real and meaningful, not tokenistic;
- the social dimension is important because peer pressure can be a positive influence where approaches are based around a social experience;
- first-hand experience of the natural heritage is important in shaping attitudes, but the outcomes depend on the context and quality of that experience; and
- young people are not all the same!

The research suggested some variations in awareness and attitudes according to a classification based on gender, geographic location and academic intention. While the results do not allow firm conclusions to be drawn, they do emphasise the point that, as with all other groups, environmental educators working with young people need to get to know their audience first.

References

McGettrick, B.J. (1999). *Introduction: Scotland the Sustainable? The Learning Process. A Report to the Secretrary of State for Scotland from his Advisory Group on Education for Sustainable Development.* The Scottish Office, Edinburgh.

Market Research Scotland (1999). Scotland's teenagers and their awareness of, attitudes to, and actions for the natural heritage: key influences and opportunities. *Scottish Natural Heritage Review* No. 99.

PART THREE

TOWARDS THE FUTURE

15 CHANGES IN LIFESTYLE AND THE FUTURE OF COUNTRYSIDE RECREATION

Jim Butterfield and Jonathan Long

Summary

1.   This chapter considers the implications of changing lifestyles and values for open air recreation over the next 20 years. Policymakers are faced with a new pluralistic individualism associated with greater diversity of both the family experience and work and leisure.

2.   Earlier life cycle studies suggested common patterns of progression which now appear to be of less relevance than taxonomies of lifestyle. Countryside recreation will reflect changes in lifestyle and associated values. Planners may have to deal with the conflict between the serious enthusiast seeking deep experiences in the countryside and the more casual users.

3.   The attractions of the countryside are contested between the continuity of an enduring relationship with nature (the 'Biophilia Hypothesis') and the insulation from nature arising from modern technology. The former suggests an environmentally conscious course, while the latter suggests increasing pressure being exerted on the more accessible parts of the countryside to offer newness and excitement and satisfy hedonist desires.

4.   We speculate on the extent to which the countryside will remain an important venue for recreation and whether current values and practices will be passed on to future generations.

15.1 Introduction

According to Castells (1998) the 'new world' taking shape at the millennium originated in the late 1960s and mid-1970s with the historical coincidence of three independent processes. These were the information technology revolution, the economic crisis of both capitalism and statism (and subsequent restructuring), and the blooming of social movements, such as libertarianism, human rights, feminism and environmentalism. He argued that *"the interactions between these processes and the reactions they triggered brought into being a new dominant social structure, the network society ... and the new information/global economy and a new culture."* (Castells, 1998, p. 356).

Whether the information technology revolution will transform open-air recreation as significantly as mass car ownership remains to be seen, but recreation cannot be immune from the influence of these economic, social and technological changes. Whether we should talk in terms of the continuity of past trends or radical change is at issue. Family walks and picnics now have to compete with new urban attractions and the ever-widening choices offered by home entertainment; some people will seek relief from the pressures of everyday life in 'green contemplation' while others will use the countryside as a venue for challenge and excitement. This latter may in turn represent an extension of their high speed living or a counterweight to the boredom and lack of control they experience in their work. We need to take account of the transformation of time and changes in work practices, family structures and the globalisation of culture, the influences of which may be paradoxical; for example, the coincidence of 'hurry sickness' with long hours of television viewing and the almost universal acquisition of sportswear with more sedentary living. Similarly, global positioning systems and instant communication can improve safety on the hills but also encourage greater risk-taking through imbuing a false sense of confidence.

This chapter draws on a 'state of the art' review of life cycle and lifestyle theories commissioned by Scottish Natural Heritage to stimulate thinking about future policies (Long and Butterfield, 1997). To begin with, we take account of demographic trends, for example the slight reduction in the overall size of the Scottish population forecast between 1991 and 2021, but with an expected increase of 31 per cent in the numbers over 65 and 22 per cent for those between 45 and 65. This is likely to be accompanied by 19 per cent fewer below the age of 40. Early retirement may continue, so that, provided incomes and mobility are maintained, we can expect an increase in demand for the gentler forms of open-air recreation. Life expectancy should continue to rise, as will, though at a slower rate, life spans. Perhaps medical advances will prolong the years available for active living. Almost 14 per cent of the population will live alone by 2021, with one-person households accounting for 35 per cent of the total number of households. Will those living alone participate less in countryside recreation because of their isolation, seek countryside recreation as a social activity, perhaps in an organised group, or look for opportunities to be gregarious in the urban areas? The demand for housing land arising from the continued dispersal of the urban population may restrict recreation opportunities in the urban fringe areas and the trend is for some of those who can afford it to look for residence deep in the countryside. Car use and dependence will continue to increase unless persuading people out of their car moves higher up the policy agenda.

The 1994 UK Day Visits Survey (Centre for Leisure Research, 1996) shows high representation of the A and B social classes in countryside recreation and the critical importance of personal mobility. Without marked changes in the present patterns of inequality, it is hard to see those who are currently under-represented or excluded changing their participation rates significantly. Many adolescents and young adults show little interest in countryside recreation. Life cycle theory suggests that they may become countryside visitors as they acquire parental responsibilities. However, a consideration of lifestyles suggests that there is room for doubt. 'Generation X', having grown up with ready access to electronic entertainment and related leisure opportunities, may take less readily to the countryside than their predecessors. However, given the demographic tilt towards the elderly, the impact of this on demand may be delayed.

15.2 The life cycle

Practitioners welcomed the life-cycle concept when it was introduced to leisure research in this country by Rapoport and Rapoport (1975) as a potentially valuable tool for the assessment of leisure needs. According to that thesis, people's lives develop along the three intertwined planes of work, family and leisure, which give rise to predictable shifts in their preoccupations, interests and activities. This process is underpinned by the search for personal identity.

The life cycle approach represented an advance over the 'stereotypical consumerist family' and dealt with the complexity, ambiguity and uncertainty inherent in leisure provision (Clarke and Critcher, 1985). Moreover, women's experiences were given equal attention to those of men, notwithstanding that for women 'with the birth of children, life becomes not just home-centred but child-centred'. However, the psycho-biological orientation undervalued the significance of variables such as social class, housing and education and the influence of stratification in leading to different patterns of living, as opposed to a common social development. Although the incorporation of life cycle analysis into planning models proved to be highly complex, it prompted managers of facilities to take account of needs that otherwise might have been overlooked.

Life cycle theory was developed during a period of greater social and economic stability than at present. However, some of the recommendations of the authors stand the test of time; for example those about closing the generation gaps, the inclusion of leisure skills within formal education, the tolerance of different lifestyles and the need for a 'people-centred' approach. But we now live in different times, with an assumption that individuals are the best judges of their own needs, although Gough and Doyal (1991) suggest that an objective approach to translating needs into policies may yet be viable. Throughout the western world, rolling back the state has been the dominant policy principle, albeit not always in practice. Personal sovereignty or pluralistic individualism may be interpreted in ways that go beyond freedom to choose in the market place and reflect more emphasis on the public domain. However, a return to paternalistic welfare remains only a remote possibility.

Life cycle theory has become less appropriate as a tool of prediction in a world of flexible labour markets, major occupational shifts, women's greater independence and prominence in the workforce, growing inequality and greater diversity in the structure and form of households. The categories and focal points in the life cycle are less fixed as a result of social and cultural change. Children take to high technology entertainment equipment more readily than their parents. Motherhood may be stretched into middle age and it becomes less exceptional for the elderly to follow vigorous leisure activities. Life cycle theory was underpinned by the assumption of relatively stable family circumstances, but is now challenged by the willingness and ability of individuals to determine their own lifestyle choices.

The information technology revolution has not resulted in the often predicted age of leisure, except perhaps for those of us in the 'Third Age'. Rather, there has been a dramatic increase in the opportunities presented by the leisure industries. Shopping hours, drinking and gaming regulations have been liberalised. Theme parks, shopping centres, heritage attractions, sophisticated home entertainment and urban cultural activities all compete for our attention and incomes. However, critics claim that the unprecedented array of possibilities may divert us from deeper forms of enjoyment, the skills for which have to be fostered and nurtured (Csikszentmihalyi and Csikszentmihalyi, 1988; Csikszentmihalyi, 1992; Scitovski, 1989). Sunday visits to the countryside no longer take place in the absence of alternatives. The availability of alternatives must have some influence on the choices made by those who grow up with them. Giddens (1991) contended that the life-cycle concept is no longer relevant by saying

"The idea of the life cycle makes very little sense once the connections between the individual life and the interchange of the generations have been broken ... [In] high modernity practices are repeated only so far as they are reflexively justifiable" (p. 146).

In the absence of the certainties passed on through custom and tradition, individuals are obliged to think and act for themselves, choosing their own lifestyles and searching for personal identities. In making their lifestyle choices, individuals take account of what they take to be expert opinion and advice. As an example of such reflexivity, Giddens (1991) refers to the wide range of self-help publications showing us how to 'take charge of our own lives' and cultivate self-awareness, particularly with reference to our health and wellbeing. Such reflexivity might encourage us to have concern for the quality of our leisure experiences, with engagement in the quiet enjoyment of the countryside to relieve stress and enhance our wellbeing. Others may use the countryside as a resource for the promotion of their health and fitness. Faced with a wide variety of options, individuals put together a self identity package, rather like filling a supermarket trolley, with what appear as disparate purchases to an onlooker but being quite coherent for the shopper. We may note that the degree of discretion and range of available choices is far from evenly spread throughout the population.

15.3 Lifestyles

"Lifestyles are more or less coherent patterns of behaviour which are freely chosen by individuals or groups of persons. A lifestyle is more likely to change according to individual preference and circumstance than are the basic norms and institutions of a culture. Lifestyle implies a person's central life interest which spills over into work, family, recreation and religion" (Devall, 1990, p. 82).

The problem is that lifestyle can encompass all or any of the observable characteristics of individuals – manners of speaking, entertainment, personal appearance, diet, expenditure patterns, occupation, leisure pursuits, choice of friends, etc. These are then categorised and used as a basis for establishing groups to provide a more sophisticated method of market segmentation than social class divisions. Some lifestyle categories have come into popular use as stereotypes, e.g. 'yuppies', 'anoraks', 'green-welly brigade', 'Sloane Rangers', 'Mondeo men', 'fitness freaks' and now 'Kidults' and 'Middlescents'. It has been suggested that rather than being freely chosen , lifestyles are purveyed to us by corporate businesses. Klein (2000) quotes the owner of Diesel Jeans as saying "We don't sell a product, we sell a style of life. I think we created a movement ... The Diesel concept is everything. It's the way to live ...". Selling the brand has become more important than selling the product; companies see themselves as 'meaning brokers', with branding pervading all aspects of the corporate culture and imprinting on consumers. Brands are no longer restricted to related products but cross over into a variety of goods and services. Klein (2000) refers to the blurring of boundaries between retailing and entertainment to construct complete lifestyle packages. People are undoubtedly influenced by the images they see in the media, but those who construct those images base them on their assessment of trends in tastes and what are taken to be the aspirations of the target group as opposed to its real behaviour. Moreover, the visual impact of lifestyle choices comes to have overwhelming importance.

Market researchers use lifestyle groups to typify consumer habits on a socio-economic basis. For example, in addition to its life stages, Mintel (1996) has also created 'Special Groups' that typify consumer habits: benefit dependants (9 per cent of the adult population), families on tight budgets (10 per cent), better off families (9 per cent), better off empty nesters (9 per cent) and working women (23 per cent). These are intended to be 'indicative of the sections of the population in a country which is polarising economically' rather than account for all of the population.

In addition to these socio-economic groupings there are now a plethora of social classifications based on psycho-demographics. Outlook was developed from the British Market Research Bureau Target Group Index and classifies people as 'Trendies', 'Pleasure Seekers', 'Indifferent', 'Working Class Puritans', 'Sociable Spenders' and 'Moralists' (Baker and Fletcher, 1987). Social value groups are a further refinement based on values and attitudes. We can speculate that different groups will have different demands for outdoor recreation activities, with self-explorers looking for solitude in the hills, experimentalists flying microlites, conspicuous consumers water-skiing, belongers going to country parks, survivors restricted to urban parks, and so on.

However, we have to accept that in practice the groups may follow the same activities but with differing motivations and we must acknowledge that we have no empirical basis on which to relate the groups to specific recreational activities. Hasson (1995) reported a similar project to monitor social change in Europe by tracking key social forces (Table 15.1).

Table 15.1. The eight key social forces identified by Hasson (1995).

Key social force	Explanation
Self development	affirming oneself as an individual
Hedonism	giving priority to pleasure
Plasticity	adapting to circumstances
Connectivity	relating to others
Vitality	exploiting one's energy
Ethics	searching for authenticity and meaning in life
Belongings	defining social links and cultural identities
Inertia	resisting change (often passively)

This monitoring suggested that during the 1980s in the United Kingdom, those under-20 moved towards the hedonistic pole and were labelled the 'boring generation'. Since 1992 the same indicators suggest that the young have been shifting towards openness to change and have become more interested in ethics and belonging, adopting principles associated with social fairness, spirituality, the environment, community and involvement in society. If Hasson (1995) is correct, this 'new' generation offers rather more scope than its immediate predecessor for SNH to interest it in issues important for our natural heritage.

Geographical systems such as ACORN (Shaw, 1984; Williams *et al.*, 1988) and MOSAIC (Experian; see http://www.micromarketing-online.com/play.htm) attempt to give lifestyle groupings a spatial dimension through analysis of socio-demography by postcode, and by linking purchasing patterns to consumer profiles (through loyalty cards). Supermarket chains can correlate occupation, residential area, vehicle ownership, etc., with product affinities. Unfortunately, the application of such methods to countryside recreation would have doubtful validity given that data on recreation activities and locations are much less 'hard' than those for recorded purchases.

Although some of the classificatory models of lifestyle have a basis in theory, most are the product of empiricism or speculation. One of the problems of such systems is that they are normally the product of someone's interpretation of some form of factor analysis and/or cluster analysis. These procedures can present different solutions from the same data set, and so the process by which the researcher selects one solution rather than another is crucial (and not quite the rigorous scientific process some analysts might have us believe). Particular procedures will depend on the purpose of the analysis, which will be unlikely to include an understanding of open air recreation. Veal (1993) regretted that much of the work on leisure and lifestyle is largely divorced from theory and challenges researchers to follow Weber (1946) and "to move beyond the simple (sic) identification of lifestyle groups to unravel the processes by which lifestyles are formed and sustained" (p. 248), and the processes by which people choose their lifestyles or have them imposed. Lifestyle choices result in wide social diversity but also reflect technologies, marketing, business organisation, and entertainment that are global in scale, blurring local and regional distinctions and the urban-rural divisions.

15.4 Lifestyle and environment

What is common to most of our present lifestyles is that they require the intensive use of energy and natural resources, such that

> *"Many of us live beyond the earth's ecological means, for instance in patterns of energy use. Perceived needs are socially and culturally determined, and sustainable development requires the promotion of values that encourage consumption standards that are within the bounds of the ecologically possible"* (World Commission on Environment and Development, 1988, p. 44).

Sustainability will require changes in Government priorities, but will also involve changes in personal lifestyles. To achieve both of these will need a significant change in public attitudes. The close contact with the natural environment that comes through open air recreation may increase people's preparedness to take heed of such warnings. In turn, conscious decisions to leave a lighter ecological 'footprint' might be examples of Giddens' (1991) reflexivity and imply people seeking alternative forms of transport, recreating nearer home and enjoying simple contact with nature. This would run counter to notions of leisure within the culture of consumerism.

Veblen (1899) coined the term 'conspicuous consumption' just over 100 years ago, drawing attention to the importance of symbolic values and social status and to the fact that productivity gains are more likely to result in extra consumption than in more leisure time. Postmodern writers place consumption and self-gratification centre stage and draw attention to the hedonism of current lifestyles, which derive their identities from consumption, its signs and symbols, its ephemerality and disposable products (Lasch,

1980). Packaged and marketed as a commodity, the countryside has to strive for public attention among the kaleidoscope of other leisure opportunities and to offer something different from the rest (Centre for the Study of Environmental Change, 1994).

The contrasting approaches to lifestyle of hedonistic consumers and reflexive environmentalists have very different implications for policy. Unfortunately, even if we were able to be certain about the lifestyle aspirations of recreation participants, we lack the empirical evidence to link them with specific countryside recreation demands. The work of Savage *et al.* (1992) is one of the few attempts to relate specific leisure behaviour to other lifestyle characteristics, categorising the middle class as postmodern, ascetic or indistinct. The postmoderns are high income earners, extravagant consumers who may engage in hedonistic, personalised forms of sport, often used to generate business contacts. The ascetic group is drawn mainly from teachers, welfare officers and health service professionals, well-endowed with cultural capital but not so well off financially and looking to the state for many of their leisure opportunities, which may include healthy activities in the countryside. The indistincts typically include managers and bureaucrats, the former likely to favour 'staid and conventional sports' such as sailing, fishing, golf and shooting. However, without addressing lower income groups, the model lacks the general applicability necessary for policy and planning applications.

Moreover, it is doubtful whether we are in a position to identify clear indicators of need and there is no longer a consensus on the role of the state in enabling leisure needs to be met. It is also doubtful whether needs for countryside recreation can be identified in the same sense as we make 'objective' statements about the need for education or health services. Nonetheless there is a longstanding view that some form of direct contact with nature should be available as part of an acceptable quality of life, perhaps making individualism less asocial and more convivial (Gray, 1996).

A further dimension of need is the varying intensity of recreational experiences. Many go to the countryside for relaxation in the company of family and friends - a social occasion in an attractive environment. Others are more single-minded and dedicated, and for them we refer to the concept of 'flow', or 'optimum experience', developed by Csikszentmihalyi and Csikszentmihalyi (1988). Individuals experience flow whenever they become completely absorbed in a task or activity in which, while abiding by rules which may be explicit or informal and implicit, they match their skills against an appropriate challenge. Flow offers a resolution to the fine balance between boredom and anxiety, and is of relevance for a number of countryside activities, particularly adventure activities, but also bird-watching, natural history, angling, painting and drawing. However, the search for it may equally lead to anti-social activity - to the excitement of 'joy riding' or the taking of illegal substances. While much informal recreation may be pleasant without incorporating flow, it is central to serious interests such as long-distance hill walking or rock climbing ('Think Pink'). These may have importance not simply for enjoyment but for personal development and, in some cases, a whole lifestyle may be built around the activity. Some individuals may achieve flow in both work and leisure, but the less opportunity for its expression in work, the more important it is likely to become for leisure; hence the requirement for providers to understand the motivation and needs of the 'serious enthusiast'. John Muir welcomed people seeking wilderness experiences.

"Thousands of tired, nerve shaken, over-civilised people are beginning to find out that going to the mountains is going home; that wilderness is a necessity ... Awakening from the stupefying effects of the vice of over-industry and the deadly apathy of luxury, they are trying as best they can to mix and enrich their own little ongoings with those of Nature, and trying to get rid of rust and disease" (Muir, 1992, p. 459; first published in 1901).

The statutory requirements of our countryside agencies are based on similar arguments pressed by those advocating National Parks during the inter-war years. The 'Biophilia Hypothesis' (Kellert and Wilson, 1993) speculates that we have an innate capacity to identify with other forms of life, and has been used to suggest there may be a scientific basis for conservation ethics. This has led to a tentative claim that the human species has an evolved capacity for positive feelings for natural environments that runs deeper than values acquired through culture alone. The suggestion is that affinity with nature has universal expression common, though mediated in different ways, across all cultures. Thus, satisfaction from direct contact with nature, and the related senses of awe and wonder, are longstanding and unlikely to be affected by modern lifestyles. Ulrich (1993) refers to the large body of research on recreational experiences that demonstrates convincingly that leisure activities in natural settings are important for helping people cope with stress (which may often be induced by the pressures of our current lifestyles). Of course, reaching those natural settings may promote stress because of the need to cope with traffic congestion and even in the natural settings people are reachable by mobile phones (now including e-mail).

Schama (1995), too, urges us to explore and identify our landscape traditions, suggesting that although

"Our entire landscape tradition is the product of a shared culture, it is by the same token a tradition built from a rich deposit of myths, memories and obsessions. The cults which we are told to seek in other native cultures - of the primitive forest, of the river of life, of the sacred mountain - are in fact alive and well and all about us if only we know where to look for them" (p. 14)

and

"Cultural habits of humanity have always made room for the sacredness of nature. All our landscapes, from the city park to the mountain hike, are imprinted with our tenacious, inescapable obsessions. So that to take the many and several ills of our environment seriously does not, I think, require that we trade in our cultural legacy or its posterity. It asks instead that we see it for what it has truly been: not the repudiation, but the veneration of nature" (p. 18).

The literature includes much on the English views of the countryside, but leaves Scottish traditions less prominent and in need of investigation.

Thus, alongside the view that agencies must adapt to changing needs and values, we have the suggestion that countryside activities may have more enduring qualities. These are not either/or positions - both exist in today's world, and hence there is the potential for conflict. Within some lifestyles there may be distinct aversions to such activities – 'biophobia' rather than 'biophilia'. To complicate matters, individuals may not fall consistently into one category or the other. Research by the Centre for the Study of Environmental Change (1994) and more recently the Countryside Commission (1997) demonstrated the variability of people's responses to attitude surveys. For example, support for restricting cars in the countryside stands alongside uncertainty about whether it is legitimate to place restrictions on cars.

Many features of current culture - the compression of time and space, insulation and protection from the rhythms of nature, the unbounded possibilities of digital entertainment - suggest the possibility of lifestyles separate from any direct contact with nature. Rojek (1995) drew attention to Zion National Park in Utah, where a drive-in cinema lets visitors experience vistas of the park and its flora and fauna without any need to leave their cars, sweat or deal with bad weather. As he says 'convenient, accessible and clean - the Zion project symbolises our absolute estrangement from Nature'. It should be noted that Zion is a wilderness area with both an extremely challenging environment and very high conservation values. Rojek's (1995) account has been described as a celebration of difference and assertion, of the collapse of moral hierarchies, together with the collapse of notions of leisure as self-improvement and self-actualisation. 'Post-modern leisure is hedonistic, inauthentic, and fragmented and is a very different phenomenon from that which constituted the objective of welfare state provision' (Henry, 1995, p. vii). Rather than the continuity of 'biophilia', such a view suggests chaotic changes in lifestyle in a world of rapid cultural change.

Orr (1993) saw human consciousness being re-shaped to fit in with a world of electronic and instantly communicated images, and a view of nature simply as dead matter to be manipulated. For Berry (1999) this represented a particular concern for children of the modern world:

"For children to live only in contact with concrete and steel and wires and wheels and machines and computers and plastics, to seldom experience any primordial reality, is a sort of deprivation that diminishes the deepest of their human experiences" (p. 82).

This is associated with the concern that too much television may inhibit children from learning about their immediate environments, with too much information learned from two dimensional representation of distant places and events and too little exploration near home (Katcher and Wilkins, 1993). The way children learn to experience nature and the countryside is important both for their personal development and for their later preference for countryside recreation. There is consequently a need for environments which children can treat as friendly places for adventure and excitement and which are safe and accessible places of freedom. Nabhan and St. Antoine (1993) referred to the 'extinction of experience', claiming that children's very ability to perceive the environment may be diminished by the replacement of direct multi-sensory experience in a richly textured 'natural' world by the world of books or the audio-visual. Our present lifestyles mean that a high proportion of children no longer make their own way to school and are discouraged from playing outside because of heavy traffic and perceived threats of violence and abuse.

Such deprivation may be a result of conscious choice of family lifestyles, but for too many is a consequence of poverty and lack of access to natural surroundings. Some children have the benefit of parents who take them to the woods and hills and a school curriculum that integrates adventure and environmental education. Experiences within the family remain important as determinants of future countryside recreation demands but we are uncertain whether the many young people who find the countryside dull and unexciting will eventually turn into adults who appreciate its values.

15.5 Conclusion

Life cycle patterns have become less readily discernible since 'Leisure and the Family Life Cycle' was formulated in a period of greater stability and certainty when there appeared to be more likelihood of lifestyle convergence. Lifestyle considerations have come to the fore, although we might usefully retain the insight that leisure interests change over a person's life course. In policy terms there is a need to respond to less homogeneous and stable family structures and recognise large variations in the quality of experience between families with similar structures.

From our own review we expect in the medium term that

- any decline of interest in general countryside recreation on the part of 'generation X' may be offset by the increase in the demographic representation of those in the 'Third Age';
- there will be no substantial increase in informal day trips to the countryside;
- there will be an increase in participation in some of the minority activities for the serious enthusiast, for which Scotland has abundant and magnificent resources; and
- for some who experience a rise in income, but no increase in time, there will be the attraction of commercially marketed developments, but the market may be quickly saturated such that the product life cycle becomes hard to estimate.

The challenge for providers will be how to take account of the plurality of lifestyles; how to cater for those whose day out will not be complete without consumer pleasure and for those who are looking for an escape from commercial pressures; how to reconcile the interests of field sports enthusiasts and those opposed to blood sports; and how to serve the needs of conservationists and those applying the latest in technology to their recreation. Attention needs to be given to the encouragement of awareness and appreciation of the countryside as well as those recreational activities which offer a deeper intensity of experience. People can be offered a wide range of choice, but challenged to exercise responsible choice. Whatever the future, it will remain important for countryside agencies to promote opportunities for people to integrate nature into their everyday lives.

References

Baker, K. and Fletcher, P. (1987). Outlook - TGI's new lifestyle system. *Admap*, **261**, 23-29.

Berry, T. (1999). *The Great Work. Our Way into the Future.* Bell Tower, New York.

Castells, M. (1998). *The Information Age: Economy, Society and Culture. Volume 3, End of Millennium.* Blackwell, Malden.

Centre for Leisure Research (1996). *UK Day Visits Survey, 1994.* Cardiff, Countryside Recreation Network.

Centre for the Study of Environmental Change (1994). *Leisure Landscapes. Leisure, Culture and the English Countryside: Challenges and Conflicts.* CPRE, London.

Clarke, J. and Critcher, C. (1985). *The Devil Makes Work.* Macmillan, Basingstoke.

Countryside Commission (1997). *Public Attitudes to the Countryside.* Countryside Commission, Cheltenham.

Csikszentmihalyi, M. and Csikszentmihalyi, I.S. (1988). *Optimal Experiences: Psychological Studies of Flow in Consciousness.* Cambridge University Press, Cambridge.

Csikszentmihalyi, M. (1992). *Flow: the Psychology of Happiness.* Rider, London.

Devall, B. (1990). *Simple in Means: Rich in Ends.* Greenprint, London.

Giddens, A. (1991). *Modernity and Self Identity.* Polity Press, Cambridge.

Gough, I. and Doyal, L. (1991). *A Theory of Human Need.* Macmillan, London.

Gray, J. (1996). *After Social Democracy.* Demos, London.

Hasson, L. (1995). Monitoring Social Change. *Journal of the Market Research Society,* **37**, 69-80.

Henry, I. (ed.) (1995). *Leisure: Modernity, Postmodernity and Lifestyles, Volume 1.* Leisure Studies Association, Eastbourne.

Katcher, L. and Wilkins, G. (1993). Dialogue with animals: its nature and culture. In *The Biophilia Hypothesis,* ed. by S. Kellert, and E.O. Wilson. Island Press, Washington. pp. 173-200.

Kellert, S. and Wilson, E.O. (eds.) (1993). *The Biophilia Hypothesis.* Island Press, Washington.

Klein, N. (2000). *No Logo: Taking Aim at the Brand Bullies.* Flamingo, London.

Lasch, C. (1980). *Culture of Narcissism.* Sphere, London.

Long, J. and Butterfield, J. (1997). Looking to the future of open-air recreation in Scotland's countryside: people's lifestyles and needs. Unpublished report.

Mintel (1996). *Sporting Activity in the 'Great Outdoors'.* Mintel, London.

Muir, J. (1992). *The Eight Wilderness Discovery Books.* Diadem Books, London,.

Nabhan, B.P. and St. Antoine, S. (1993). The loss of flora and fauna: the extinction of experience. In *The Biophilia Hypothesis,* ed. by S. Kellert and E.O. Wilson. Island Press, Washington. pp. 229-250.

Orr, D. (1993). Love it or lose it: the coming biophilia revolution. In *The Biophilia Hypothesis,* ed. by S. Kellert, and E.O. Wilson. Island Press, Washington. pp. 415-440.

Rapoport, R. and Rapoport, R.N. (1975). *Leisure and the Family Life-Cycle.* Routledge and Kegan Paul, London.

Rojek, C. (1995). Leisure and the Dreamworld of Modernity. In *Leisure: Modernity, Postmodernity and Lifestyles, Volume 1,* ed. by I. Henry. Leisure Studies Association, Eastbourne. pp. 3-12.

Savage, M., Barlow, J., Dickens, P. and Fielding, T. (1992). *Property, Bureaucracy and Culture.* Routledge, London.

Schama, S. (1995). *Landscape and Memory.* Harper Collins, London.

Scitovski, T. (1989). *The Joyless Economy.* Oxford University Press, New York.

Shaw, M. (1984). *Sport and Leisure Participation and Lifestyles in Different Residential Neighbourhoods: an Exploration of the ACORN Classification.* Sports Council, London.

Ulrich, R.S. (1993). Biophilia, biophobia and natural landscape. In *The Biophilia Hypothesis,* ed. by S. Kellert, and E.O. Wilson. Island Press, Washington. pp. 73-137.

Veal, A.J. (1993). The concept of lifestyle: a review. *Leisure Studies,* **12**, 233-252.

Veblen, T. (1899). *The Theory of the Leisure Class.* Macmillan, New York.

Weber, M. (1946). Class, status and party. In *From Max Weber,* ed. and translated by H.H. Gerth and C. W. Mills. Oxford University Press, New York.

Williams, E.A., Jenkins, C. and Nevill, A.M. (1988). Social area influences on leisure activity - an exploration of the ACORN classification with reference to sport. *Leisure Studies,* 7, 81-94.

World Commission on Environment and Development (1988). *Our Common Future (the Brundtland Report).* Oxford University Press, Oxford.

16 SPORTING ESTATES AND OUTDOOR RECREATION IN THE HIGHLANDS AND ISLANDS OF SCOTLAND

Andy Wightman and Peter Higgins

Summary

1.   Sporting estates are the dominant type of landholding in the Highlands and Islands of Scotland. Their status, character and role, however, continue to be poorly understood.

2.   Hunting as a leisure activity is inadequately integrated into strategies for outdoor recreation as a consequence of the intimate linkages between it and the sporting estate phenomenon.

3.   Hunting is important to the rural economy but the economics of sporting estates are frequently unrelated to the efficient exploitation of the hunting economy.

4.   Public policy remains confused and frustrated by an inadequate analysis of the sporting estate phenomenon.

16.1 Introduction

This chapter explores the nature and character of Highland sporting estates and their relationship with outdoor recreation. The Highland sporting estate has long provided a focus for debates about land ownership and land use and a degree of tension has developed concerning the legitimacy and role of such landholdings.

Underlying this tension has been a set of assumptions about the nature and role of hunting as a recreational pursuit, the economic benefits associated with hunting, and the nature and role of sporting estates as the main landholding framework within which mountain recreation takes place. In order to clarify the nature of what is being negotiated and the motives of those taking part, it is imperative to have a better understanding of the sporting estate phenomenon.

16.2 The sporting estate

In 1811 there were only six or seven deer forests which were actively managed for hunting (Clutton-Brock and Albon, 1989; Orr, 1982). By 1873, however, the number had risen to 79 and by the end of the 19th century there were between 130 and 150 deer forests covering a million hectares (2.5 million acres). The greater part of the region had been converted into a vast outdoor playground for the upper stratum of British society. By 1906, deer forests extended over around 1.4 million hectares (3.5 million acres). By 1957, the last date for which accurate figures are available, there were 183 deer forests covering some 1.13 million hectares (2.8 million acres) of Scotland (Orr, 1982).

By the end of the 19th century, sporting estates dominated the Highlands and Islands. They were created as physical, legal and social constructs. Boundaries were delineated, infrastructure (hunting lodges, roads, fences) built, and large numbers of gamekeepers and domestic staff were employed. Uniforms (the estate tweed) were designed to clothe employees based on designs unique to each estate.

The contemporary Highland sporting estate is typically around 6,200 hectares (15,200 acres) in extent with boundaries created in the 19th century from older and more extensive traditional landholdings. It will have a lodge built to accommodate the proprietor and visiting hunters (incorporating a gun-room and typically in 'Scots Victorian baronial' style). It will employ gamekeeping staff and will typically be owned by a man from a family with substantial business or financial interests. The owner will visit infrequently and will often employ a professional estate agency firm to administer and manage the estate.

Today, there are around 340 sporting estates in the Highlands and Islands of Scotland covering around 2.1 million hectares (5.2 million acres) of land, which represents over 30 per cent of the total privately-owned land in Scotland and over 50 per cent of privately-owned land in the Highlands and Islands (Wightman *et al.*, in press). These estates therefore represent a significant influence on how land is used in the region.

16.3 Research questions

Whether it be from an environmental perspective (debates about red deer numbers and wild land management), a social perspective (the role sporting estates play in rural development), a recreational perspective (conflicts between hunting and other forms of outdoor recreation), or a political perspective (debates about land reform), sporting estates are the focus of widespread interest and contested values. Despite this, however, and despite the frequency with which sporting estates feature in rhetorical discourse on the subject of rural land ownership and land reform, very little is understood about the nature and distribution of sporting estates, how they operate, their economic performance, or the motivations of their owners. Little has emerged by way of data, analysis and review of the economic, social and environmental impacts and roles of the modern sporting estate.

This is a weakness which has confused and frustrated public policy towards sporting estates and outdoor recreation generally. The aim of the research reported here is therefore to understand better the phenomenon of the Highland sporting estate (its nature, character, purpose and role) and the function it fulfils in outdoor recreation (including hunting). In particular we want to develop a better understanding of

- the status of hunting as a leisure pursuit,
- the relationship between hunting (the activity) and sporting estates (the legal framework),
- the internal economic dynamics of sporting estates,
- the character, motivation and outlook of sporting estate owners,
- the views of the wider private and public sector regarding sporting estates, and
- how hunting, sporting estates and outdoor recreation are represented in contemporary discourses.

Our preliminary findings bear out the impression that sporting estates, hunting, outdoor recreation and tensions over both land ownership and use in the region have together built up a catalogue of perceptions and world views which have become embedded in public perceptions of such issues and which are reiterated with little empirical foundation. Two particular facets of the discourse which are worth exploring in more detail are, first, hunting as leisure and, second, sporting estates as benevolent rural institutions.

16.3.1 Hunting as leisure

The critic's lament, that vast acreages are turned over to playgrounds for wealthy elites, in part reflects the perception of hunting as a frivolous and unproductive activity compared with agriculture. Mirroring this view of hunting as play is the terminology developed by devotees of hunting which refers to 'country sports' and 'field sports', even 'pastimes' to describe the range of hunting pursuits. The widespread use of the word 'sport' (e.g. as in 'sporting estate') in particular testifies to a long-held recognition promoted by hunting interests themselves (and evident from the literature) that hunting is a form of recreation.

Public bodies have, however, adopted a range of attitudes and positions regarding hunting as a form of outdoor recreation. SportScotland recognises most forms of angling (coarse, sea, game, salmon and sea trout, and wild brown trout) but on apparently ethical and moral grounds does not recognise deer-stalking, grouse-shooting and other forms of field sports which involve the shooting or hunting of live animals.

On the other hand, whereas Scottish Natural Heritage's principal concern is with 'informal' recreational activities such as hill-walking, cycling, horse-riding and canoeing, it does recognise field sports as a form of recreation, e.g.

"other countryside recreations, such as field sports, are part of commercial or private land use" (Scottish Natural Heritage, 1994, p. 5).

The same policy paper concluded that

"... in large areas of upland Scotland recreation is now the main land use, either as a private and commercial use for field sports or in public use - or the two combined" (Scottish Natural Heritage, 1994, p. 76).

Partly because of such ambivalence, the debate over the legitimacy of sporting estates and their contribution to the Highland economy has become entrenched and sterile. In order to break out of this impasse, it is useful to recognise that the intimate relationship between hunting and sporting estates is neither inevitable nor necessary. Hunting as a leisure pursuit, or as an economic activity, does not require the sporting estate phenomenon to survive and thrive. Other European countries have a strong and powerful hunting culture but no sporting estates to compare with the Scottish experience.

In Scotland, however, a powerful and seemingly incontestable discourse has been propagated that suggests that hunting and sporting estates are indeed intertwined and that sporting estates are not just playgrounds for wealthy hunters but make a significant contribution to the rural economy.

16.3.2 Sporting estates as benevolent rural institutions

Assertions relating to the economics of hunting and sporting estates form a central part of the argument advanced by landed interests in defence of the sporting estate. Sporting estates are portrayed as benevolent rural institutions. Understanding the relevance of this discourse is an essential part of analysing the role of the sporting estate and the implications for the recreational land use economy. Put briefly, the argument in defence of the existing division and use of land is that hunting is a valuable component of the rural economy. Sporting estates, in particular, lose money and the rural economy is supported by the inflow of capital and revenue which, were it not forthcoming, would lead to the economic collapse of many remote rural areas. From the little evidence that exists, however, such claims appear questionable (Wightman and Higgins, 2000).

Mountaineering is quite clearly the more valuable recreational land use in the uplands of the Highlands and Islands (Table 16.1), given that only a proportion of the £72.3 million spend and £53.0 million income from sporting shooting may be attributed to either the uplands or to the Highland and Islands. These figures represent the macroeconomic impact of hunting as an activity. They suggest that it is a useful revenue earner for rural areas although perhaps not as critical as some would like to believe.

Table 16.1. Economic impact of hunting (sporting shooting) and mountaineering (data from McGilvray *et al.*, 1990; Highlands and Islands Enterprise, 1996). It should be noted that hunting data include overseas participants, lowland shooting activities and applies to the whole of Scotland. In contrast, mountaineering data are restricted to the Highlands and Islands and to hillwalking above 750 m (2,500 ft), technical climbing, ski-mountaineering and high level ski touring. It excludes overseas participants. Monetary data are in millions of pounds sterling.

Economic indicator	Hunting (whole of Scotland)	Mountaineering (Highlands and Islands only)
Participant expenditure (£m)	29.6	158.0
Direct expenditure (£m)	72.3	163.7
Employment (FTE)	7,200	6,100
Income generation (£m)	53.0	53.0

What is of equal, if not greater, interest in the context of this research is to explore the role that sporting estates play in this economy. Typically such landholdings are portrayed as loss-making enterprises dependent on their survival upon subventions of finance from the external wealth of their owners. It is difficult, however, to obtain any data to verify such assertions since sporting estates make no official economic returns of any kind and are notoriously wary of divulging any information on their activities or economic performance. However, one estate was recently forthcoming in its plans for the future. Letterewe Estate in Wester Ross produced a 10-year Management Plan in September 1998 (Letterewe Estate, 1998).

What makes the Plan interesting is its presentation of the estate as a benevolent institution which makes heavy operating deficits, as outlined in Table 16.2. Interestingly the figures imply more than the usual simple annual revenue losses and suggest that investment income foregone on the asset value (i.e. the income the owner would have received if it were invested elsewhere) represents a further benevolent contribution to the local economy. On this basis the total 'loss of income' to the owners is £680,000 per annum.

Table 16.2. Some economic indicators for the West Highland Letterewe Estate (from Letterewe Estate, 1998).

Income, expenditure, etc.	Amount (£)
Present estimated market value	8,000,000
Average annual income	130,000
Average annual costs	250,000
Yearly out-of-pocket loss	120,000
Loss of income on asset value at 7 per cent per annum	560,000
Total loss of income to owners per annum	680,000

However, what the figures do not reveal is that the underlying asset (the land) has undergone significant capital appreciation. On the basis of the purchase price of the estate (which was bought in different parcels since 1978 for a total of £3,405,000) and a current value of £8,000,000, the property has grown in value by 7.8 per cent per annum. In 1999 alone such growth will yield a capital appreciation of £624,000, a figure which outperforms the opportunity cost of investment elsewhere and which is more than sufficient to finance ongoing annual operating deficits.

Thus, on the basis of the available evidence, not only does hunting make a relatively minor contribution to the economy of the Highlands and Islands, but sporting estates, far from being the benevolent loss-making concerns propping up the Highland economy, actually represent a valuable form of recreational capitalism and profitable asset base.

16.4 Policy implications

Such research does not only throw up some interesting sociological, economic and cultural questions but has significant and meaningful policy implications in the fields of outdoor recreation policy.

For example, on the question of access to the hills, the Access Concordat and other advisory literature highlights the need for freedom of access to the hills being subject to reasonable constraints for management and conservation purposes (Access Forum, 1996). The guide produced jointly by the Scottish Landowners' Federation and the Mountaineering Council of Scotland advised hillwalkers that contact should be made at critical times of the year and the visitor should be prepared to accept, on occasions, an alternative route in order to avoid disrupting the essential work of an estate. In the same publication the period from mid-August to mid-October is given as the most critical time (Mountaineering Council for Scotland and Scottish Landowners' Federation, 1996).

Given the fact, though, that the major management and conservation purpose of deer stalking is the control of overall deer numbers, and that it is the hind population which is the critical factor in determining recruitment rates in a population, it is the October to February hind season that is, from a conservation and management perspective, the critical period. Highlighting concerns over the stag season has more to do with protecting the commercial value of stag stalking and the private enjoyment of sporting estate owners. While such concerns are perfectly legitimate, but politically sensitive, their submergence in favour of arguments based on a rather spurious conservation case simply serves to confuse the real policy issues further.

Recreational impacts are also subjected to partial treatment as a consequence of this confused stance. The Access Forum (a consensus grouping of landowners, managers and recreation groups) produced a code of good practice for walkers, *Care for the Hills*, which stressed, for example, the need to avoid widening paths and the desirability of using public transport (Access Forum, 1997). However, hunting is not covered by any equivalent code. The construction of bulldozed tracks and the use of motorised vehicles in hill areas to facilitate hunting activity, which has grown in recent decades, is thus implicitly accepted despite such developments having had a far greater impact on the Scottish hills, particularly in sensitive areas such as the Cairngorms. Such contradictions have their origins in the confused understanding that exists over hunting as a leisure pursuit and the role of the sporting estate.

16.5 Conclusions

Hunting is a leisure pursuit but has intimate linkages to management of the environment, property rights and land ownership, class, and rural power structures. Such linkages have enabled vested interests who wish to defend sporting estates to employ a melange of myth, conjecture and assertion to underpin the continuing hegemony of the sporting estate.

At the same time the economic contribution of hunting and the contribution of sporting estates to the economy of the Highlands and Islands remains poorly understood. On the one hand the real economic performance of sporting estates is frequently misrepresented. On the other hand, the economic importance of hunting is frequently downplayed by those antagonistic to the sporting estate regime.

In the emerging policy discourses concerning land reform, access, environmental protection, land management and rural development, claims and counterclaims are being made regarding the legitimacy and role of the sporting estate. With such important new roles being negotiated for the countryside, it is more important than ever that a clearer understanding of the sporting estate phenomenon is forthcoming. Only then will it be possible to find the new balance that is so eagerly being sought between rights and responsibilities.

References

Access Forum (1996). *Scotland's Hills and Mountains: a Concordat on Access*. Scottish Natural Heritage, Perth.

Access Forum (1997). *Care for the Hills*. Scottish Natural Heritage, Perth.

Clutton-Brock, T.H. and Albon, S.D. (1989). *Red Deer in the Highlands*. BSP, London.

Highlands and Islands Enterprise (1996). *The Economic Impacts of Hillwalking, Mountaineering and Associated Activities in the Highlands and Islands of Scotland*. Highlands and Islands Enterprise, Inverness.

Letterewe Estate (1998). Letterewe Management Plan 1999-2009. Unpublished.

McGilvray, J., McRory, E., Perman, R. and Stewart, W. (1990). *The Economic Impact of Sporting Shooting in Scotland*. Fraser of Allander Institute, University of Strathclyde, Glasgow.

Mountaineering Council for Scotland and Scottish Landowners' Federation (1996). *Heading for the Scottish Hills*. Scottish Mountaineering Trust, Edinburgh.

Orr, W. (1982). *Deer Forests, Landlords and Crofters*. John Donald, Edinburgh.

Scottish Natural Heritage (1994). *Enjoying the Outdoors. A Programme for Action*. Scottish Natural Heritage, Perth.

Wightman, A. and Higgins, P. (2000). Sporting estates and the recreational economy in the Highlands and Islands of Scotland. *Scottish Affairs*, **31**, pp. 18-36.

Wightman, A., Higgins, P., Jarvie, G. and Nicol, R. (in press). The cultural politics of hunting. Sporting estates and recreational land use in the Highlands and Islands of Scotland. *Culture Sport Society*.

17 NEW ACCESS LEGISLATION IN SCOTLAND

Richard Davison

Summary

1.   This chapter describes the proposals for new access legislation in Scotland that were developed through the national Access Forum. The proposals are founded on a consensus between recreational groups, land managing groups and public bodies.

2.   The chapter also describes the key needs for change and the package of proposals, which include rights, responsibilities, a major programme of promotion and education, better management and new resources. This package is markedly different from the proposals for England and Wales, which are now enacted through the Countryside & Rights of Way Act 2000.

17.1 Introduction

The next couple of years will see new access legislation being enacted in Scotland. This legislation will form a modern and balanced framework for much greater investment in the provision of new facilities and in the management of access. This paper describes the process involved in developing these proposals, assesses the need for change to existing access arrangements and summarises the main proposals put forward by the Access Forum and Scottish Natural Heritage (SNH).

17.2 Developing the proposals for new access legislation

In 1997, a Labour government was elected and one of its manifesto commitments was to give people greater freedom to enjoy the countryside. Under the Scotland Act 1998, access to the countryside is a devolved issue and so the proposals for legislation have developed separately in Scotland from those in England and Wales. This has resulted in a much wider review of access arrangements and a very different, more comprehensive set of proposals in Scotland compared to England and Wales.

The Government recognised that "… *Scotland has distinctive laws and traditions relating to access, which are different from those in England and Wales, and it would not be appropriate to consider this issue on a Great Britain basis. We need measures appropriate to Scotland, and this is something [we] would expect the Scottish Parliament to address*" (press statement by the Scottish Office in 1997).

In October 1997, the Government asked SNH for advice on appropriate changes to the law relating to access in Scotland and to consult both land managers and recreational interests. The Government suggested that SNH might wish to use the existing Access Forum to assist in this work and that the work should be completed by the end of 1998 (press statement by the Scottish Office in 1997).

The Access Forum was established in 1994 to debate and resolve access issues at a national level (Scottish Natural Heritage, 1994). A separate group, called the Access Forum

(Inland Water), was established in 1996 to explore access issues relating to recreation on inland waters. The term 'Access Forum' is used throughout to cover both of these groups. The membership of the Access Forum includes land managing interests, recreational interests and public bodies (see Annex 17.1).

The Government confirmed that the review in Scotland was to cover all types of countryside and was not to be restricted to open countryside or to one or two recreational activities (as in England and Wales). Another important feature of the process was the involvement of the Access Forum. By doing this, all of the key parties had a direct participatory involvement in the development of the proposals. This went well beyond a purely consultative approach.

The process involved looking at the issues, identifying the reasons why change was needed, assessing various options and developing proposals. Four key tasks undertaken specifically for the review were

- public consultation on what the main needs for change were and what changes were needed in the law with a report on the responses published (Scott Porter Research & Marketing Ltd., 1998);
- consultation with practitioners in local authorities, land management and user groups on technical issues, including how the current law is used and what advantages and disadvantages it offers;
- a study of access arrangements in Norway, Sweden, Denmark and Germany (Peter Scott Planning Services, 1998); and
- the commissioning of a legal opinion from Professor Douglas Cusine of the University of Aberdeen, with detailed comments by Scottish Wildlife and Countryside Link.

Table 17.1. Timetable of the process (as seen in January 2001)

Date or anticipated date	Action
October 1997	The new Labour Government asks SNH to start the review
March 1998	A consultation leaflet is issued by the Access Forum
October 1998	The Access Forum submits its proposals to SNH
November 1998	SNH submits its advice to the Scottish Executive and publishes the proposals
February 1999	The Government accepts the proposals as the starting point for drafting the legislation
February 1999	The Government asks SNH and the Access Forum to draft a new *Scottish Outdoor Access Code*
June 1999	White Paper on Land Reform published
September 1999	Draft Code submitted to SNH by the Access Forum
October 1999	Draft code submitted to the Scottish Executive by SNH
Late 2000	Revised draft Code submitted to the Scottish Executive after further discussion of key unresolved issues
February 2001	The draft Bill and draft *Scottish Outdoor Access Code* are expected to be put out to consultation (for 12 weeks)
Spring 2001	The consultation period is due to end
Autumn 2001	The draft Bill is expected to be laid before the Scottish Parliament
Spring 2002	The legislation is expected to receive Royal Assent

The timetable of the review is set out at Table 17.1. Legislation is currently being drafted by the Scottish Executive and it is expected that a draft Bill, together with a draft Scottish Outdoor Access Code, will be put out to consultation in early 2001.

17.3 The need for change: the existing situation

An essential step was to consider why changes to existing access arrangements were needed. In doing this, particular attention was given to the needs of people wishing to visit and enjoy the countryside, and of those who own and manage land and water. The Forum also considered the trends that have affected the countryside and its use for land management and recreation. The key issues are summarised in the following three sections.

17.3.1 Changes in society and the countryside

People's ability to enjoy the countryside depends on a range of physical (e.g. the availability of paths and tracks, signposting), social (e.g. the ability to travel into the countryside) and psychological (e.g. uncertainty about where to go) factors. For many people, the countryside can be an intimidating and unwelcoming place and their enjoyment of the countryside can depend greatly on the availability of secure and welcoming routes. One survey (System Three Scotland, 1991) found that 62 per cent of those interviewed were concerned about not knowing where they were allowed to go in the countryside.

Despite this, participation has increased greatly in recent decades (Greene, 1996, 1998) through a combination of factors, such as increasing car ownership, greater wealth and more time available for leisure. This same period has also seen new recreation activities, such as jet skiing, windsurfing and mountain biking, and the remoter parts of Scotland becoming ever more accessible through road improvements. Participation is expected to increase over the next 20 years, partly because more people are retiring early and on better pensions. Car ownership in Scotland is increasing at a faster rate than elsewhere in the United Kingdom and this might encourage more people to visit the countryside more often (Farrington and Robinson, 1997).

Most informal recreation takes place on privately-owned land or water and which is used for a variety of purposes, such as farming, forestry or field sports. Most land managers run businesses based on these uses and depend on them for their livelihoods. The Access Forum concluded that the interactions between access, recreation and land management are very important.

During the 20th century, agriculture has become more intensive, particularly in the lowlands, and subsidies have encouraged the creation of ever larger fields. More recently, encouragement has been given to set aside land and to leave field margins for conservation. Forestry has been encouraged through tax incentives and grants. Urban areas have expanded and new roads developed. Over time, these changes have resulted in the disappearance of many paths and tracks, particularly close to towns and cities (Rowan-Robinson, 1994).

The pressures on land managers have grown in recent decades and this has lead to the more intensive use of land. With higher capital values in stock and equipment, the result is often increased concern amongst farmers about the public being on farmland. The perceptions and actions of land managers can also be influenced by factors such as location, land quality, personal views on privacy and nuisance, and their experience of those who seek access (Crabtree *et al.*, 1992).

Some recreational impacts do occur, particularly in the urban fringe, and can include disturbance of livestock by dogs, damage to walls and fences, gates being left open and cars being parked badly. Some land managers also face more criminal activities, such as fly-tipping and vandalism. These impacts can all cost time and money to resolve, though there is broad agreement that such behaviour is often by a small minority. The deepest concerns about access are held by those who have not experienced much recreational use on their land. The Access Forum concluded that many of these issues could be resolved by greater investment in the provision of paths and by the better management of access.

17.3.2 Problems with the existing legal framework

The Access Forum agreed that an effective legal framework should provide clear and secure access to the public – so that they know where they can go and what they can do – and adequate safeguards for land managers. The Access Forum concluded that the existing legal framework fails on both counts.

The main basis for access in Scotland is that of implied consent and this equates with a long-standing tradition of tolerance and respect towards the need for people to move freely through the countryside (Rowan-Robinson and Ross-Robertson, 1995; Blackshaw, 1999). To many people, this implied consent almost amounts to a right - and certainly to a freedom - to roam; others would argue that it does not come close to a right or freedom as a landowner can change his mind at any time and ask someone to leave and would be within his rights to do so. Although such access provides many of the opportunities for open air recreation, it does have a number of significant weaknesses. These include the facts that access

- is not secure - a person could be asked to leave at any time, and so provides an inadequate basis for promoting use or investing in the provision of facilities or in management;
- is not openly welcoming, particularly as many land managers do not wish to have such access signposted or promoted;
- is favouring those people who have confidence in using the countryside (e.g. those with a reasonable knowledge of the law and of the countryside) and so for those lacking confidence or knowledge this type of access limits them to places that they know well or where they are likely to be welcomed; and
- is uncertain, in that it is not clear if the implied consent of a landowner applies to an entire property, to all types of recreational activity or to all likely visitors.

The current legal arrangements also allow for the assertion of public rights of way on land and rights of navigation on water. Rowan-Robinson (1994) and the responses to the consultation leaflet (Scott Porter Research & Marketing Ltd., 1998) highlighted several problems with such rights. First, they are not always relevant to modern day needs, particularly as they are asserted in order to secure passage through the countryside rather than for informal recreation. Second, as they bring into conflict the rights of the landowner and the public, they can require expensive court action to reach a conclusion. Third, the requirements for assertion vary considerably, with evidence of 40 years of use required for a right of navigation and 20 years of use for a right of way. Whereas a right of navigation, once asserted, cannot be lost, a right of way on land can be and can be challenged at any time by the owner (in England and Wales, once a right of way is on the definitive map it is permanent). Fourth, the absence of any definitive map means that there is no certain record of the existence or user status of a right of way. Finally, and again unlike in England and Wales, there are no duties on local authorities to signpost and maintain rights of way once asserted. The main outcome of these problems is that most rights of way in Scotland do not have the certainty or permanence of those south of the Border.

The Countryside (Scotland) Act 1967, which gave local authorities powers to secure access, create facilities and manage recreation, is strongly based on a voluntary approach in which the agreement of the land manager is required. In practice, these powers have had relatively little use as they can take months, sometimes years, to utilise and there is a concern amongst local authorities about having to pay compensation. As a result, local authorities have been constrained by the current legal framework and the inability to secure long-term, assured access, particularly along paths and tracks (Rowan-Robinson, 1994).

17.3.3 The lack of good path provision

This outdated legal framework has resulted in a significant lack of access opportunities available through secure legal rights, particularly close to towns and cities, and for cycling and horse riding. In Scotland, there are almost 7,000 known rights of way, covering a total distance of almost 15,000 km (Scottish Rights of Way Society in partnership with Scottish Natural Heritage, 2000). About 84 per cent of these routes are only claimed as rights of way, though many of these are not in dispute. Few rights of way have been asserted for cycling or horse riding and only about 800 km are known to be legally available for such activities.

By comparison, there are about 169,000 km of rights of way in England (Countryside Commission, 1998), most of which are recorded on publicly-available definitive maps, are signposted off public roads and are maintained. Of these routes, at least 37,000 km are known to be legally available for cycling and horse riding (about 23 per cent of the total compared to 5 per cent in Scotland). In Wales, there are about 38,000 km of rights of way of which over 7,000 km are known to be legally available for cycling and horse riding (20 per cent of the total) (Countryside Council for Wales, 1995). Although the densities of rights of way in relation to population are not so different, in Scotland some 60 per cent of rights of way are in 6 of the 32 local authority areas, accounting for only 23 per cent of the population (Scottish Rights of Way Society in partnership with Scottish Natural Heritage, 2000).

17.4 The need for change: looking to the future

Having assessed the existing situation, the Access Forum considered what sort of arrangements might be needed in the future. The needs that were identified are summarised in the following six sections.

17.4.1 The need for a modern legal framework

The current legal arrangements are out-of-date and do not provide the basis for giving people greater freedom to enjoy the countryside or for helping local authorities to manage access and recreation. The lack of clear and secure rights makes it difficult both to promote responsible behaviour by the user and to justify investment by the public sector. The Access Forum therefore concluded that a modernised legal framework, which provides greater clarity and certainty, is essential.

17.4.2 *The need to provide better access close to where people live*
In Scotland, the provision of secure access generally close to where people live, and paths for walking, cycling and riding in particular, is very poor compared to other European countries (see Peter Scott Planning Services (1991) for information on provision in other countries). Initiatives such as 'Paths For All' have made significant progress in the last few years (Paths For All Partnership, 2000) but there is still a huge gulf between current provision in Scotland and that available elsewhere.

17.4.3 *The need to have a better balance of rights and responsibilities*
At present, people are expected to behave responsibly even though they are unsure about where they can go and what they can do. The successful promotion of responsible behaviour depends on there being a better balance between rights and responsibilities and on people having a good understanding of the need to behave responsibly. A key element of this is the need to strengthen the links between people and the outdoors. Access legislation in Scandinavia, for example, is closely and positively linked to the conservation of the countryside that is being enjoyed.

17.4.4 *The need to involve local people in access provision and management*
Local people, including land managers, are often not involved in access provision or management. The Access Forum concluded that a key need, particularly compared with elsewhere in northern Europe, is to improve the sense of responsibility for, and stewardship of, the natural heritage and countryside generally by public and local communities.

17.4.5 *The need for better management and additional resources*
Establishing a modern legal framework, which balances rights and responsibilities, will help to justify greater investment in new facilities and in management. The introduction of a statutory right of access, for example, will increase the need for the better management of access in some places. Inevitably, additional resources will be required but the benefits of such investment will be considerable.

17.4.6 *The need to help deliver a wider policy agenda*
Getting access arrangements right will help the Government to deliver a wider policy agenda. By providing better quality access provision and management, more people should be encouraged to visit Scotland, and to return, and this will help to support stronger rural development. Providing easier access and more off-road routes for walking and cycling will help the Government to persuade people to make less use of their cars and thus deliver a more sustainable transport system. Importantly, better access and facilities will enable more people to get more active, by walking or cycling to work, to the shops or to school or for pleasure, and will complement the efforts of Government to promote a more active population and thus reverse the extremely poor health record of Scotland's population. Finally, providing good access, particularly close to where people live, will help those

without a car and those with disabilities to enjoy and appreciate the countryside and thus help the Government to implement its social inclusion policy.

17.5 The proposals for change

The Access Forum and SNH concluded that the existing law cannot be used to provide people with greater freedoms to enjoy the countryside. A distinctive new approach is needed which is underpinned by a modernised law designed to meet Scotland's needs. A package of proposals (Scottish Natural Heritage, 1998) has been put to the Scottish Executive, covering rights, responsibilities, information and education, management and resources. These are summarised in the following sections.

17.5.1 Rights

The key proposal was for a statutory right of access to all land and water, exercised responsibly, for informal recreation and passage. The aim was to introduce a wide-ranging right, thus avoiding tricky definitional issues, and stress the need for it to be exercised responsibly, i.e. the emphasis should be on how the right is exercised and not on where it does or does not apply. This right would

- extend, with a few exceptions (see below), to all land and inland water in Scotland;
- be available to any person, either on their own or in a social group (such as with family or friends) or as part of a club outing;
- extend to any time of the day or night (though the degree of responsibility increases at night time); and
- be available for a wide range of informal open air recreation activities and for passage.

Several qualifications on the right of access were recommended which aim to protect the interests of other people and the outdoors. As proposed, the right of access would not extend to

- any building or its curtilage, or places where public access is already proscribed by the law;
- field sports (including angling) or any motorised activity on land or inland water;
- taking anything away from the outdoors;
- the provision of facilities and services to support an event or similar activity, or to the provision of areas for starting or finishing an event or activity, or to any event which requires the suspension of land management operations; and
- anyone behaving irresponsibly and causing damage or significant disturbance (the law already provides sanctions against many forms of irresponsible behaviour and these will continue).

17.5.2 Responsibilities

The draft *Scottish Outdoor Access Code* defines responsible behaviour as "... acting with awareness, care and responsibility, and following the Scottish Outdoor Access Code and the law, in order to avoid damage and disturbance to the interests of other people and to the outdoors" (Scottish Executive, 2001). Explaining what this means, particularly on the ground, is the role of the new Code. A draft of this Code has been prepared and will be put out to consultation alongside the draft Bill. The Code will indicate how the right of access is expected to operate in most situations, and will provide the reference point for the much shorter codes which, at a later stage, will be needed for general public use. The Access Forum recommended that SNH should have a duty to promote both the Code and responsible behaviour generally.

The Code should be an evidential document (similar to codes for health and safety and for disability discrimination). When someone is not following the Code and, after being asked to modify his or her behaviour, fails to do so and damage or significant disturbance occurs, that person would take him or herself outwith the right. In this situation, the land manager would be entitled to ask the person to leave.

The draft Code also sets out the responsibilities of land managers. The main requirement is that people should not be obstructed, interfered with or intimidated from exercising the right of access. Generally, though, the draft Code encourages a positive, welcoming approach to access and it explains that land managers will be able to manage how people exercise the right. This could include, for example, asking people to follow an alternative route whilst a management operation is underway.

Liability is a key issue for many land managers. The Access Forum recommended that the legislation make clear that people exercising the right of access should do so at their own risk. However, land managers would still be liable for any of their actions which were deemed reckless or negligent.

The Access Forum and SNH also proposed that public bodies, particularly local authorities, will have a critical role to play in making the right of access work on the ground. They recommended that all public bodies must recognise, accommodate and protect the right of access and the responsibilities set out in the Code in their policies, plans and actions. Local authorities are expected to have new duties; these should include a duty to establish at least one local access forum covering their areas (these forums would have membership drawn from all key interests and would have a strong advisory and consultative role); to facilitate and plan for access in their areas (possibly through a subject plan); and to identify a core path network for their areas and ensure that it is well-defined, accessible, protected and managed.

17.5.3 Information, promotion and education

Providing good information, and then communicating it to the right people at the right time, is essential as it will help people to make better, informed decisions about when and where to go in the outdoors. Communication might involve face-to-face contacts as well as information boards, leaflets and telephone answering services (for example, the Hillphones service (Access Forum, 1997) provides up-to-date information on deer stalking activities to hillwalkers).

The Access Forum and SNH recommended that services like the Hillphones service should be expanded. An access website and a telephone helpline have been proposed. A national campaign of promotion, information and education will be needed and this is already in development.

17.5.4 *Management*

With the introduction of a statutory right of access, the emphasis is expected to shift away from whether or not someone has a right to be in a particular place to how people should exercise the right and how this use is managed. It is anticipated that there will be four levels of management. First, by explaining what is meant by responsible behaviour, the new Code will help to minimise the likely scale of instances where some sort of more formal management is needed. Second, a framework for the introduction of more formal management at busier or more sensitive places will be provided through the proposed access plans and by the local access forums. Third, land managers will be able to manage how people exercise the right whilst specific management operations are underway. Finally, there will be the use of more formal management powers by publicly accountable corporate bodies, such as local authorities and SNH, where a greater degree of robustness in the management regime is needed.

Local authorities already have a range of powers to provide facilities in the countryside. It was recommended that local authorities should have new powers to remove signs and obstructions, and wider powers to employ ranger services over any land or water as well as to create management rules and byelaws over any land or water.

17.5.5 *Resources*

Finding some extra resources will make the difference between the improvements to access provision and management being minor or significant. Getting it right would generate significant benefits for Scotland and help to deliver the wider Government agenda set out in section 17.4.6. Early estimates of the likely costs suggested that additional funds of about £14 million each year would be needed.

Apart from calling on Government to find these additional resources, the Access Forum also recommended that adjustments should be made to the way in which existing public funding is used to support land and water management activities. These adjustments should ensure, for example, that both grant support for agriculture, forestry, fisheries and local economic development, and taxation arrangements, support the aims of the new access legislation. It also suggested that local authorities and central government should give a higher priority to expenditure on access and set targets for allocations from appropriate budgets, including roads, for leisure and recreation.

17.6 A comparison with the approach in England and Wales

The Countryside and Rights of Way Act 2000 is now in force in England and Wales. This Act introduces a right of access to various types of open country (mountain, moor, heath and down) and to common land, and reforms various rights of way procedures.

In England and Wales, there is a much denser network of rights of way, particularly through farmland and close to where people live (see section 17.3.3), supported by a stronger legal framework than exists in Scotland. This framework is not without its shortcomings and hence the reforms provided for in the new Act. Compared to Scotland, there is a much smaller area of open countryside in England and Wales though it is historically important (for example, the mass trespasses in the 1930s) and often remarkably close to large urban areas (the Peak District, for example, lies within a few miles of both Manchester and Sheffield). Thus, Government decided to introduce legislation providing for a right of access to open countryside and strengthening the rights of way procedures.

In England and Wales, people will have a right to walk on any area of mountain, moorland, downland or heathland which is shown on a map as open country. A key task, therefore, is to map open country. The Act sets down a procedure for this work, which includes consultation on draft maps and an appeals process. Once the extent of open country is agreed and mapped, the right can be exercised. Given the fragmented nature of open country in England and Wales (especially downland and heathland), mapping will represent a real challenge.

The Act also allows for a range of restrictions to be placed on the exercise of the right. Importantly, landowners are entitled to close off areas of open country for up to 28 week days (and for longer with the approval of the Countryside Agency or National Park Authorities). A process for receiving applications, making decisions, and then recording and informing the public of any closures or restrictions is being developed by these agencies.

The approach, therefore, leans more to the regulatory, with the details set out in legislation, than does the approach recommended in Scotland (which relies on a more flexible, non-legislative process). However, there are some proposals which are similar to those in Scotland. For example, there is a strong emphasis on the need for responsible behaviour by recreational users and landowners, supported by codes of practice and education. A national Access Forum has been established in England, and the Act requests local authorities to establish local access forums in their areas to consider access to open countryside and rights of way provision.

17.7 Conclusions

Whilst the process of securing new access legislation in Scotland is taking much longer than in England and Wales, there is every chance that a new, modern and flexible framework for access to the whole of Scotland's countryside is attainable within the next two years. The approach is flexible and wide-ranging, and is based on the consensus reached by the Access Forum and Access Forum (Inland Water). It is vitally important, though, that all elements of the package - rights, responsibilities, information and education, management, and resources - are implemented. This, in turn, will bring real benefits to Scotland in terms of stronger rural development, more sustainable transport, greater social inclusion and better health of its population.

References

Access Forum (1997). *Care for the Hills.* Scottish Natural Heritage, Perth.

Blackshaw, A. (1999). Implied permission and the traditions of customary access. *The Edinburgh Law Review,* **3**, 368-380.

Countryside Commission. (1998). *Rights of Way in the 21st Century.* Countryside Commission, Cheltenham.

Countryside Council for Wales. (1995). *Managing Public Access. A Guide for Farmers and Landowners.* Countryside Council for Wales, Bangor.

Crabtree, R., Appleton, Z., Thomson, K., Slee, W., Chalmers, N. and Copus, A. (1992). *The Economics of Countryside Access in Scotland.* Scottish Agricultural College Economics Report No. 37.

Farrington, J.H. and Robinson, K, (1997). Personal mobility, transport and the dominance of the car. Unpublished report.

Greene, D. (1996). Leisure day trips to the Scottish countryside and coast, 1987-1992. *Scottish Natural Heritage Research, Survey and Monitoring Report No. 10.*

Greene, D. (1998). Leisure day trips to the Scottish countryside and coast, 1994. *Scottish Natural Heritage Research, Survey and Monitoring Report No. 42.*

Paths For All Partnership (2000). *Strategy 2000-2003.* Paths For All Partnership, Alloa.

Peter Scott Planning Services (1991). Countryside access in Europe. *Scottish Natural Heritage Review No. 23.*

Peter Scott Planning Services (1998). Access to the Countryside in Selected European Countries: A Review of Access Rights, Legislation and Associated Arrangements in Denmark, Germany, Norway and Sweden. *Scottish Natural Heritage Review No. 110.*

Rowan-Robinson, J. (1994). Review of rights of way procedures. *Scottish Natural Heritage Review No. 9.*

Rowan-Robinson, J. and Ross-Robertson, A. (1995). Implied permission for access. Unpublished report.

Scott Porter Research & Marketing Ltd. (1998). Access consultation: analysis of responses. *Scottish Natural Heritage Research, Survey and Monitoring Report No. 134.*

Scottish Executive (2001). *A Draft Scottish Outdoor Access Code.* Scottish Executive, Edinburgh.

Scottish Natural Heritage (1994). *Enjoying The Outdoors: A Programme For Action.* Scottish Natural Heritage, Perth.

Scottish Natural Heritage (1998). *Access to the Countryside for Open-air Recreation: Scottish Natural Heritage's Advice to Government.* Scottish Natural Heritage, Perth.

Scottish Rights of Way Society in partnership with Scottish Natural Heritage (2000). Mapping and recording the Rights of Way of Scotland project. *Scottish Natural Heritage Research, Survey and Monitoring Report. No. 130.*

System Three Scotland (1991). A survey of public attitudes to walking and access. *Scottish Natural Heritage Research, Survey and Monitoring Report No. 4.*

Annex 17.1.   The Access Forum and Access Forum (Inland Water)

The membership of the Forum is small in order to promote effective working; is balanced, so that there are roughly equal numbers of recreation groups, land management interests and relevant public agencies; and is representative, mainly of the 'umbrella' organisations which can inform and consult their own memberships about the Forum's work. The organisations represented are listed below.

Access Forum

Chairman (Roger Wheater)
Association of Deer Management Groups
Convention of Scottish Local Authorities
Forestry Commission
Mountaineering Council of Scotland
National Farmers' Union of Scotland
Ramblers' Association Scotland
Scottish Countryside Activities Council

Scottish Crofters' Union
Scottish Landowners' Federation
Scottish Natural Heritage
Scottish Rights of Way & Access Society
Scottish Sports Association
Sportscotland
VisitScotland

Access Forum (Inland Water)

Chairman (Roger Wheater)
Association of Salmon Fisheries Boards
Convention of Scottish Local Authorities
National Farmers' Union of Scotland
Royal Yachting Association Scotland
Scottish Anglers' National Association
Scottish Canoe Association

Scottish Landowners' Federation
Scottish Natural Heritage
Scottish Sports Association
Sportscotland
VisitScotland
Water authorities (East of Scotland Water Authority)

18 DELIVERING THE NEW COUNTRYSIDE RECREATION AGENDA IN SCOTLAND

John Thomson

Summary

1.   The proposed new general right of responsible access will transform the context for action to improve countryside recreation opportunities. The new agenda, particularly on low ground, will focus on understanding and planning for recreational needs; establishing and maintaining new infrastructure, especially Core Path Networks; and defining and encouraging responsible behaviour.

2.   In the hills there are the added challenges of identifying carrying capacity in areas of high conservation value and of protecting wild land character. In all settings novel pursuits will inevitably pose new problems.

3.   The key to meeting all of these challenges is better and more sophisticated management, founded on well-targeted research and experience-gathering. But such management must respect people's desire to explore the countryside for themselves. To succeed it must be firmly grounded in an understanding of human behaviour.

18.1 The new legislative basis

In more ways than one, the enactment of the proposed new general right of responsible access will mark a watershed in the history of outdoor recreation in Scotland. Most importantly, of course, it will usher in an era of enhanced opportunities for both land- and water-based activities. The new legal framework that it will create will be geared to the recreational aspirations and needs of a 21st century society, rather than the work and travel patterns of a long-gone society. It will provide a firmer basis for reconciling recreational use of the countryside with the multitude of other legitimate land and water uses. And it will explicitly and emphatically link rights with responsibilities for all parties to what constitutes a momentous new social compact.

But the change in the agenda of policy makers and access managers should be no less dramatic. From frustrating attempts to illuminate the deep obscurities of the current legal basis of access, and investigations into access law and practice elsewhere in Europe, policy makers will be able to turn their attention to teasing out in detail how the ever-increasing range of outdoor leisure pursuits are to be practised within the new legal framework. Access managers, relieved of the burden of clarifying the status of claimed rights of way and of the endless negotiations often required to create even minimal new access provision, will be able to set about with vigour the task of establishing the new infrastructure required both to meet user expectations and to resolve any tension between informal recreation and other uses.

This chapter explores some of the practical challenges that this new environment will generate. In particular, it tries to flag up areas where research – most of it very much of the applied variety – will be needed to inform both policy choices and action on the ground. It goes without saying that most of the investigation that will be required will relate to aspects of human behaviour. There will continue to be issues of a more technical kind - about techniques of path construction for example. But the new agenda will focus strongly on two essentially behavioural questions, namely

- what do people want by way of recreational opportunities and facilities; and
- how can their behaviour when pursuing their chosen activity be influenced to ensure that it is appropriate to the circumstances?

Neither of these questions has been explored in any depth in the past. Indeed it would be fair to say that open air recreation generally is a poorly researched field. Despite the efforts of a handful of pioneering individuals, notably Joy Tivy and Terry Coppock, it does not have a large academic following and the attention that the research councils have paid to leisure is in no way commensurate with its significance as a social phenomenon. Nor are there publicly funded research institutions dealing with leisure which remotely compare with those which exist for the natural sciences or even other land uses. In Scotland, most of the research relating to open air recreation has been funded by a few public agencies – Scottish Natural Heritage (SNH), Sportscotland (formerly the Scottish Sports Council) and the Scottish Tourist Board – and has been almost exclusively functional in character.

The reasons for this relative paucity of effort are by no means clear, especially given the contribution that tourism and leisure-related enterprises make to the national economy and to rural communities in particular. But whatever the explanation, the situation that has resulted means that there are plenty of opportunities for ground-breaking new work.

18.2 Planning and providing for access

The original recommendations from SNH and the Access Forum, which have informed the new legislation (Scottish Natural Heritage, 1999; Scottish Executive 2000), proposed that local authorities should be given a much stronger duty than hitherto to plan and provide for informal recreation in the countryside. Central to the discharge of this duty would be the identification, through a planning process of some kind, of the so-called Core Path Network. The extent and nature of these Core Path Networks were unlikely to be prescribed in great detail in the legislation itself. But they would have a key role to play, both in encouraging less experienced, confident and physically able people to venture out more and in reconciling recreation with other land uses, especially in the enclosed, lowland countryside.

Such networks could be expected to incorporate a large number of existing tracks and paths, with new links being constructed mainly to create the type of circular routes that are most in demand. With this in mind, SNH has already commissioned work to establish how best to compile a comprehensive inventory of the current infrastructure and is currently considering its findings (Ordnance Survey, 2000). The networks will need to cater not only for walkers but also for cyclists and horseriders, and for the physically less able. But of course not all elements of each individual network need be suitable for all these users. It will be essential at the outset of the planning exercise to assess the scale of demand for each type of activity, so that provision can be made accordingly.

For such assessments to be credible, they have to be prepared in close consultation with local people, who in most circumstances are likely to make up the majority of users. The proposed local access forums (Scottish Natural Heritage, 1999) may well have a role to play in the process. However, in areas of high tourist demand, local consultation of this kind will not be enough. Nor indeed will currently expressed demand necessarily be an accurate guide to potential demand, particularly in places where the limited opportunities available in the past may have discouraged participation. In planning ahead, access managers will also need to take account of long-term demographic trends, such as the increasing proportion of elderly people in the population.

Relatively sophisticated planning of this type will not be new to local authorities. They have for long had to undertake it in their statutory planning and social service functions. But experience of applying it in the field of countryside recreation is relatively limited (Scottish Natural Heritage, 1997), which is one reason why SNH has over the past year been working with seven pilot local authorities to explore this and other practicalities of implementing the new legislation (Land Use Consultants, 2001).

Other issues that the identification and establishment of Core Path Networks are likely to throw up will be of a more technical character. There are trade-offs to be made, for example, between the initial costs of construction and ongoing maintenance costs. There is the long-debated, but never conclusively settled, question of the acceptability of multiple use. Even these apparently more factual issues have their perceptual dimensions. Are the type of surfaces commonly found in and immediately around urban areas appropriate in the deeper countryside? How far will people accept attempts to segregate them by fencing from the farmland through which they are passing? How far, indeed, will the underlying purpose of re-connecting people with their natural environment be satisfied if they are so separated?

Once again, almost all of these questions have been addressed to some degree in the past. But all will take on even greater relevance as the scale of investment increases and our understanding of them will have to be regularly reviewed and updated.

18.3 Encouraging responsible behaviour

The third element of the new access package, alongside the modernised and clarified statutory basis and the enhanced physical provision, will be a major effort to encourage responsible behaviour. The main target of this campaign will not be the tiny minority of deliberate troublemakers, who are unlikely to be deterred from their criminal or near-criminal activities by a mere educational programme, however well-conceived. Rather, it will be those who might create problems for others out of thoughtlessness or ignorance.

The centrepiece of this drive for improved awareness and understanding will be the Scottish Outdoor Access Code. An advanced draft of this document has already been prepared by SNH, working closely with the Access Forum, and it is the subject of consultation by the Scottish Executive alongside the draft legislation (Scottish Executive, 2001). The text cannot be finalised until all of the detailed provisions in the legislation have been determined by the Scottish Parliament. The real challenge, however, lies not in framing the guidance in the Code but in disseminating it. SNH has already commissioned research designed both to gather baseline data about the current level of awareness and to inform its choice of techniques for promoting the messages in the Code (NFO System Three, 2000). Once the campaign is underway, it will be necessary to monitor its effectiveness - both its immediate impact in terms of raising awareness and its ultimate efficacy in promoting responsible behaviour on the ground (see also Allison, this volume).

There is, moreover, the question of how to ensure that behaviour on the ground reflects the precepts in the Code itself and in the family of supporting Codes foreseen to cover a range of individual activities and settings. There is emphatically no easy answer to this. All parties to the Access Forum, including SNH, have always been adamant that the legislation should not bring with it any new criminal sanctions. The creation of new offences would run directly counter to the overall spirit of the proposals, which is to lay the foundations for a more harmonious relationship between recreationalists and the owners and managers of the land and water that they use.

But if the heavy-handed approach is not the answer, what is the alternative? In part it must lie in the more effective enforcement of the existing criminal law. But overwhelmingly it must rely on guidance and mediation on the ground. This means better information and more rangers. It may well involve some blurring of the distinction between visitor management professionals and those whose primary task is managing land or water for other purposes. We need to be prepared to innovate and experiment with different approaches; all else apart, it is unlikely that the same regime will be appropriate, for example, in rural Aberdeenshire as in the urban fringes of Glasgow.

18.4 Open hill access

Hitherto, this chapter has concentrated very much on the task of improving low ground access. This is certain to be the main focus of activity in the wake of the new legislation, not least because it is the setting in which the need for improvement is most acute. But it would be quite wrong to infer from that prioritisation that issues associated with informal recreation in other areas can or should be set to one side. The opportunities for open hill access in Scotland are unparalleled elsewhere in the United Kingdom and part of SNH's wider responsibility must be to maintain and enhance these opportunities in a manner that also takes due account of the very high nature conservation and scenic values that attach to much of the land concerned.

There can be no doubt that in this context the elusive concept of carrying capacity will once again come to the fore. The obligations placed on the Government by the Birds and Habitats Directives (Anon., 1979, 1992) will trigger this. But once again there is no magic formula or single management technique that will resolve the issues that arise, only the need for a multitude of very tricky judgements. It is very much to be hoped that on the relatively rare occasions when such fine balances have to be struck, those making the decisions will take as their lodestone the principle that conservation and recreation are complementary, not opposite. Commitment to conservation objectives is built by welcoming people into an area, not turning them away. SNH is currently demonstrating its own commitment to that philosophy in its new policy for National Nature Reserves.

In many settings the limits of carrying capacity may in any case be set far more by perception – by the quality of the experience on offer – than by physical attributes. One aspect of the task of managing Scotland's mountains and moorlands which is likely to gain in prominence in years to come is the question of how best to protect the less tangible qualities that many of these areas possess. These qualities, such as the sense of remoteness and wildness, are increasingly scarce elsewhere and are under threat everywhere with, for example, the onward march of telecommunications – not only the structures that support it but also the instantaneous communication that it brings. Must those who hold Scotland's wilder landscapes particularly dear simply accept that the qualities at risk are doomed and are, in any case, measured largely in relative, rather than absolute, terms? Or should they be seeking greater recognition for their value and developing mechanisms for safeguarding them effectively? Again there are no easy answers. At the very least, those with responsibility for the future of Scotland's countryside should be trying to improve their understanding of the perceptions themselves, and of the human needs that underlie them, as well as the nature and extent of the current resource and the options available to give expression to the significance that society attaches to it.

18.5 Novel pursuits

In a chapter that attempts to look forward, it would also be wrong to ignore the fact that the range of recreational activities in which people engage expands continually. Much of this expansion is driven by technological innovation, supported by growing general affluence. The introduction of new activities into what is already quite a crowded field always carries with it the potential for conflict. This is especially true where the resource required to support the new activity is itself quite limited in extent, as for example with inland water.

In many cases it may be easy to assimilate the new activity alongside existing ones. But in others there may be real difficulties and even total incompatibilities. If such problems are to be kept to a minimum, or better still averted, we need constantly to be looking ahead and trying to anticipate and mitigate any conflicts that may threaten. Such informed 'crystal-ball gazing' must also form part of our future agenda – small relative to the other parts perhaps, but of high importance nonetheless.

18.6 The challenge of management

If there is a single thread that stands out most strongly from this whole complex skein, it is that of management. The concept of countryside or visitor management is of course far from new, as in a variety of contexts people have long recognised the need to reconcile conflicting objectives. But in a world where human influence is ever more pervasive, the range of human activities ever wider and the sheer number of people participating in them ever greater, that need becomes even more pressing.

It carries with it, of course, a requirement for resources, both financial and in terms of specialist skills. Maintaining both the physical infrastructure - the paths, tracks, gates, stiles and signage – and the human infrastructure – the ranger services, recreation planners and access forum support services – that will be needed will be expensive. So too will paying farmers and other landowners to keep the countryside in the condition that recreational users will wish to see. Whilst it would be only proper for the public purse to pick up most of this bill – and probably inevitable that it should do so – it is unlikely that public funds alone will be sufficient to carry out the task to the standard that is desirable. Everyone involved in managing for countryside recreation will need to be creative in searching out ways of supplementing the public funds.

But huge as the challenge of securing adequate funding for management will be, it is not in the final analysis perhaps the most testing one. That will be the challenge of managing without over-managing: of managing 'with a light touch'. Most recreational users of the countryside are drawn to their pursuit by a desire to explore their surroundings for themselves. Degrees of confidence vary widely, of course, and relatively few will derive their main satisfaction simply from self-reliance. But a sense of freedom lies at the heart of the experience that almost everyone seeks. Respecting and preserving that quintessential element whilst at the same time guiding in such a way as to avert a whole range of potential conflicts will demand great sophistication and subtlety. Above all it will require a profound grasp of 'what makes people tick'. Therein lies the greatest single challenge of delivering the new countryside recreation agenda.

18.7 Research needs

This chapter has highlighted a number of areas in which research effort will be needed in support of the legislative changes, both to inform implementation and to monitor the outcome as reflected in visitor behaviour and impacts both on the natural heritage and on land managing interests. It is at least arguable, however, that as open air recreation assumes greater importance as a use of land, there is a need to go further and to consider what broader themes require investigation, to aid understanding of the phenomenon itself and the forces which drive it. Three broad themes provide a possible starting point.

First, there is a need to stabilise the data gathered about participation in open air recreation. Over the years there has been an understandable tendency to develop and refine the studies undertaken, with the result that despite 30 years of survey effort there are no continuous trend data. If this regrettable state of affairs is not to be perpetuated, it now behoves all of the bodies with a strong interest in the subject to get together and agree on a standard survey methodology which, adhered to over many years, will provide the long-term picture that is needed.

Second, the time has perhaps come to move beyond the essentially empirical approaches to recreation policy and practice that have been pursued hitherto and to move towards a more probing type of research enquiry. This would seek deeper insight into the factors which influence recreational behaviour. It would yield a better understanding of people's detailed practices and expectations of open-air recreation, provide the basis for more structured trials of alternative ways of managing, and illuminate more fully the physical impacts of recreation on natural and managed land. It should also make it possible to articulate more effectively the benefits that arise from the many and varied activities involved.

Finally, such efforts to deepen understanding of recreational practice need to be complemented by others designed to provide a better understanding of the social factors that determine participation in open-air recreation. Society is changing rapidly, both demographically and in terms of social norms and expectations. What implications do these changes have for the countryside experiences that people will seek in the future? How much is now driven by fad and fashion, and by commercial interests of various kinds? Can it be assumed safely that the values that have traditionally underlain countryside recreation will continue to prevail?

These are deep questions and the answers may well prove elusive. Investigations into them should not displace practical observation and experimentation. But as the recreation world becomes ever more complex, it is vital to develop the breadth of understanding required to support the sophisticated management that this chapter has identified as so essential to the evolving scene in Scotland, with its new countryside recreation agenda.

Acknowledgement

In preparing this chapter I have drawn heavily on the deep knowledge of my colleague John Mackay who, over the years, has done more than anyone to push forward the countryside recreation research agenda in Scotland.

References

Anonymous (1979). *Council Directive of 2 April 1979 on the Conservation of Wild Birds (79/409/EEC).* European Commission, Brussels.

Anonymous (1992). *Council Directive 92/43/EEC of 21 May 1992 on the Conservation of Natural Habitats and of Wild Fauna and Flora.* European Commission, Brussels.

Land Use Consultants (2001). Local Authority pilot project, research findings and guidance: final report. Unpublished report.

NFO System Three (2000). Survey of behaviour associated with access and informal recreation. Unpublished report.

Ordnance Survey (2000). National baseline inventory of paths & tracks, phase 3 report: evaluation of feasibility study. Unpublished report.

Scottish Executive (2000). *Draft Land Reform (Scotland) Bill: Consultation Paper.* The Stationery Office, Edinburgh.

Scottish Executive (2001). *A Draft Scottish Outdoor Access Code, Public Access to the Outdoors: Rights and Responsibilities.* The Stationery Office, Edinburgh.

Scottish Natural Heritage (1997). *Countryside Recreation and Access Strategies: Guidance for Local Authorities.* Scottish Natural Heritage, Perth.

Scottish Natural Heritage (1999). Access to the countryside for open-air recreation: Scottish Natural Heritage's advice to Government. Unpublished report.

19 Role of Research in Environmental Education in Scotland, with Particular Reference to Responsible Access

Sheena Wurthmann and Ruth Grant

Summary

1. Influencing values and attitudes, and encouraging behavioural change, are elements that distinguish environmental education from environmental studies. It follows that educating about responsible access is one theme within environmental education.

2. In Scotland, research in this field is patchy and lacking essential baseline information for measuring change. Most research has focused on the formal sector but environmental education is a life-long need, delivered through both formal and informal methods.

3. More work is needed on policy and practice especially in informal education for a range of audiences, providing data that gives confidence to practitioners.

4. Research capability needs to be built up through more open contract procedures which encourage the formation of multi-disciplinary teams.

5. Environmental education can learn from practice in other sectors such as health education.

19.1 Introduction

This chapter aims to address a series of questions that arose during the Scottish Natural Heritage's conference, throughout which there was a theme of research data being used to support decision-making, practice and management. This was illustrated in a number of ways, not only for access to the countryside but also for health choices and attitudes to road safety.

Responsible access to the countryside implies that formal and informal recreation takes place in a manner that is compatible with employment in the countryside, including production from agriculture, fisheries and forestry, and that land managers respect the public right of access. It follows that there is a need for research which addresses issues of current knowledge, values, attitudes and behaviour and also addresses changes brought about through programmes to improve responsibility among all those involved in access. In situations like this, where environmental education is used as a tool to stimulate change, baseline data and the ability to measure change are needed. The data should be based on sound research, carried out by independent researchers and suitably peer-reviewed. This raises five questions.

-   Do we know what research has been carried out, and the quality and relevance of that research for the Scottish situation?

- Do we know the questions that research should be addressing?
- Are we addressing research to the complete audience in terms of age, interest and type of participation?
- Do we know who are the practitioners of environmental education?
- Do we have an independent research capability in how people learn about the environment (the pedagogy of environmental education)?

The rest of this chapter addresses each of these questions in turn.

19.2 Do we know what research has been carried out?

Lavery and Smyth (2001) reviewed Scottish environmental education as seen by the political parties and the devolved Scottish Parliament. They include a bibliography that reflects a wealth of writing on environmental education and sets the Scottish experience within the global context. This may suggest that, for Scotland, environmental education research is well-grounded. However, examination of the text and references shows that much of the research has been focused on Scottish experience on environmental education policy. The authors do not include researched information on the pedagogy and practical implementation that is essential to support decision-making and practice in delivering environmental education as a lifelong experience. Work in Scotland is rarely compared directly in appropriate methodologies with important work in North America, Australasia and Europe such as that of Andresen (1984), Tranter (1986) and Wiley and Humphreys (1986).

Cottingham *et al.* (2001) indicated that basic pedagogic research is well-established in geography as a subject discipline, but similar work has not been carried out in earth and environmental sciences. This is seen as a vital need in order to achieve research-based, decision-making in all aspects of environmental education. Scottish work has been evaluated, predominantly by practitioners considering their own work or by reporting on projects. Fundamental questions about knowledge, values, attitudes and behaviour have rarely been addressed.

Within the discipline of environmental education, educators are confident and comfortable with knowledge drawn from earth and life sciences. Recent benchmarking exercises for earth science, environmental science and environmental studies in higher education have found academics in agreement about the academic discipline, knowledge and understanding, as well as practical skills. There is a difference of opinion, however, in the priority of the selection of the topics studied and the depth of study needed.

The Quality Assurance Agency for Higher Education throughout the United Kingdom is now looking for higher education to deliver knowledge, understanding, skills and competence; values, attitudes and behaviour are all included in the curriculum. It is not expected that lecture courses cover all of these areas, but rather that students have the opportunity to learn about them. This is very familiar territory for practitioners in environmental education, and for health and outdoor recreation educators. Environmental education should be an inclusive, integrated educational process. But is this just an educational platitude?

The evidence for baseline knowledge, skills, attitudes and behaviour is seldom independently researched to enable measurement of the changes that are taking place. In similar circumstances the early intervention programmes for literacy (Pirrie, 1999) are notable in the use of management research organisations to monitor effectiveness and value for money of the intervention. One example of similar work relating to the environment is the limited research on public attitudes to the natural environment done by System Three (Brown, 1999).

From this review it became apparent that basic rigorous research into the current knowledge and understanding of learners at all stages has not been carried out in Scotland. The selected methodologies for delivering learning are usually based on intuition and on feedback from learners rather than independent peer-reviewed research. This is supported by the rigorous review by Rickinson (2001), where the author has found that environmental education theory and research appeared to have overlooked the learning and the learners. Rickinson (2001) highlighted the need for the evidence base in environmental education research.

19.3 Do we know the questions that this research should be addressing?

From the media and political sources we are familiar with the need for literacy and numeracy in a knowledge-based economy. However, we are less clear on the forms of literacy and their importance for human survival and sustainability worldwide. Orr (1992) described this as ecological literacy and has developed a philosophy and pedagogy. He addressed these issues in the context of the North American university liberal arts tradition of education and learning on the campus. In his discussion he used Bloom's (1987) concept of 'great books' to be read. Translating 'great books' and literature to the environment and sustainability, Orr (1992) produced a formidable reading list that is worthy of not only four years in liberal arts education but four years in a library. However, environmental educators are agreed that this is only part of education for ecological literacy (Scottish Office Environment Department, 1995). Direct contact with the natural environment must be present somewhere.

It is interesting to visit a primary school and look at what the children are learning and the process of educating. The visitor will recognise the reading, writing and arithmetic that is taking place. Learning the alphabet and arithmetic tables still takes time and is a struggle for some. The 5 to 14 year curriculum in Scotland (for students from early primary school to junior secondary school) includes environmental education as part both of science and of personal and social development. It is a cross-curriculum theme that includes knowledge and understanding as well as values and dispositions (the term favoured in formal education).

Several attempts have been made to document levels of environmental literacy in formal primary and secondary education. However, none of these researches appear to use the clarity of 'reading ages' and 'stages in mathematics' skills developed in national testing, national examination successes and league tables. This is a challenge for research because environmental education is seen as a vehicle for other forms of education (such as science) rather than a discipline in its own right.

An example of the questions that should be addressed is 'what is the current level of knowledge of, and attitudes to, the conservation of the environment among the voting public?'. To be able to develop public support for the work of environmental bodies such as Scottish Natural Heritage, we need to have solid and reliable data on the need for education, promotion and campaign work. These are interrelated activities but use different strategies, methods and materials. The public aspect is the promotion or campaign, but the background should be the education and learning support system. At present nature conservation and environmental education groups do not usually carry out rigorous research to address the basic questions. Environmental education in general is lagging behind the work done by the Health Education Board for Scotland (HEBS) to establish its separate campaigns for teenagers, young adults and the middle aged (the 'Gavin Hastings' campaign; see Allison, this volume). It is clear that the need for such research to support the promotion of the proposed Scottish Outdoor Access Code has been identified and a start has been made. Research is now being commissioned into the current knowledge, values, attitudes and behaviour of the Scottish population with regard to access to the countryside for recreation. This baseline information is essential to the development of a campaign or educational programme for selected target audiences. Without this information it is impossible to measure change resulting from any programme to initiate change in attitudes and behaviour. Evaluation of work, which does not have this background information, is flawed. Only in the field of interpretation is research more focused. It is constructed to provide the information needed to measure change brought about through the provision of interpretation. Understanding of visitor profiles and needs, definition of measurable interpretive objectives, and evaluation, are encouraged. The evaluations are valid and valued by practitioners.

19.4 Are we addressing research to the complete audience?

The audience for environmental education is the whole population. At present the research on environmental education has focused mainly on the formal sector with the early stages of school as the prime target. Lavery and Smyth (2001) identified three groups in the population: promoters, practitioners and recipients. Depending on circumstances, individuals will change from one group to another, but this grouping gives a useful segmentation of the total population, although further division or distinction of recipients is needed, for example, to differentiate between formal schooling and informal community education, or between different interest groups. In *Learning for Life* (Scottish Office Environment Department, 1995), it was pointed out that recipients were very fortunate if they received environmental education in a structured and progressive manner. The provision of environmental education was patchy and the outcome of this meant that knowledge and understanding was lacking coherence and progression. Since 1995 little has changed in either formal or informal education at any level. If there is little structure and consistency in formal education, there is no policy and practice for informal and community education. The audience, for whom these provide the only educational opportunities, is poorly served.

The disparity between the ideal coherent approach to learning and understanding and what is actually happening is put into focus with the example of the education service at the Royal Botanic Garden, Edinburgh (I.D. Edwards, pers. comm.). The service produces education packs and materials for schools who visit the Garden as well as for classroom use. The team found that schools were familiar with tropical rain forests and well-versed in the biodiversity to be found there. However, they had no knowledge of temperate rain forests of Scotland, so the Garden developed a travelling show to address this topic.

19.5 Do we know who are the practitioners of environmental education?

Teachers, teacher educators and lecturers are easily identified in formal education as practitioners. However, there is no guarantee that an individual progressing through compulsory and post-school education will necessarily have had sufficient contact with practitioners and promoters to become environmentally or ecologically literate.

Other practitioners include the countryside rangers, education officers in non-governmental organisations, museum and community educators. These are the practitioners most commonly in contact with the general public. Beyond this list there are many professionals who, through their employment and recreation, act as informal environmental educators. There is, however, no method of identifying, recognising and supporting these people.

Environmental educators, both formal and informal, work hard to deliver what they understand as an appropriate curriculum, using a range of materials and approaches that they see as working well. They are not supported by evidence that the curriculum is appropriate for the students and that it progresses their knowledge and understanding in a coherent way, nor that it influences attitudes and behaviour, if that is the aim.

Practitioners also need support in practical aspects of teaching using first-hand experience. The field component of environmental education is cited as an important element in the learning process but we lack Scottish research evidence to back up this assertion and a mechanism to identify and disseminate good practice to teachers and students.

19.6 Do we have an independent research capability?

For this type of research we need both an environmental and an educational capability. The research which is done frequently considers the environmental or the educational elements and extrapolates rather than integrates the findings. This is not a satisfactory or satisfying basis for the implementation of research into practice.

The need for integrated approaches has to be clear in the process of bidding for research funding and in the research brief. Environmental education has benefited from commissioned research carried out by the non-governmental organisations such as the Worldwide Fund for Nature and the Royal Society for the Protection of Birds. However, the Research Councils do not fund this type of research and it is left to the educational and environmental ministries of government and their associated agencies to contract this work. History indicates that tendering for these contracts has not followed a fully open and transparent system, such as open advertising, which creates the opportunity for new groups and teams to participate. The multi-disciplinary approach, as demonstrated by a transport team (Stradling, this volume), enhances the methodologies and insights available. The tendering process can encourage the 'cheapest' option rather than considering value for money. It does not facilitate the development of teams, as the cost increases as more people are involved. Part of the philosophy of developing research is developing the research capability.

Independence of the researchers in terms of allegiance of their organisational base is recognised as enhancing the objectivity of the approach. Universities are good sources of this independent and objective approach but they are not the only agencies for this work. Business-based organisations have important groups of researchers that can address multi-disciplinary research questions effectively and efficiently, but not cheaply.

Our experience suggests that there is a research capability for environmental education in Scotland which needs to be fostered with interesting and challenging projects, encouraging appropriate synergy and co-operation. The challenge is to the funders, either in government or agencies, to address the research community with the projects and the funds to provide the knowledge base and enable policy decisions based on good data and their interpretation.

19.7 Where do we start?

The research of the Health Education Board for Scotland, mentioned in section 19.3, identified key health issues such as drugs (including smoking and alcohol) in young adults, cardio-vascular health in adult males, cancer, and fitness in adult females. For a similar research programme in environmental education we need to identify the problem areas. Responsible access would be a good starting point. Do we have data on the current knowledge and understanding of the proposed legislation? What is understood by climbers, bikers and casual tourists as 'responsible access'? Does the visitor's definition of access match the landowner's definition? As a result of answering these questions, do we need to make changes? How can environmental education methodologies be used to encourage these changes? What research is needed to demonstrate the effectiveness of environmental education programmes?

The HEBS's promotions appear as advertisements in the media, but these are supported by educational resources and help (see Allison, this volume). Following the pattern set by HEBS, environmental education to promote responsible access needs a thorough examination and basic data collection and analysis. This research must be independent and based on rigorous methodology. Social science research has made major developments in methodologies to identify cultural, economic and other biases in research; these must be used in this research. From this work it will be possible to identify the equivalents to drugs, diet and exercise as the key points on which to focus in research for responsible access.

This is the approach that was taken in Norway (Vistad, this volume). The Norwegians based their planning for access on good research when they developed their strategy. The research showed that adult males (young and old) used the countryside for outdoor pursuits. Adult females showed a gap in participation about the age range of 'young mothers'. This is the key to family participation in the outdoors and enjoying the countryside. Making paths and access to the countryside family friendly, and developing routes that are suitable for short walks with small children, has shifted participation. The question in Scotland is 'What do we know about who is using the countryside for recreation and about how they use it?'. Recent experience, when access to the countryside was denied during the foot and mouth disease outbreak, suggests that there has been an underestimation not only of the numbers of people who frequently visit the countryside but also of the economic contribution they make to the rural economy. It has also demonstrated that, with clear messages, good information and public understanding of an issue, the public will respond responsibly.

Intuition is not an appropriate tool for research. Scottish Natural Heritage is clear that good, research-based knowledge supports decisions in protecting and managing sites and species. The same standards, using social and educational research methodologies, are needed to look at public knowledge, understanding and perceptions in Scotland. This rigorous approach will allow us to develop with confidence an ecologically literate community and nation. This will enable us to learn to live sustainably.

References

Andresen, L.W. (1984). Field studies at the University of New South Wales. *A Quarterly (Australian Consortium on Experimental Education),* **9**, 4 –7.

Bloom, A. (1987). *The Closing of the American Mind.* Simon and Schuster, New York.

Brown, E.G. (1999). Visitor behaviour on Mousa SSSI. Unpublished report, Scottish Natural Heritage.

Cottingham, C., Healey, M. and Gravestock, P. (2001). Fieldwork in the geography, earth and environmental sciences higher education curriculum: an annotated bibliography. *Geography Discipline Network* (www.chelt.ac.uk/el/philg/gdn/disabil/fieldwk.htm).

Lavery, A. and Smyth, J.C. (in press). Developing environmental education: a review of a Scottish project I – international and political influences. *Environmental Education Research.*

Orr, D.W. (1992). *Environmental Literacy – education and the transition to a postmodern world.* State University of New York Press, Stony Brook, New York.

Pirrie, A. (1999). "Supposing": reading between the lines: an allegorical account of contemporary debates on literacy. *British Journal of Educational Studies,* **47**, 4.

Rickinson, M. (2001). Learners and learning in environmental education: a critical review of the evidence. *Environmental Education Research,* **7**, 208 – 317.

Scottish Office Environment Department (1995*). Learning for Life - A Scottish Strategy for Environmental Education.* HMSO, Edinburgh.

Tranter, P. (1986). The value of field trips in tertiary education: guidelines for planning a successful field trip. Unpublished manuscript, Department of Geography, University of New South Wales, Duntroon.

Wiley, D.A. and Humphreys, D.W. (1986). The geology field trip in ninth grade earth science. *Journal of Geological Education,* **33**, 126-127.

PART FOUR

CONCLUSION

20 CONCLUDING PERSPECTIVE

Michael Scott

Summary

1.   New access legislation is being introduced in Scotland. This concluding chapter picks out themes from elsewhere in the book about the opportunities that this creates and some of the problems that will have to be solved.

2.   To achieve a positive result for both people and the natural heritage, we need to learn from the past, learn from other people's experience, understand social research into countryside access, and transcribe all of that ethos to Scotland.

20.1 Background

The challenge of summing up this conference was put into sharp focus by the particular circumstances of that day in September 2000. Fuel blockades had closed Grangemouth and the other major oil refineries, resulting in empty petrol stations which threatened to bring all road transport to a halt. Rumours circulated at the conference that even the trains were going to run out of fuel that evening. This situation helped to emphasise the heavy reliance of outdoor recreation in Scotland on private, rather than public, transport. Against that background, all that was possible in concluding the conference was to offer a few simple thoughts, which, at the time, did equal injustice to the authors of all of the papers.

As Markland (this volume) emphasises, the conference was the ninth in a series organised by Scottish Natural Heritage (SNH). That recreation and access issues had been left as a leading topic to ninth in this sequence is in no way a reflection on the importance given to the subject. The conference simply could not have happened eight years previously. In the discussion sessions, Robert Aitken noted that several of the issues covered by the conference have been discussed many times before, but until a few years ago these discussions were regarded almost as incitement to rebellion. But by 2000 they were at the mainstream of public policy, giving the topic of the conference, and this volume, legitimacy as a subject whose time had come in the wider political arena.

It was important to emphasise that the current debate on wider countryside access in Scotland had not been instigated by SNH. Rather, SNH had been asked by Scottish Ministers to take forward work on the subject, after a commitment made in the Manifesto of the Labour Party at the first devolved Scottish parliamentary election in May 1999. Markland (this volume) describes the broad consensus that had developed on the proposed 'right of access to land and water in Scotland for the purpose of informal recreation and passage, exercised responsibly'. That last phrase is critical to the consensus and, in a sense, is the central topic of this volume – providing guidance and best practice on how to encourage and ensure responsible recreational access. Davison (this volume) describes the process of reaching that consensus, through the Access Forum and the Access Forum (Inland Water), and he outlines the proposals for transcribing that consensus into what he describes as a modern law to meet modern needs (the detailed legislative proposals for countryside access in Scotland were eventually published, as part of the draft Land Reform (Scotland) Bill, almost six months after the conference on 22nd February 2001, and they are therefore beyond the scope of the conference and this volume).

One of the oft-repeated phrases in the Scottish Parliament is the need for 'Scottish solutions to Scottish problems', but in developing such national perspectives it is important not to lose sight of the practice elsewhere. It was therefore valuable to have a briefing at the conference from Paul Johnson on the Countryside & Rights of Way Bill for England and Wales (the Countryside & Rights of Way Bill subsequently completed its passage through Westminster in November 2000 and received the Royal Assent the following month; its main provisions came into effect on 30th January 2001). This established the principle of a right of access only to registered common land and open country, a principle that would be extremely difficult to translocate to the much more expansive open spaces of Scotland – at least without requiring a GPS system as an essential accompaniment to any walk! That made many of the participants at the conference all the more appreciative of the distinctively 'Scottish solution' that was being discussed here.

20.2 Some problems

It was evident at the conference that everything was not 'sweetness and light' in terms of the response of all parties to the Scottish proposals. The consensus on responsible access was a fragile one, with some participants at the conference keen to debate the proposals and their impact on the rural economy, but it was made clear that this was beyond the scope of the conference. Nevertheless some of the interjections from the conference floor, unfortunately not captured in this volume, were a cold shower of reality on the practical issues that had still to be addressed.

There were many issues still to be resolved: on public liability for access on private land, on access to water, on access to cropland, on access after dark, and, perhaps most intractably of all, on access with dogs. But it was emphasised that publication of the draft legislation would offer the appropriate occasion for debating these issues. In the meantime, the aim of the conference was, in effect, to provide better information for that debate, when it came.

Previous volumes in the *Natural Heritage of Scotland* series have focused primarily on science and research issues. One of the questions for the conference organisers to resolve was whether there is a 'science of access'. As several papers made clear, there is such a science. It is a social science, perhaps imprecise compared to the physical and biological sciences, but no less relevant for that. SNH's mission statement is "working with Scotland's people to care for our natural heritage". Previous volumes in the *Natural Heritage of Scotland* series have been based around aspects of the natural heritage; this volume concentrates much more on the words 'people' and 'care', in seeking to define the key concept of 'access exercised responsibly'.

20.3 The knowledge base

The conference made clear that there is plenty of research to underpin our understanding of access issues and to help us determine the way forward. Hunt (this volume) describes research on how people enjoy the natural heritage. At the conference, he invited participants to 'perch on the edge of their seats' as he revealed the fascination of statistics, although it was consoling for some of the conference participants to discover from his paper that half of the people asked to give a 'contingent valuation' to countryside recreation refused to answer! Some things, surely, are above financial value.

Costley (this volume) describes research into the attitudes, perceptions and expectations of both the public and land managers. This perspective is valuable for everyone working in the field, but many of the points he makes should not come as a total revelation. After all, whether or not we have responsibilities for managing access, almost everyone attending the conference – and probably anyone reading this volume – also participates in countryside recreation. His paper is therefore not about managing 'them', but about managing 'us', and it is thus of very direct relevance to every Scot, every visitor to Scotland, and indeed every visitor to the countryside.

Taking that theme forward, one of the conference workshops was about the expectations of tomorrow's recreationists, thinking about the 15–16 year old age group (Fenn, this volume). There are many ways in which countryside managers should seek to influence this important age group, but an important lesson of the workshop was that we should also learn to listen to this group of young people, because they have much to teach us.

On the pre-conference field visit, participants saw at first hand why we need to get the balance right between recreation and conservation, whether in Loch Lomond and the Trossachs – set to be Scotland's first National Park after more than 50 years of advocacy and debate – or in the urban fringe of Glasgow at Hogganfield Loch. Lister-Kaye (this volume), in referring to his 'violin with a broken string', argues for the vital need to build respect for nature and wildness into our culture. He emphasises the fragility of wildlife habitats and how precious is the thrill of experiencing nature at first hand. I certainly can still recollect vividly the first occasions on which I saw an otter or a pine marten in the wild. Neither was on an organised wildlife expedition and neither was anywhere near a footpath. The best 'close encounters' with Scotland's natural heritage have always relied on the freedom to roam that has been a cherished tradition in the wild land of Scotland – a tradition which the proposed access legislation seeks to regularise and enshrine in law.

20.4 The people dimension

There is, of course, a concern that too many people can destroy that thrill, and damage the very thing they are travelling to the countryside to enjoy, but Sidaway (this volume) offers the sensible perspective that, in the relatively small number of circumstances where there is such impact, its effects usually are localised. He argues that the local effects of recreation are manageable, but we need the right information first. Proper scientific monitoring of the natural heritage is clearly a wise precaution wherever pressures are high. However, that monitoring is useless unless there are also back-up powers to control and reverse any damaging impact that the monitoring reveals. As an example of this, SNH has sought to build both the monitoring and the back-up powers into the Visitor Management Plan associated with the controversial funicular railway on Cairn Gorm. This should ensure that the increased summer and winter trade the funicular seeks to attract does not result in damage to the integrity of the important nature conservation interest of the European 'Natura' habitats and species around it.

The usual assumption in recreation management is that we are catering for existing demand, perhaps with a slow growth in new demand. Butterfield and Long (this volume) seek to put that into context by considering the implications of changing lifestyles on open air recreation. They conclude that it is not possible to make definitive projections in a competing leisure marketplace, but they also emphasise the need for scientific methodology to define different lifestyle types.

Allison (this volume), in discussing the promotion of healthy behaviour, offers two different messages of direct relevance to the conference theme. First, she shows that recreation is not all demand-led; sometimes it can also be opportunity-led. She talks about the major drive to encourage a healthier lifestyle for 'fat'n'flabby' Scots, and one of the best ways of addressing that is by encouraging recreation in the countryside. That makes it particularly important to focus efforts to improve access provision on the countryside around towns, so that the brisk 30-minute walks encouraged by Scottish rugby star Gavin Hastings in the promotional video can be enjoyed by the largest numbers of people in surroundings as appealing as possible.

The second, incidental perspective from Allison (this volume) is equally pertinent. She illustrates how a highly professional campaign (in this case promoting healthy exercise), carefully targeted at particular sections of the Scottish population, can begin to have a marked impact for the good. A vital component of the shared understanding from the Access Fora is the need to promote responsible behaviour in the countryside, and, in particular, to promote the Access Code. Promoting such a Code will also require a professional, targeted campaign, and this will undoubtedly benefit from the expertise and experience of other campaigns, including those mounted by the Health Education Board for Scotland which Allison describes.

Two of the workshops explored other ways of promulgating the message of 'a right of access, exercised responsibly'. One looked at the North American experience of access codes and the use of simple 'icons' to convey messages about good behaviour in the countryside (Jones, this volume); however, the workshop did not attempt to identify an icon which could be used to represent responsible behaviour! The other workshop looked at the importance of using education to reduce conflicts between different recreation users, especially in inland waters. The combination of the sort of understanding considered in these workshops and the type of highly professional campaign illustrated by Allison (this volume) should go a long way to meeting some of the understandable concerns that remain about public behaviour in the countryside.

Carter (this volume) describes research on how to change recreational behaviour and provides valuable guidance. He sees interpretation as a fundamental tool in achieving the 'holy grail' of responsible behaviour, but he also emphasises that it is vital to ensure that the interpretation is promoting the correct message, rather than massaging what was originally a fundamentally wrong decision. The last thing people taking recreation in the countryside want is to be aware that they are being managed, so this is never an easy balance to achieve.

Those who attended the conference, in particular, will appreciate having the chapter by Foley *et al.* (this volume) so that we can take more time to come to grips with their deep discussions of cultural capital. The very fact that there is a Department of Hospitality, Tourism and Leisure Management at Glasgow Caledonian University is surely an encouraging sign that these important matters are now being addressed in a systematic and professional way.

20.5 Promoting responsible behaviour

At the time of the conference, it was clear that, despite all of the relevant experience available, the promotion and encouragement of responsible behaviour in the countryside is going to be a challenging task. One of the suggestions is that the agreed Outdoor Access Code should come to have 'evidential status' in the Courts, equivalent to the Highway Code. It is useful therefore to have Stradling's (this volume) perspective on promoting responsible behaviour on the roads, even if it is rather depressing to learn that surveys show the Highway Code itself to be almost irrelevant, compared to personal motivation. His finding that 77 per cent of drivers surveyed feel that they are entitled to use their cars wherever and whenever they want shows what a huge task lies ahead in promoting a genuinely sustainable transport system in Scotland. He makes it clear how valuable it would be to have a similar psychological analysis applied to those who take access in the countryside, and perhaps the results can be reported upon at a later SNH conference!

Scotland is not alone in facing many of these issues. There is value in comparing and contrasting our experience with that of other countries. Vistad (this volume) focuses on *Allemannsretten* in Norway, offering a fascinating and useful perspective. Norway may well have much in common with the Scottish Highlands, but his perspective is perhaps rather less relevant to the heavily farmed and developed landscapes around Scottish cities, and the culture of Norway is very different from that of Scotland. His chapter stimulates thinking, but does not provide answers; we still need to seek 'Scottish solutions to Scottish problems'.

Similarly, Marion and Reid (this volume) present information about the *Leave No Trace* programme in the United States; this offers many valuable lessons on getting across the message about responsible behaviour in the countryside through education, interpretation, and the management of public perceptions. But, again, the USA is a very different country from Scotland, and we cannot transcribe Marion and Reid's experience directly to Scotland; we need to create our own messages.

20.6 Looking to the future

In particular, both Norway and the US are big countries with a lot of open, 'wild land'. Scotland is a much smaller country, used more intensively, but it is widely recognised that sustaining the fragile rural economy is vital to sustaining the qualities of the Scottish countryside that are most valued. Although there is a long Scottish tradition of freedom to roam, what has always proved a problem is getting access over enclosed land to reach the open countryside, and that is one of the issues which it is hoped the new legislation will address. It is also no coincidence in this context that the proposed Scottish access legislation has been intimately linked with plans for land reform.

This book offers many ideas for taking forward changes in recreational access in Scotland. Thomson (this volume) offers SNH's perspective on delivering the new countryside recreation agenda. Although the delays in taking forward the legislation are frustrating for all involved, he hopes that the time might be used productively to continue to develop the imaginative thinking that already lies behind the developing concordat on access. Only time will tell how strong that concordat has proved to be, but in September 2000 it was certainly evident that there still was a major job to do in ensuring wide acceptance for the proposals that were being put forward at that time.

In his highly visual presentation to the conference, Richard Williamson (this volume) vividly illustrated how stereotyped are our visions of country users. It is true that the estate he works for is large and therefore perhaps atypical, but it is also one with land on the urban periphery where many of the greatest pressures on land are perceived as happening. It was therefore refreshing to read his pre-conference abstract.

"Let's get real, we are after all only talking about a walk in the countryside. There are no real access problems for land managers, only perceived problems and these arise from our blinkered, stereotypical, boxed view of looking at things" and *"The biggest change required will be in mindset or attitude. We all need to take off the blinkers, stop thinking in stereotypes and get on with the business of delivering a multi-benefit countryside".*

That somehow seems the most appropriate and positive message with which to end this book. It was clear in September 2000 that access legislation was going to happen in the near future. That legislation could either happen well, or it could happen disastrously. The challenge for everyone with an interest in the field is to ensure that it happens well. To do that, we need to learn from past experience, to learn from other people's experience, and to transcribe that ethos to Scotland. We need to build on the understanding that comes from sociological research into countryside access. Above all, we need to learn to work together, whether we are a sheep farmer or a staff member of SNH, whether we are an estate manager or a local authority employee, or whether in any of these roles we too are a recreation user. That is the challenge in moving forward the access legislation that is being introduced in Scotland.

INDEX

Note: most references are to Scotland, except where otherwise indicated.

Bold page numbers indicate major topics. *Plates* are indicated by *italics*

Printed by The Stationery Office, 10/01 c5